About the au

Well, here we go, brace yourselves!

Being a self-taught, award winning, exhibiting portrait artist, celebrant, justice of the peace and writer all started from very humble beginnings in regional New Zealand. I was the youngest of six, a large, loud, loving family and I had to fight for my parents' acceptance and spent my time continuously proving my worth at any cost.

My bushman dad and stay-at-home mum gave us everything we needed to build our own lives and move forward as a family or separately.

Discovering life outside our town became my mission and I was gone as soon as I was old enough to run!

The rest came with hard work, solo parenting, and self-teachings... Did I get it all right? Probably not, however, I gave it my absolute best shot and made the decisions with the resources I had at the time.

My media career and work as an artist gave me a road map, a plan to work with and my life, family and friends compliment everything I did/do.

As someone I respect once said, I "went hard and went early" to make sure I had enough time to fit everything in, and luckily, I'm still on that journey to this day with everyone I love at my side.

THE BUSHMAN'S SON

TERRY FERGUSSON

THE BUSHMAN'S SON

Vanguard Press

VANGUARD PAPERBACK

© Copyright 2022
Terry Fergusson

The right of Terry Fergusson to be identified as author of
this work has been asserted by him in accordance with the
Copyright, Designs and Patents Act 1988.

A CIP catalogue record for this title is
available from the British Library.

ISBN 978 1 80016 360 7

*Vanguard Press is an imprint of
Pegasus Elliot MacKenzie Publishers Ltd.*
www.pegasuspublishers.com

First Published in 2022

**Vanguard Press
Sheraton House Castle Park
Cambridge England**

Printed & Bound in Great Britain

Dedication

Dedicated to my parents,
Stubb and **_Myrna Fergusson._**

And to my favourite human,
Kyle Fergusson-Hughes,
"I love your face".

Acknowledgements

"The Girl from north Clyde" — Denise Williamson
Gloria Alsop Fergusson — Photographs
Marilyn Dawson — Family History
Lesley Newland — info and photographs
Valerie Doidge - Insight
Yvonne and Joe Hedley — Photographs/History
Exhibitions Gallery Auckland & Wellington
The Rotorua Daily Post
NZME

It's okay to look back at the past... just don't stare...

I wish that I had learnt to live my life unapologetically earlier in the piece. It all makes total sense to me now. Not fitting in or conforming means always having to win people over constantly to push the fit and, if it didn't work, it seemed totally devastating at the time.

This is my story… As it was — no frills or bleaching… Just my experience and how it happened. there's a lot in here about the people around me that tried their best to keep all the pieces of the puzzle together and some that didn't. I shared this entire experience with them.

This is my interpretation of the facts as I recall them.

Top song in 1967 — *To Sir with Love*

Some of my earliest memories were being, I suppose, a toddler, or there about, living in our mill house at Hutt Timber mill in Tokoroa where our father worked… I remember being able to see the television from where I was sleeping in my room. Well, that's what's stuck in my head so whether it's a memory or not, I'm not sure. Anyway, Mum and Dad where the first people on our street to actually have a television so, complete with blue cellophane over the screen to apparently offer up a better picture, they would have all the neighbors over to watch the topical programme at the time — news, sport or entertainment. I guess because they were all hardworking people — timber workers, bushmen, etc., they would struggle to stay awake, *especially* my parents! They would wake up an hour or so later and all the guests had disappeared home after turning off the telly and closing the door behind them. Pretty trustworthy in a house where the six of us kids were sleeping!

Six kids in the sixties and a three-bedroom state-style house, no insulation, an open fire for heating and a coal range/woodburning stove for cooking, which also heated the hot water. I'm sure there was an electric switch to heat the hot water but when you are a family of eight, it was a luxury we just couldn't afford or just wouldn't consider when you lived in a timber town in a timber mill village surrounded by forest, which meant an endless supply of firewood… free or otherwise.

The telly wasn't our only source of entertainment at Hutt Timber village… We still had the radio with its various news programmes and Sunday morning stories… But, along with that, our house was always full of music. Mum always loved music, any kind, any way… But especially country music. She would sing and dance around the house frequently while doing housework or in between rounding us kids up. Music would waft through the house… She loved Loretta Lynn, Jim

Reeves, Patsy Cline, *Georgy Girl* by The Seekers, *The Twist* by Chubby Checker… Complete with dancing with a towel with my older sisters to get the movement right, and a lot of Elvis thrown in for good measure. She came from a family that sang with piano, ukulele and guitar right into their old age…

I think that music was an escape for my mum and always was… It made her happy and gave her a release from being constantly bombarded by six needy children… The youngest being two — that was me — and a husband that loved her but also loved rugby, drinking with mates and pig-hunting just as much.

Our dad, affectionately known as "Stubb" because of his bullheadedness, was the only son of Arnie and Effie Fergusson and had two younger sisters, Noeline and Shirley. Nana was a seamstress and an educated southern woman whilst "Ern", as we called him, was a pioneering man from the far north. Quite amazing how they managed to meet from opposite ends of the country, fall in love at the late age of twenty-nine and thirty, and marry.

Nana Effie was very much a prim and proper lady, complete with gloves, pearls and matching handbag and Ern was a part-Ngāpuhi bushman. I guess there's a lot of truth in the phrase that opposites attract. Our dad, being their only son, was apparently a very spoilt mummy's boy who had to be placed on the kitchen bench while his mother was peeling the spuds for dinner as he couldn't stand to be any distance from her, and in their eyes, he could do nothing wrong.

Our mum, Myrna, was a shy woman when we were young… Sociable, but shy… She earned the name "scary crow" early on from friends and family… She loved her family… Us and her siblings, etc.

She was the nineteenth child from a family of twenty. Same parents — no twins. My grandmother, Gertie, had twenty separate pregnancies with her husband, George, in Tolaga Bay and Gisborne.

Gertie's mother, Evelyn Goodley, was a midwife and would arrive by horse to deliver most of the babies — her grandchildren.

The family consisted of Myrtle, Mona, Elva (Lev), Vera, Ben, Ivan, Nolan, Enid, George, Neville, Alexander (Alec), Melvyn (Nig), Joan,

Zelda, Velma, Esma, Oriel, Milton (Bandy), Myrna (my mum), and William (Bill).

Mona and George died as infants, and Esma was stillborn… We were told that she was so perfect and beautiful so wasn't meant for this world.

George and Gert loved each other very much and *obviously* had a very active sex life… George always said that he married the most beautiful girl on the east coast and believed that until the day he died. Gert apparently would say that all her husband had to do was hang his trousers over the end of the bed and, boom, she was pregnant again! He was always touching her and singing to her *You are my sunshine*, *Little green valley*.

Perhaps these romantic times where strategically planned in case he was out drinking with mates and leaving her alone with so many children to feed. Gert may had been little in stature but made up for it in strength as she would hurl his plated dinner across the room when he frequently arrived home drunk. My aunty, Velma — the fifteenth child — remembers her and some of the other kids at home hiding in the cupboard from the screams of Gert to George. She recalls her mother exclaiming that he was spending all the money on boozing with his mates when the money was needed to feed the kids… Gert screamed at George that there was no cash left for meals so she would have to grab a knife and cut their throats! Obviously, the children were bloody terrified and that prospect and all started screaming in the cupboard. I think Gert got her point across, but the behavior continued. But their adoration for each other got them through until death parted them.

They met in Tolaga Bay, outside of Gisborne, where George lived on the family farm with his parents, Benjamin and Elizabeth Jolley, and older brother, Charles. Gert, born in Freemans Bay, was the eldest child in her family of nine children — four daughters and five sons. I guess it was work that brought them to the bay with parents, Harry and Evelyn Goodley.

Harry operated the punt to get people and transport across the Uawa River in the village… George, twenty, and Gertrud, eighteen, met in that small community and were married at the Reverend Hounsell's home in

Gisborne and settled on the Jolley family farm in a small house they built with the help of the family, just down in the valley next to George's brother Charles' house and their parents in the original homestead. Their first eighteen children were born on that very farm… Which is still owned by descendants today.

My grandparents, George Jolley and Gertrude Goodley, on their wedding day.

It would have been a fantastic place to grow up and especially during the depression, where everything was rationed, as the farm would provide. Velma would often tell stories of climbing the trees on the farm in the orchard to steal apples and other fruit, as their Uncle Charlie refused to part with it, and would chase them off,

Many of Mum's older siblings would talk often about their childhood memories living in the bush. These tales were written about in my cousin Denise's book, *A Girl from North Clyde.* She quotes her mother, Enid, one of the older Jolleys, and a wonderful, kind lady who would give me chocolate and money when we stayed with her when we were kids. Enid also mistook a dark freckle on my nose for fly shit, or so she said, and scrubbed and scrubbed until my nose skin bled. This left a scab, much to my mother's horror when she picked me up, but, thanks to my dear aunty Enid, once the scab fell off, the freckle was gone! I was about six or seven.

Anyway… Enid and her siblings would talk about spending five to six months twenty miles into the bush, living in nikau whares. The children spent their days cutting supple jack growth to clear the way for their father and other bushfellers.

At this time, there were only seven of the Jolley children. The youngest were placed either side of a horse in a pikau, which was a sack split down one side and slung across the saddle. These pikaus were used for carrying their supplies and babies on their twenty-mile journey. Apparently one of the kids' biggest fears was being lost as it was always a present danger. In the latter years, the family had a car but mainly they had to use a horse to move supplies in and out.

Zelda would tell me how, when they would sometimes head into town with their mother, Gert, and that she was caught short and needed a toilet — well, long drop, actually, in those days, and being about seven or eight years old — she resorted to squatting between cars in the main street of Tolaga, only to be spotted by her mother and thrown back on the horse and sent home with a rather red slapped bum.

Gert was a small woman with black hair and dark skin… Through genealogy tracing and later DNA matches, it turned out that she was actually from Spanish descent, hence her olive complexion. Most of her children inherited this olive skin, including my mum. And some of the boys were often taken for Māori.

Christmas with the Jolleys was apparently always a very traditional event and Grandad Benjamin would liven up every Christmas morning by appearing just before the family festivities and start skipping along the trail from the old house, dressed from head to toe in one of Elizabeth's dresses, and all the many children present would shriek with delight and the grown-ups present would giggle along with the not-so-surprising annual gag.

Some of the older Jolley children rode to Whangara school — approximately eleven miles away — every day and Gertie would teach the younger children at home via correspondence. My Aunty Velma would recall in later years how they would escape Gertie's lessons at the big kitchen table when she would have to attend to certain chores. They would run off and head outside to play for the rest of the day, only returning when their father returned from working in the surrounding bush.

George worked as a bushman in many different places around the area. He worked in the Mangaheia Valley, inland from Tolaga Bay, as well as Tutamoa. For many years, the family lived around the area of Takapau station, where the older sons — my uncles — worked alongside their father in the bush.

Benjamin and Elizabeth stayed put on the farm with their sons well into their later years and subsequently died leaving the entire farm to older brother, Charles... Things, weren't great and that action wasn't well received, from what I've been told over the years.

George was a distinguished sportsman who represented the east coast on numerous occasions in cricket, rowing and rugby. He was also well-known all over Gisborne, for his woodchopping, winning many competitions. I'm unsure how he provided for his large family from that point, but Elva told us that he continued his passion for sports, with rowing championships being one of his favorites. She mentioned that they would watch him start on the bridge, then scream down to the finish line before the river emptied out to the bay to see him finish.

After their years in Tolaga Bay and districts, the family moved to Gisborne. For this trip, they had to supply their own horses to transport all their worldly goods because the stagecoach at the time could not take them all in one load.

Stormy weather — Ethel Waters 1933

Gisborne is where Gertie gave birth to her last two children — my mum and Uncle Bill. The house they lived in wasn't far from a grocery store owned by a certain Humphrey family, who were so good to the Jolleys, I imagine, when it came to credit and food, etc.

When my grandmother, Gert, was pregnant with Uncle Bill at forty-six, Mr Humphrey said to the expectant parents that, if the child was a boy and they named him Humphrey, he would gift them a red suit for the infant. So, yes, it was a boy and my uncle's full name was William Humphrey Jolley! After the shop owner, himself. Cute!

Humphrey's Store — Gisborne NZ

Later, the family would move to Opotiki, where George would again work on a farm. In the fifties, they moved to Mamaku, near Rotorua, to retire near their children. They both had endured a hard-working life, rearing a very large family in that isolated area around the east coast.

My nana, Gertie, had given birth to twenty children in twenty-six years, and was forty-six when she had the youngest. She never knew the luxury of having a washing machine, a fridge, vacuum cleaner or even hot water without lighting a fire, but she always had the time for a cuddle or a hand rub by the fire.

I was told that she was a gentle, loving person and in her later years, would very much look forward to the weekends when one of her children would invariably turn up to visit them with food or gifts. She would apparently always make scones just in case someone turned up. Sometimes their children would convince them to visit them in Napier, Wairoa, Paeroa or Tokoroa and Matamata, but mostly the family would go and visit them at home in Mamaku.

Any photos that Gertie had, she would write on the back of them as she loved to look at them over and over.

My sister, Heather, remembers visiting her nana, Gertie, in Mamaku when she proudly had in her possession a rather large gobstopper... Gertie was horrified that the child would choke on such a large sweet so took it outside, placed it on the chopping block she used to cut kindling, and chopped it in half. My sister was obviously mortified about her grandmother's actions and never forgot it! Safety first for her friends and family was always apparently a priority for this loving couple.

George would sing songs to his Gertie, and whoever else was present, with great gusto, such as *The Wild Colonial Boy*. He also loved poetry and would recite long poems like *The Albatross*.

They were both interested in politics and often talked about the Great Depression of the 1930s. They were absolute Labour Party stalwarts and had photos of Labour prime ministers, Michael Joseph Savage and Peter Fraser, on their walls along with the family photographs.

Grandad George Jolley died in Rotorua in 1961, leaving a devastated and rather confused Gertie alone. She had the symptoms of dementia or Alzheimer's at the time, which I guess could've softened the blow of losing her soulmate. My Aunty Joan would tell us that those symptoms got so bad that she would wander off looking for her George, thinking that her husband was late back from work or, even worse, at the RSA or pub. After a couple of these episodes, Joan would have to tie a stocking around the gate to hold it closed, preventing Gert from escaping and searching for her lost love. Then she would stand at the gate, unable to pass, and would stop people and ask them if they knew where George was. One neighbor called one evening in tears, relaying his heartbreaking conversation with her.

It certainly was incredibly sad and torture for her family to see her rapidly decline both mentally and physically. She died eleven months after her George... My mum always said that Gert died of a broken heart and I now understand that she probably did.

Gert Jolley pictured after George's death, 1961.

Because George and Gert had both died before I was born, and I was constantly listening to stories about them and looking at photographs of both of them, I would often wonder what they would've been like to know. Gertie's image fascinated me as a child and sometimes I would think I saw her walking past our house or smiling at Mum when I was in town with her.

There was one woman in particular that I was convinced was my Nana Jolley... It was at the various A & P shows we would go to as children. There was an elderly woman who use to operate a small merry-go-round with her husband. I would stand and stare at her, thinking that perhaps she was actually still alive but always too petrified to talk to her, let alone ride on her contraption... She was elderly so eventually disappeared from the shows as I got older. Crazy, I know, but it was the closest I would ever get to laying eyes on my mum's mummy — dear Nana Jolley — Gert.

I remember at school my friends would talk about their two sets of grandparents... One from each parent. All I had were my Fergusson Nana and Ern, who were fantastic grandparents, but I must admit, I felt a bit robbed not having what everyone else had and it was the late Jolleys that let me down, well, that's how I saw it as a boy.

Mum was pregnant with my brother, Rex, when her dad died and preggers with me eleven months later when she lost her mum... She always told us that she was embarrassed to go back to the funeral home as the undertaker would think she was still pregnant from the year before!

She got the news of her father's death in 1962 when her and Dad were camping in Opononi in the far north. No mobile phones back then so the bad news was communicated via the camp office. They called Dad over to the office and he then walked back to the campsite where Mum was waiting for the outcome of this very urgent phone call. She was devastated and apparently cried all the way from Northland back to Mamaku, just outside of Rotorua, where they lived at the time. She was in her 30s and her mum and dad had gone.

Her siblings — the seventeen that made it to adulthood — became even more important to Mum than ever. They were all so close and we knew them all. I never realized that all these people that were in our lives where actually our uncles and aunties and then there was the cousins... I have over eighty of them thanks to the Jolleys.

Losing her parents when she was still a young woman made my mum hold fast to her own immediate family. She reigned in our lives as a point of security and awareness. She trusted very few and was always suspicious of strangers and their motives. Mum always keep us kids close and if we were out of sight or away, she would always know exactly where and with who.

She was an insecure woman and worried constantly about us… They say that it's just a mother's lot and you are only as happy as your unhappiest child, but a lot of Myrna's problems started when she was a girl growing up in rural NZ. Her parents worked on farms and sometimes deep in the bush where George worked as a bushman and Gert would work in various cookhouses, preparing meals for workers and her family. If there wasn't enough to go around everyone, she would simply say that she had eaten earlier and pass her portions on to someone more needy in her eyes… Or so I was told.

Our mum would often tell us these stories about growing up rough and even remembered living on dirt floors and never having toys or even a doll to play with. However, during life in one of the bush camps, her dad, George, appeared with dolls made of wood, which he had handcrafted for Mum and Oriel, one of her older sisters. She would smile when she relayed the story to us, saying that she was so excited to have a doll that she could dress, look after and play with.

However, when it was time to leave the bush camp and head back into town — Gisborne, or there about — George would insist on throwing the dolls away as he was embarrassed that others would see what his younger daughters had to resort to when it came to toys, etc. She would say that they would cry and cry for their makeshift wooden dollies, which I'm sure were made with a lot of love and skill by a man who was desperate to provide for his massive family, but too shy to let others witness how poor they actually were. Later in life, Mum and a lot of her sisters would all have a collection of dolls in their homes. This need was obviously born from these events.

The Napier earthquake in 1931, which devastated the city and region, also had an effect on Mum's parents. George and Gert were based in

Gisborne at the time and Mum would've been just twelve months old or less and some of her older siblings, such as Joan, Velma, and Zelda, were attending school at the time the violent jolt hit. Gert, on her own with son, Ivan, took cover and waited for the shaking to stop. George was at work so Gert rushed Ivan away to fetch the girls from school and bring them home safe... Ivan ran to the school to ensure his young sister's safety only to be nearly knocked down by Joan who was breaking the speed of light and jumping fences in a single bound... Not even noticing her concerned brother on the dirt road!. She arrived home to her mum, Gert, and was asked where her savior brother was... 'Never saw him,' Joan gasped. Ivan arrived home eventually with the others at school and the family waited out the shaking... Aftershocks galore!

My Aunty Joan always loved relaying that story to me, saying that she was faster than an Olympic runner. It surprised me that she had the lung capacity after the tales she told me in later life about her and Ivan smoking dock leaves rolled in newspaper, down the back of the farm, away from their parents' watchful eyes. It would've been so harsh but I guess tough times call for tough measures.

Growing up in this family environment meant the younger girls in the family working from a very young age and travelling around the country with parents who were constantly looking for work. Velma would tell me how she was woken in the early hours on her day off from helping Grandad in the milking shed as Joan had been given the sack for being so bad-tempered towards disobedient cows and kicking them or pulling their tails to get the reaction she wanted. Velma always said that she did it on purpose so she wouldn't be allowed back and whoever was in bed at the time would have to fly into action... No milking machines in those days, all done by hand... Back-breaking work and not for the faint-hearted, apparently.

Sentimental Journey — **Doris Day with Les Brown and his orchestra, 1945**

A lot of my Mum's older siblings had married and left home by the time the younger members of the family arrived. Some of the older girls had their own families and a few of the boys had enlisted and gone to war.

One brother in particular, Melvyn, had a nickname that wouldn't be very PC by todays standard because of his dark appearance… A very handsome young man who loved his family and was determined to serve his country. Much to the horror of his parents and siblings alike, he went missing during conflict and they all waited for word on whether he survived or not. Mum would often talk about how she would see her mum, Gertie, sobbing in the woodshed so no one could see her, or so she thought, as she obviously wanted to keep a strong, positive shield up so nobody would worry. Gert and George would often hold each other and cry with the agonizing worry that this situation presented.

Months later, word finally came through that Nig had been captured by the Nazis and was placed in one of the Stalag work camps. He remained there for a number of years, doing hard labour and witnessing horrendous atrocities to prisoners but managing to keep his head down and survive until the liberation. Mum said that when he finally returned home, he was a different man, obviously changed by what he had seen and endured. He never discussed or disclosed much at all about the war effort to his family because I guess it was just too horrendous to relive. However, mum would tell us that he was starved almost to the point of death along with his fellow prisoners and witnessed the guards making the prisoners run as fast as they could and then releasing German shepherd guard dogs on them to bring them down.

Such violence and torture would've been hard for him to work through and there wasn't a lot of help for returning servicemen in those days to help deal with the ordeal, mentally or physically. He struggled until his death from Alzheimer's.

The war was hard on all the Jolley family... It affected them all in some way. My mum, Myrna, was only a girl when war broke out in Europe. Her older sisters, Joan and Zelda, had been manpowered to help in Wellington Hospital as nurse aids. During this time, American and English soldiers had descended on NZ as part of the home defense and to help the war effort with manpower, etc. They offered to build a superhighway from Wellington to Auckland, but apparently the NZ government at the time declined as it was thought that the bodies could be put to better use... And that they were!

Joan and Zelda, being young, attractive girls with classic good looks and a hell of a lot of country charm fitted right in the social sect of the time. It was a world away from the manual labour they were submitted to as children in the Hawkes Bay area. They and their close friends were always on the invite list when it came to wartime events in the capital city.

One day they were invited to head down to the Wellington waterfront as a friend's brother was arriving back from the war on a ship with hundreds of other servicemen. So they braved the crowds and managed to get right to the front and, hanging onto the wharf front's large railings and gates, they managed to see who they were there to welcome home.

It just so happened that news cameras were there onsite filming for the weekly newsreels that played out at cinemas around the country. Giving war updates, news and entertainment updates. Sitting in a theatre, weeks later, Joan and Zelda were confronted with images from that day starring themselves! Joan was in awe as she saw her own beautiful face flash up on the screen... Her very own close-up. She would mention her surprise well into her old age. Luckily for us, this reel still exists, and we get to see a moment in time where my dear aunties looked so incredibly young and happy without a care in the world.

Alas, for Zelda and Joan more trying times were ahead... Joan, my aunty with the movie star looks, was no stranger to controversy. From a young age, she was doted on by her parents and was tiptoed around just to keep the peace and not upset her. Joan's fury when not getting her own way was well-documented. She wrote the book on sulking and would sometimes lock herself in a room refusing to come out for days on end and would ignore her mother's wails, pleading her to "please eat", but to no avail. This strong, dare I say bullheaded, woman refused to agree until her terms were met, or at least all the guilty parties, according to her, were all extremely sorry and apologetic.

By the time Joan had started her war effort alongside her sister in Wellington, she had already given birth to my cousin, Valerie, in Pukekohe, where she was sent from Napier to stay with sister, Oriel, until the baby was born. Val's father was seventeen and Joan was twenty-three — quite the scandal. My Aunty Zelda would often relay the story about the two of them getting ready to hit the town but if Joan couldn't get her hair to look just right, she would throw her hands in the air and say, 'That's it! I'm not going!' And that would be the end of the night's plans for both of them.

Joan being Joan, and still being a young woman, her daughter was soon spending most of the time with her grandparents, George and Gert, whom she adored, and the feeling was absolutely mutual. G and G offered Valerie a stable upbringing... Something that Joan wasn't able to at the time and, to be honest, it seemed that Joan wasn't all that interested in supplying it.

So here she was in Wellington city... Living and working freely, and she meets an American soldier, William, and falls in love. He adores her and wants to marry her and whisk her away but, as every wartime story seems to mention... The soldier has to go to battle and would return for her afterward. Their relationship became physical and William left to fight in the war in the Pacific. Joan stayed behind in Wellington. She wrote to him and he wrote back. Then there was nothing... Silence. Joan, during this period, found out she was pregnant and then came the communication that her young, American dream was missing in action, presumed killed.

William, who was killed in action.

In the 1980s, she opened a small box and showed me the contents. It was the letters and photographs she had sent him but had been returned. She told me even then what a loss she felt. She truly was a *forgotten casualty of war.*

So here she was, a single woman in the 1940s, pregnant for the second time. Certainly not an ideal situation. Her and sister, Zelda, did their best to conceal the pregnancy by getting Joan's corset as tight as possibly to keep her latest bump from being seen in public.

Image: Zelda and Joan pictured with Zelda's husband in wartime 1940s Wellington.

Meanwhile, back in Tuai, where her parents lived at the time and where George was working at the local power station, her sister, Velma, who had married while quite young a few years before, noticed that Joan's letters had become irregular and even Zelda wasn't very forthcoming with much communication. Velma told me that this just didn't make sense to her and since she was getting no response or answer to numerous phone calls or letter, she'd had enough and booked a ticket to Wellington to sort these two girls out.

She arrived in the capital and made her way to Joan and Zelda's accommodation, but they aren't there. Velma's next option was the hospital where they worked and just as she was about to give up, she spotted Zelda coming down a flight of stairs. Both sisters froze for a moment then, without a word, Zelda spun on her heels and ran straight back up the stairs she had just come down. Velma was in hot pursuit, wondering what the hell was going on. Zelda was no match and Velma, desperate for answers, saw Zelda disappear into a hospital room... She flung the door open to see Joan propped up in the bed, holding a newborn baby girl — my cousin, Yvonne — and dear Zelda standing next to her as white as a sheet.

So, there it was — the reason for the silence. Nobody else knew a thing about this new baby with an American soldier father, gone to the list of WWII dead. Since Joan was legally still an unmarried woman, it made sense to keep this under wraps and pass the newborn to Velma and her new husband, Aubrey, to raise as their own, so that's exactly what happened. Joan told me in later years that she really didn't want to part with this beautiful, blonde baby girl and actually felt a bit bullied into it, however, a single parent in the forties left Joan with little choice.

Mum said she looked at this new baby when it came home with Velma and blurted out that she knew whose baby it really was... She was quickly put in her place with a slap from her mother, Gertie, and told never to mention it again, but she knew the truth.

The ups and downs of life's challenges didn't stop there for Joan. She coped with the separation from her second born daughter and went on to meet a fair-headed man from the deep south of New Zealand. The war was over, and she was ready for love.

She travelled via bus to spend time with this new man and all was going well. I'm sure that she and he had marriage on their mind, however, her new beau had a mother who didn't approve of the idea of her beloved son aligning himself with a woman of ill repute so did all she could to sour the relationship. Joan mentioned to me that her potential new mother-in-law would glare at her and she always felt extremely uncomfortable.

As fate would have it, Joan returned to her home in the north and subsequently found that she was with child for the third time and, once again, was unmarried! She wrote to her new partner, informing him of the unexpected but happy news, but no reaction came… She tried phoning his mother, only to be told he was unavailable — away, busy, unreachable. A frantic Joan kept trying until my cousin, Brian, was born and then gave up, thinking that her southern man had totally bailed on her and arranged his mother to be gatekeeper.

Once again, she was left holding the baby…

This is the tragedy of the whole situation and it turns out that he had never seen any letters or received any messages from frantic phone calls as he had been in serious accident and had been laying in an induced coma for months and his "bitch of a mother" — Aunty Joan's words, not mine — had destroyed all letters telling of the imminent birth.

She was a resilient woman by this stage and returned to Mamaku where her eldest daughter — my cousin, Valerie — was living with George and Gert. She spent time with them but ended up living with my parents. Mum and Dad soon saw a matchmaking opportunity and introduced Joan to Dad's best mate, Andy.

Andy — short for Anzac as he was born on April 25th — had live in the small village of Mamaku all his life and was quite the catch when it came to potential husbands in the small community. He became completely besotted with this classic beauty, Joan Jolley. He knew all about her past and decided that, not only did he want to marry her, but also take on the children she still had with her.

There was much opposition from Andy's traditional parents, upset that their son was marrying a woman who wasn't as pure as they would have liked or expected. However, the wedding went ahead with my mother so excited that she made the cake for this intimate affair — it was thought that this was the best approach at the time and they went to the courthouse in Rotorua for a quick ceremony. There is possibly a handful of snaps taken on that day and it was quick with no fuss to keep it all under the radar. The children — Val and her brother, Brian — took on Andy's surname, much to Gertie and George's horror as Val had carried their surname up to that point — it broke their heart. 'The name Jolley has been good enough for her so far in her life — why change it now!' exclaimed Gert.

So here she was, finally married and her family intact... Meanwhile, in the deep south, Brian's father recovered and found out the truth about all the communication from Joan but it was too late as she was married and settled with Andy... Love wasn't there initially with Andy, she told me later in her life, but it was the right thing to do and she grew to love him. They lived well together, with Joan wearing the pants and Andy complying with all rules that were subject to change without notice.

My cousin, Val, left home as soon as she was able, leaving Brian to be the thorn in Joan's side. She treated him in a way that nowadays would be called abuse… She would sit him on the potty and make him stay there until he pooped and if he didn't, she would walk past and slap him around the ears calling him all sorts of names — horrific.

This dislike for each other grew as the years went on and the dislike turned into hatred — a hatred that lasted all their lives… Unbearable to watch or be around. Brian eventually left his mother behind but his love for Andy — the only father he had ever known — kept him distantly around. His real father popped up in later years, much to Joan's horror, as she had never told her son the truth that Andy was actually his stepfather… He was devastated by the news and pleaded with my mum, Myrna, asking her to say that it wasn't true and that surely, she was his real mum and not *her*!

This was the nail in Joan's coffin and after Andy died in the mid-nineties, he completely cut his mother off, not even returning when news of her death reached him. The damage she had done had cut so deep that he was actually glad she died and would only return to dance on her grave. However, I loved her so much and she was adored by her grandchildren… She was beautiful and complicated, and her death left a hole in my life.

Zelda, during that wartime in Wellington, was a social butterfly and would adapt to any social situation… Drinking and chatting with the rich, posh and famous, or at the local public bar with other wartime workers.

During this time, she met an Englishman, Arthur Alfred Taylor, more commonly known as "Sonny". He was a patient in the very hospital where she worked, suffering from appendicitis. They fell in love, were married and had a daughter late in 1946, planning to return to England to settle post-war. However, my Aunty Zelda refused to leave her siblings and parents, so they divorced. It took ten years for a divorce to come through from Sonny and she had met her next partner, John, years before it was finalized so their first two children were born out of wedlock. She was a very private person and only her nearest and dearest were taken into that confidence.

John and Zelda went on to raise another two children before she tragically lost him in the late sixties — he was only forty-nine. She was to marry for a third time and grew old with her new husband, affectionately known to her as "Dickie"

She really was the life of the party and always kept us entertained when we were visiting. Alzheimer's took her from us, and the world really did become a little less funny and less entertaining when we lost her in 2006. The white casket and the release of bright red balloons on the day was a big salute to Zelda's fun-loving party nature.

Zelda (second from right) pictured with friends in Wellington.

The first tits I ever saw were Zelda's! Mum and I were visiting her in Hamilton, where she spent most of her married life. We were in a friend's swimming pool when I heard my rather comedic aunty yell out, 'Hey, Terry... Look! I'm Miss New Zealand!' When I looked up, there was my glam aunty in a bikini with her top off and posing like a beauty pageant contestant.

Mum yelled, "Zelda, put those fried eggs away!" Such entertainment.

Aunty Velma would also tell me when Zelda would stay with her in Napier, she would serve cups of tea in the morning to her sisters as a topless waitress... Yup, again with no top on.

She loved to party and loved a drink but couldn't really handle either. She would crack rude jokes... Scream out the window at other motorists — my first exposure to road rage before we even knew what it was. I'm painting a pretty bad picture of my dear Aunty Zelda but, no, she was a great woman, a wonderful mum, who survived a lot of tragedy in her life but saw the humorous side of absolutely everything. Her and mum together were bad and would egg each other on to be worse, especially over a bottle of Asti Spumante.

I was five years old when I had my tonsils out in Waikato Hospital and while I was in there, Mum stayed at Zelda's. They called up to see me on the third day after the operation and were told I wouldn't be coming out for another day or so. The naughty twosome headed home and cracked a bottle of their favorite tipple when the phone rang saying I was being checked out. Oops, no way they could drive back so I was bundled in a taxi by the hospital staff and sent off to auntie's house. I was five years old and all I remember about the trip is how big the back seat was to me and clutching onto my overnight bag.

I arrived OK and Zelda and Mum put me straight into bed and told me to rest. I would've but the chatting and cackling laughter made me want to join them, so I did. They were such good fun separately but another level when together and she would often appear in her bikini again and dive in with me floundering about with mum who always swam in a dress to hide her big bum, or that's what she thought at the time.

I so loved those school holidays with Mum and Aunty Zelda in Hamilton... I was so happy hanging out with them. They *always* kept me entertained and included so I felt a sense of belonging with women from an early age... Oh, and yes... She had a Para pool in her backyard.

Another poignant moment I experienced at Zelda's house in Hamilton East was about a decade or so later, in 1986, when we were again visiting with some other relatives... It was the 8th March 1986, to be exact, and Halley's comet appeared for the first time in around seventy-five years… We stood in her back yard and watched the phenomenon. At that moment, I realized how different the world would look next time it passed us by in 2061. My mum and dear Zelda would all be gone and even I would be dust. It was a moment of mortal awareness and sadness that I would experience again later in life, devastatingly.

The Jolley family played a huge part in my family's life. The closeness of Mum to her siblings really did give us a huge amount of love in our lives growing up. We knew them all and were involved in all aspects of this huge family, whether we wanted to be or not. We took the good with the bad and the gracious with the indifferent, but mostly it was great fun. But as I got older, I started to lose them one by one.

My parents' wedding in Mamaku, Rotorua. 22nd July 1950.

Mum and Dad left Mamaku in 1956 and headed to Tokoroa, where there was a promise of work and housing. A lot of milling and bush work had started to slow down in the late 1950s, so moving away was the only way to stay employed and move forward.

Morning town Ride — The Seekers, 1968

My three older siblings were born before the move, so they packed up their small family — Heather, Gloria, Raymond and Jeannie the cat — and headed to the south Waikato.

37 Murray Road, Hutt Timber village was situated adjacent to the Hutt Timber mill and processing plant at the southernmost end of the Tokoroa township that boomed into being during the 1950s.

Our mills house at Hutt Timber village, Tokoroa.

It attracted people and families from all around the country with the prospect of high wages and fresh land. Mum and Dad's plan was to go for a year then return to Rotorua to be close to Dad's parents, Effie and Ern, and what was left of Mum's family.

It was a small and close community, with lots of kids to play with and adults for get-togethers, dinners and parties. My parents slipped into their new life easily and made lifelong friends right there in that small mill village

My sister, Desma, was born next in Tokoroa maternity... Then my brother, Rex, then me, eleven months later. The story goes that Mum had Rex, who was two months old and felt quite unwell so went to the doctor... The news was so shocking to her that she went home and whacked Dad! Her older sister, Oriel, told her about the contraceptive pill after I was born as she had been on it for a couple of years before — Mum was furious that she hadn't mentioned it before... Thank God she hadn't, or I probably wouldn't be here.

The three older kids always said that they were happy with their smallish family, then the next three of us showed up and spoilt everything. How bloody rude!

A typical 1960s family photo — Us Fergie kids, 1960s.

The closeness in age between Rex and myself means that we are the same age for about a week each year. We were similar in stature, so our mum always liked to dress us the same — like twins — much to Rex's horror as he really didn't want to be associated with me on any level other than teasing — poking, prodding and general ridicule. It was as if he got a sense of satisfaction from hearing me squeal and cry out for help, which meant Mum coming to the rescue.

I've been told that his general dislike for me came as Mum went into labour and headed to the maternity hospital to give birth to me. He and the rest of the kids were sent off to our Aunty Oriel and Uncle Mick's farm just outside of Tokoroa to stay until Mum got back and Dad was home. Apparently, he became very close to our sister, Heather, who acted as a surrogate mother during the absence.

When it was all over and Mum returned home with a new baby, Rex wouldn't go to her at all and glared at me for taking up all his mother's time. This was the start of a strained and sometimes cruel relationship between the two of us that lasts to this day. I totally understand that as a young child resentment can fester and last a lifetime, like Joan and her son, Brian, but I truly believe that we were both victims of circumstance with feelings that should have been dealt with decades ago.

A rather normal day with me being teased and Rex taking my new bike.

So that was it, our family was complete, three girls and three boys and me the last on the Fergusson line-up. Complete with twinkly blue eyes and dimples to boot. I spent a lot of time on my mother's hip… The dimples definitely came in handy if I was ever cornered for being badly behaved and spoilt, which I have to admit happened frequently.

I remember being slightly separated from my siblings at this time because of my closeness with my mother… I went most places with her and would scream if I was left behind. From this early age, I felt an affinity with women and especially Mum's friends or relatives. It was with them I felt my most comfortable and relaxed. I understood their conversations and the emotions around them… Chatting about their respective spouses and all the giggling laughter and cups of tea and the smell of cigarette smoke filling the room. In those days, most people smoked and there was always a blue-grey line of smoke in the room where these wonderful friends got together. I was never far from the action and was even the center of attention a lot of the time, along with mum's friends' children who were lucky enough to be admitted into this sacred realm.

My siblings were usually otherwise engaged, either at rugby or pig-hunting with Dad, or playing around the timber stacks behind the houses. Included in the multiple high stacks of wood was the working sawmill and the arsenic dipping troughs used to treat the timber before export or building. Not the safest of environments for kids to play, however, it provided hours and hours of entertainment.

The mill village forged friendships that would last through my parents' lives… Not all, of course, as some just naturally faded away but others stayed true and solid through the coming decades.

There would be different celebrations for the village families around specific times of the year, such as Easter, Christmas, New Year, etc., and especially for the kiddies. Us!

There was a village hall just down the gravel road from our house and it must have been a few days before Christmas day when I remember Mum sorting out a costume for me for the village kids' Christmas lunch celebration. 'C'mon,' she said, 'let's get going.' The thought of being separated from her was daunting for me and she was talking fast and humorously to keep me occupied so as not to fret about the upcoming separation. I was handed a cup and a plate with a sticking plaster underneath where she had handwritten my name in pen so I wouldn't lose it. This was then all put in a small bag that I had to carry. We walked out of the house and down the road. I remember holding her hand tightly and I listened to her reassuring conversation as we got closer to the hall.

We walked in and it was a Christmas wonderland (or at least that's how I remember it) complete with fairies, presents and a rather scary Santa. Mum must have slipped out and my desperation at being abandoned must have waned as I remember her coming to pick me up in rather record time. It must have been a few hours, but I hadn't notice as Santa and the fairies must have kept all us rather clingy children entertained to the point of screaming and stamping our feet at the thought of going home.

Us kids had made lots of friends in the community, especially my older sisters. Gloria, however, was often in trouble for causing some kind of ruckus or losing her temper at someone's house and storming home, much to Mum's horror. It happened frequently as she obvious never could suffer fools, even from this young age.

On one of several occasions, there was a knock at the door. Mum opened it to see Mrs Nicholson standing there with her son, Chris, who, in Gloria's words, was a spotty-faced whining little shit who constantly annoyed her. 'Look what your daughter has done to Christopher!' she exclaimed. Mum looked down at his freckled, rather annoying face and saw two rather large welts across his tear-stained cheeks. 'She whipped him with her skipping rope again!' Mrs Nicholson screamed.

My mother took a deep breath. 'Well,' she said, being rather sick of seeing this forlorn, rather sarcastic woman on her doorstep again with her rather cheeky, loudmouth son, 'he probably bloody deserved it.'

Mrs N, looking rather stunned with no words coming to her in retaliation, grabbed Chris by the hand and walked down the back steps… Then she swung around and with her parting breath, bellowed, 'Well, Myrna, you're nothing but a common heap!" *A common heap*? What even is that? For years and years, it would come up in conversation and we would laugh hysterically about the day Myrna got called a common heap.

Mrs Nicholson and Mum had a strained relationship, however, at the end of her life, our mum was there visiting her and looking after her as she slipped away…

My parents continued to be social butterflies while living in Hutt Timber village, which was completely normal for a young couple in their 30s, but none more so than Dad. He took the extreme measure of constantly trying to keep up with his mates — drinking, partying and more drinking.

One week, he disappeared on a Friday evening after his shift at the mill with his ex-Mamaku mates and left mum at home with the six of us — the oldest being thirteen and me, the baby, at approximately two years old. Mum was distraught when Dad finally showed up on the Sunday afternoon, with his mate, Gordon, in tow, expecting a hearty meal to be simmering on the coal range and a doting wife to be sitting at home in an apron holding his slippers… It was quite the opposite! Myrna lost her shit and gave him a decent dressing down and quite rightly, too! Gordon then piped up and called our mother an old dragon… What? With that insult, Mum rushed into the bedroom in tears and started packing. My sister, Gloria, remembers it clearly and because of her feisty nature, planned to rush at Gordon with as many expletives as she could muster (remember, it was the 60s and she was about twelve years old). 'Don't you call my mother a dragon, you bloody bastard!' she screamed. Gordon left the house and never came back and Mum, for the rest of her days, wouldn't even be in the same room as him and fair enough, I reckon. However, Dad somehow talked her off the ledge, and all settled down… For a while anyway. My mum at that point realized that she would always have to deal with this kind of behavior at some level throughout the rest of her marriage… Quite a daunting prospect for a mother of six.

Dad, being the guy he was at that time, always seemed to have an image to uphold… That of a sporty lad who was always up for a good session with mates. I'm not implying that he shrugged off any fatherly duties, just that he obviously wanted to maintain that particular persona.

Living in the village was also Mum's brother, Alec, and his family — arguably her favorite sibling. As I have mentioned before, the Jolley family were extremely close and he must have kept one eye on her during our time living there and noticed most things.

Dad and Alec worked together in the sawmill and an argument broke out between the two in-laws. This heated disagreement soon turned to fisticuffs and they planted each other to the point that they both hit the ground. Apparently, they were either caught by the management or reported to the bosses. Long story short, my father was sacked, and Alec was kept on as, apparently, he was better mates with the mill hierarchy than Dad was. Dad festered about this for a lot of years and never forgave his brother-in-law for pointing the finger. Just after the incident, Dad saw Uncle Alec helping that certain mill manager responsible for Dad's sacking in his garden and acting like bosom buddies... This added fuel to the fire and the two never spoke for more than four decades, much to Mum's horror and disappointment.

So there it was — no job, a wife at home, 6 kids and homeless as the house came with the job... Good work, guys! I'm not sure how long we had to vacate the mill house on Murray Road but the hunt was on to find an income and a roof over our many heads.

As far as I can remember, or was told — it's hard to decipher between what is memories and what's information when you are so young — my father was offered a well-paying job working in the bush, cutting posts, etc. A dream job for him as he always loved being out there in the forest and making stuff happen — he was once again a bushman.

As we had to vacate the mill house ASAP, Dad and Mum planned to build a new home on the north side of Tokoroa. Bigger, better and slicker than any of us had had before. Four bedrooms, a separate toilet, electric stove and a chippie, complete with an open fire in the lounge for more heating. We thought we were bloody royalty. I don't remember the move at all, but I just remember being there.

San Francisco (Be Sure to Wear Flowers in Your Hair) — 1967

The street was part of a new subdivision with a brand-new primary school a few minutes' walk down the road. We had the second house to be built in that street, so we were surrounded by empty paddocks full of long grass that I remember running through, pretending that I was in a scene from the many glamourous movies that I had watched with my mum. It was also great for hide and seek and general rough and tumble with my brothers and sisters.

One by one, the other houses in our new-found personal farm/street started popping up and spoiling our acres of natural playground and shortcuts to friends' houses and shops where we would drag boxes of empty Coca-Cola and Leed lemonade bottles for a few cents refund. We would immediately spend it on small packets of mixed lollies, which we would almost certainly eat on the way home so we wouldn't have to share with any of the others.

We would be left alone with the eldest so our parents could go out to the club with friends, etc. Heather and Gloria, being young, sophisticated women, or so they thought, would be into the booze cabinet, drinking Mum's blackberry nip and gimlet vodka. They would also line us younger ones up and make us put a lit cigarette in our mouth and say, "suck it like a straw". Of course, we would cough and hack with eyes watering and feeling rather dizzy from the nicotine hit. 'Now,' Heather would announce as she stood there puffing on her cigarette, 'you can't tell on us for smoking coz you have been too!' Well, that was certainly enough to buy our silence.

Fighting amongst ourselves was a regular occurrence at 21 Paraonui Road and was usually between Heather and Gloria or Rex and I. Raymond and Desma were the quieter sect and were constantly stuck in the middle of the ruckus. Gloria would slam doors and scream, then would play Jimi Hendricks or Jethro Tull so loud that the windows would rattle. Her bedroom door was slammed to hard so many times that the handle disintegrated, and dad refused to replace it as punishment so she couldn't lock herself away in one of her fits of rage. To get away from the rest of us, she would climb into the roof space through her wardrobe and spend hours up there getting some peace from the rest of us little shits and our uncool parents. She would eventually turn up when the aroma of that night's dinner wafted through the attic space

Heather would annoy Gloria to the point she — on one occasion — pulled out Dad's hunting 202 and threatened to pull the trigger. Unfortunately for G, but fortunately for H, Dad always removed the bolt. Sometimes things were thrown between sisters just to shut each other up.

On one occasion, a full tin of beans was flung. Heather ducked just as mum walked past and she took a direct hit to the head... Down she went... 'OMG you've killed Mum!' she screamed as we all flocked around to see if she in fact was dead... Thankfully not, but there was blood, screaming and crying and that impact left a nasty scar.

There, of course, was a price to pay for this action and it was set up by the words, "Your father can sort you out when he gets home.' That was a sentence you *never* wanted to hear and put the fear of God into you!

Soon after, my older sisters had discovered boys and there were no shortage of suiters hanging around my young, rather attractive sisters. Dad was rather oblivious to the goings-on, however, our mother always had one eye on them, who they were with and what was happening. Mum always assumed the worst and thought that these girls were always up to no good... Not really the case... Well, kind of not.

Around about this time, Heather and Gloria decided to try their luck in Auckland so packed their bags and hitchhiked as all attractive young girls did in the late sixties/early seventies. Mum was apoplectic but away they went in miniskirts so short that they use to call them "fanny pelmets". They got jobs in a clothing factory in Mount Eden called Sunny Knitwear with a couple of their girlfriends also from Tokoroa. They told me in those days that they were out every night with no money for food, so all lost a lot of weight... Every teenage girl's dream. From flat to flat they went... Moving on when the rent got too overdue. From Mount Eden to Grey Lynn to Ponsonby and more.

Ponsonby and a lot of the central suburbs were close to being city slums in those days, with crime rates that were through the roof, however, my sisters and their mates always managed to scrape by with little disruption.

Although there was one night when they were all together, walking up Queen Street. Gloria had had an argument with the other girls so was lagging behind the others as a mark of protest against her mates and sister in a rather sulky slow walk. At that moment, a car full of young men swung in toward her and they leaped out, grabbing her and forcing her toward their waiting vehicle. Now, I will tell you the turn of events shortly... All I will say is that Gloria's reputation was that of a firecracker, a spitfire, a fighter with a fuse shorter than my first haircut. Put it this way... They grabbed the wrong sister as Heather would have screamed then cried then fainted dead away, but not Gloria! Once she realized what was happening, she fought them off, kicking one in the shins, then the other, more aggressive offender got the hardest kick she had ever kicked right in the balls. As he went down in a heap of excruciating pain, she whipped off her rather large solid platform shoes and smashed him on the head. The howls and screams came from these wannabe attackers and those sounds made Heather and her friends aware of what had just happened. They turned around just in time to see the guys heaped on the footpath in the middle of Queen Street and crawling back to the parked car, with Gloria running up the road with her shoes in hand. As I mentioned earlier, these guys really did pick the wrong girl! She told us this story often with great pride saying that she kicked the guy so hard that she was sure that he would never father children.

Our dad loved to relay this story to his mates amidst roars of laughter as the would-be attacker never really stood a chance, however, the sobering thought about this whole incident is that the outcome could've been totally devastating.

The girls' big city experience was soon to come to an end as most of the group had been fired for not turning up to work and a multitude of other reasons. Gloria, who was fifteen, was the only one who kept her job and her wages went to rent and food... None of these things were very important to the group.

It was about then that the owner of Sunny Knitwear called our dad purely out of concern that the "young one was the only one still employed", and that he really didn't know how they were surviving. Well, as any parent would react to that kind of information, Dad called them and told them to pack their things as he was about to hit the road to Auckland to bring them home. I remember being in the car and arriving to collect the forlorn sisters. I don't remember any conversation or who else was in the car, but I can imagine that it was a very quiet trip back to Tokoroa.

Refusing to be labelled as Tokoroa girls, they soon found another option to escape the trap and avoid the branding. A mutual friend had headed down to the Mahia Peninsula, south of Gisborne. They could stay with their mate and had visions of getting jobs as fruit pickers — nothing to lose, huh.

Well, through their friend, Heather was introduced to local lad, Joe Kara, of Ngāti Kahungunu. He was a complex Māori guy who had been whāngai'd from a very young age, so his parents were actually his uncle and aunty. He was an incredibly shy guy with dark skin and hair down to his waist.

The relationship seemed to be going OK when Heather discovered she was pregnant so tried to keep it quiet as long as possibly when the girls returned to Tokoroa. Enid, one of mum's older sisters, quickly caught on to Heather's condition and questioned her. 'Are you pregnant, Heather?'

'No!' she replied, but it did eventually have to come out as her waistline expanded.

Remember that it was 1970 and our parents were mortified and wanted to avoid the shame, which is crazy in hindsight as Mum's sister, Joan, had been through the same thing but it was handled with ease and dignity. Our mother's first action was to insist on adoption, but this was met with a sound "no" from everybody involved. 'Well, he'll have to marry you,' Dad exclaimed!

Joe was still on the east coast, waiting for the Tokoroa explosion to go off and settle, when he got the call from Dad with the decision and instruction. I've been told that he leaped into action and physically leaped into a taxi, which took him from Wairoa to Tokoroa! I can't imagine what that cost him, but it must've been Dad's tone of voice that made him realize he had to act there and then.

He finally arrived and popped the question — Heather agreed, and they were married not long after the birth of my parents' first grandchild — a boy. I was an uncle and I was only eight years old. This child and the adoration that circled him really did mark the end of my very short time as the center of attention. I never realized it at the time so much, but as I got older, I realized how I really had to take a back seat due to this new arrival.

Heather and Joe's wedding, 1970 — family pic.

The wedding, I remember, was thrown together with us all playing a part. Joe cut his long tresses, Gloria as bridesmaid, and the rest of us fussing around doing other jobs to make sure the whole production went well. The actual day consisted of the Tokoroa Pirates Hall decorated with punga ferns on the walls. Heather married in a pink dress as wearing white was just taking the piss and the minister at the church would definitely frown about that, or so it was thought. My grandfather, Ern, flung a throwaway remark that the happy couple shouldn't be at the reception, but home, looking after the baby… Heather cried and Rex and I mooched around the hall, drinking all the dregs so the family photo taken on the day shows the two of us showing the effects of too much beer! It was all a bit like a bad movie with an OK ending — done!

It was about this age that I realized that I was a little different than other boys and especially the boys in my immediate and extended family. As I got older, the differences opened up not just as a small divide but more like the Grand Canyon. I was always spending more time with my sisters and their friends. I would love to be with them when they sat around smoking seductively, trying on new clothes they had sewed themselves, chatting about the latest music and talking about boys. It was so glamourous, and I was a captive audience of one.

I had a major problem with bed-wetting, and it didn't get any more infrequent as I got older. The only thing worse than not being able to stay over at friends' houses or relatives' houses without an apology or a plastic sheet, or declining school camps or anything that involved an overnight stay away, was the embarrassment and constant ridicule from my brother, Rex. He seemed to really enjoy it and would use it along with "poof" or "pansy" at every opportunity. Obviously, it made him feel good to put me down. Teasing is part of being a kid, or so they say, but Rex really got off on it… I really had to pay for being around, or at least that's how he made me feel. Mum tried everything to help me stop, like not letting me drink anything after four p.m. in the afternoon and waking me up every few hours during the night to take me to the toilet, but in the morning, I was usually wet up to my neck in my own urine. The mornings that I did wake up dry were cause for celebration! Thankfully, I eventually grew out of it at thirteen years or so… What a relief… An end to the ridicule — well, not quite.

My parents' relationship during this period of family life had its ups and downs, although Dad had settled down more and entertained his mates more at home, rather than disappearing out on the town with them, much to Mum's relief. They partied a lot with their friends, which were mostly other couples and a lot of this was done at home where we could join in by entertaining with jokes, singing or tricks for money, from easy-to-trick drunks.

Sometimes I would play the house DJ on Mum's record player, taking requests and logging them in order by writing them on a piece of lunch paper. Other times, it was full-on singing with a mate's guitar until the wee small hours. Our mum, though tipsy as hell, would always make sure we were set off safely to bed before the party got rough (one of her favorite sayings). Us younger ones would listen to the music from bed and sometimes would crawl up the passage way to sneak a look at who was dancing with who, or who was making an absolute dick of themselves… We were never disappointed.

Our parents were avid Labour Party supporters and we were raised to have an extremely left-wing view of the political world. This stemmed back to Mum's parents, George and Gert, being the same, along with Dad's parents, Arnie and Effie. Nana Effie told me once that, during the Great Depression, the Tory leader or politician at the time was asked what to feed the working class as they were starving and food was in desperate short supply. He was quoted as saying, "feed them grass". She always had a look of anger and disgust when she told me that story and it always ended with her saying, 'And that's why you must *never* vote for the Tories!' Bless her.

Although, during this period, our dad spent more time at home with Mum and the rest of us, he refused to give up his club nights, which were most Fridays and sometimes Saturday evenings if Mum refused to go with him. He went anyway to sit and drink as much Waikato beer as possible and it was always a competition to see who could outdrink who.

Some nights, when he was late home, Mum would ask us to call the club and have him paged. When he wouldn't come to the phone, she would cry and say she had had enough of his shit and wanted to pack up and leave. Of course, we were mortified, as where would *we* go? Sometimes my brother, Ray, would drives us down to the club to get him to come home and we would wait at the front door, asking people who were entering to ask Stubb to come out. Eventually he would but was not happy about it… Or he would make us wait until he finished his last jug that mysteriously kept getting refilled.

Looking back, it was an extremely upsetting position to be in for all involved. I held a major grudge against him for being so inconsiderate, firstly to Mum and to us as a family… I just didn't understand the importance of drinking and bullshitting with his mates, rather than being at home with us, and mum crying was something that I just couldn't tolerate.

Alone Again (Naturally) — Gilbert O'Sullivan, 1972

I started to feel like an outsider as I didn't find "boy" things entertaining or the "boy" jokes funny. I didn't want to go hunting, I didn't want to play sport, especially rugby, which I just really didn't understand at that time. My parents didn't understand so my mum pushed me into hockey and soccer. 'Well, you have to play some kind of sport, Terry," she would say… The ridicule I received from brother, Rex, and co. was humiliating but on the field, I went, praying that the ball would never come my way as I would surely fuck it up to the point of laughter on the sideline. This kind of mental abuse became the norm the older I got, and I was always prepared for it, whether it happened or not.

I felt a sense of disappointment from Dad, who just pretended it wasn't happening. I even had to get a ride to soccer from the neighbor whose son played, as Dad was busy on the sideline of my brothers' many rugby matches.

I became very chubby in my pre-adolescent years and struggled to find anything I was good at until a report card mentioned that I was great at art. Mum picked this up and ran with it. A story that I often tell at my exhibition openings in the last few years is that of Mum taking me into town to the Tokoroa stationers, where the smell of expensive paper and pens, paint and crayons, affected me to the point I never wanted to leave. She bought me pencils, erasers, paints and cartridge paper, which was not cheap and was an absolute pleasure to work with. I never forgot that special day when I realized that she believed in me and made it happen. Sketching and drawing became my medicine and relieved anxiety and tension. This was something I could do on my own. No team members, no coach, no ball. Whew!

I continued on with my art and regularly used it as a way to spend time alone in a rather full and rowdy house. Heather and her new husband and child lived with us also, moving into the lounge and setting it up as their bedroom. So many people in a four-bedroom house with one toilet and a bath. How did we cope? In today's world, we just wouldn't. Eventually, they moved into their own flat, which was a bit of a treat as we had another family household to visit, albeit a tiny one.

I remember life returning to a kind of normality, mainly that we had our lounge back and that Mum and I could once again snuggle on the sofa, watching old movies where she would explain who the actors were and whether she thought they were talented enough or liked them at all. In very old movies, when it screened a close up of, say, Grace Kelly or Doris Day or a similar beauty, the picture would always turn a kind of fuzzy, sort of as if it was trying to make you react in a different way. When I questioned this with Mum, she said it was because the subject was so beautiful that the camera just couldn't cope or function properly. It was years later that I heard that in the golden days of Hollywood movies, the director would smear Vaseline or something similar on the lens to make the starlets close-up shot look different than anything else they had just filmed. I preferred my mother's explanation… It was far more romantic.

I also had my great aunties around in these days — my nana Fergusson's sisters — Vera, and Cassie, who lived in Auckland. I remember them as glamourous women, like nana, dripping with pearls, blue hair, horn-rimmed glasses and complete with fox furs. However, Cassie was a little more risqué and regularly wore trousers and dyed her hair a shade of auburn. The trousers were more to cover up the fact that she had a wooden leg as she had ignored earlier warnings to get her ulcerated leg checked years before and it went septic to the point that you could apparently smell it when you entered her house.

'Here he comes!' these old aunties would shriek. 'Here comes lover boy!' This was their pet name for me, as I constantly wanted to be around them, kiss them, sit on their knees and listen to the latest gossip, which there was plenty of because they would chat and chat and chat. I loved my time with them and I loved them dearly. As each of them disappeared, I felt a real sense of loss as those moments with them around were some of the happiest I had felt up to that point. It was an environment that I felt I belonged to, before, once again, I was forced to play outside or join a team sport or make an effort in something else that I just didn't want to do.

We would spend a lot of time in Auckland in the days of the aunties and stayed with Dad's cousin, Eunice, and hubby, Rex. Their kids became our best mates in the big city and I was amazed that they had so much entertainment right on their doorstep but still had time for their "country cousins", as Eunice affectionately called us. We would all stay together in a three-bedroom house in Mangere and the four adults would leave us kids to be responsible while they headed out for dinner and drinks. Six of us and four of them — Shelley, Adele, Gail, and Graham, who was the only boy and a massive sook, even more than I was and I was the best at tantrums.

When we got bored, we would go through the phone book and make prank calls to random people with random names, like phoning Mrs Salt and asking for the pepper, or the good old favourite, 'Hello, is your fridge running?' Great fun until we got a phone call from the post office, who ran the telephone exchange, insisting on talking to our parents. Not a happy ending for us.

We would play all sorts of sporty kids' games like climbing trees, hide-and-seek, etc., but Gail and I were experts at hopscotch and skipping, which I'm sure she cheated at constantly but never admitted to. Shelley was very quiet and reserved, however, Adele, being a little older, would be heading out regularly to the latest mall to smoke and meet boys with my sister, Desma, in tow. I remember pleading with them to let me go but I was too young and too uncool to hang out with them and no doubt I would've blabbed about the goings on. Those holidays were such good fun and forged lifelong friendships. I yearned for a big city life away from the small town I felt tied to — I never wanted to go home after fun holidays in the big smoke.

School was a challenge for me… Although I always managed to have a group of friends, I was always a little timid and kept skipping around the outskirts of events, conversations or any activities. I remember my first day at Tokoroa North School. Mum got me ready with new cloths and a snazzy haircut and was constantly trying to keep me excited about the prospect of branching out alone into the big scary land of classrooms, teachers, structure, playgrounds and lots of other kids that I didn't know at the time and wasn't really interested in meeting.

On *that* day the walk up to the gate took about two or three minutes as we were only a couple of houses away from this big, overwhelming place. I remember being led into the classroom and being introduced to a middle-aged woman with a kind face and soft voice. I had one eye on her and the other on my mother as the teacher took me forward to meet the rest of the class. I saw Mum slip away out of the classroom door... I remember a feeling of desperation which was quickly replaced with delight when I saw some of the activities the other kids were doing, so I decided to stay and see what happened... Just this once!

The bell rang for interval and, thinking that I had probably had enough for the day, I sauntered off, out the school gates, leaving my brand-new school bag complete with a packed lunch that consisted of wild pork bacon sandwiches, an apple, and a small pack of raisins behind with the rest of my new classmates. My mother was so shocked when I walked into the kitchen at home, exclaiming that it wasn't so bad, but I'd had enough for the day and wouldn't be going back any time soon. Before I even knew what hit me, I was spun around and marched straight back to class in time for the end of interval... My mother didn't muck about. I stayed put as I knew that sneaking home again wouldn't be all that wise.

No sooner had I started school than I fell ill. I remember the nausea I experienced and being too sick to get out of bed. I'm sure my mum thought initially that I was faking it because getting me to school every day was on her top ten challenges list at that time. I also remember feeling so bad that I was constantly throwing up to the point that blood appeared in the bowl and I was turning more yellow with each passing day. Mum rushed me to Dr Rawley — the same doctor that had delivered all 9lb, 4oz of me just over five years before.

All I remember is trying to stay awake in the car and feeling really ill as Mum flew into every corner... She was never a slow driver and couldn't abide motorist who were! There were numerous tests and bottles of medication galore that had to be forced down me by any means possible. I would fight with anyone who was on duty to administer said drugs, usually because of the foul taste and texture. Yuck!

A couple of days passed and I was still flat on my back in bed, unable to move, when the phone call came. It was hepatitis and all manner of people arrived at our house. I was quickly moved into a separate room... Dr Rawley was there most days and my parents also had a visit from the health department to follow up on how on earth I contracted it! They checked through the house, the drains and anywhere that the infection could've come from, but to no avail. The school was notified, and the necessary precautions taken. My parents were shocked and mortified, especially my mum, who worried what everybody would think of her and that her house was dirty enough for one of her children to contract such a disease.

It is a mystery to this day to how I caught hepatitis, but it stays in my memory how sick I felt at that very young age. My school mates missed my participation in class and when they were told that I wouldn't be back to school for at least three months, they all banded together and drew pictures, made cards and flower arrangements and all were delivered by my teacher with the kind face and the soft voice. I felt so special and couldn't wait to get out of bed and back to the classroom. Quite the turnaround for me.

I made a full recovery and returned to school a bit of a celebrity after my brush with death... Of course, I talked it up a bit to make it sound more dramatic... Never let the truth get in the way of a good story.

It was at that time that I cemented some lifelong friendships and because Tokoroa was a small town, those friendships usually took you through primary, intermediate and high school. My buddy, David, was one such lifelong friend. He suffered from a genetic disease that made him quite frail and unable to participate in much rough and tumble sport or activities. I was always the kind of kid to back the underdog or be fiercely protective of people who couldn't do it themselves.

David and I bonded and became the best of mates. He lived on his parents' dairy farm, which was within bicycling distance of our house. His mum and dad seemed older than mine but were always welcoming. Their house was small and a little untidy and his mother, Lucy, had a special lounge that was hardly used and was impeccable... It was as if it was lost in time with its floral carpet, curtains and doilies. If I was staying the night, I would often wander in there just to see if anyone was there or if anything had changed. I was enchanted by it.

When we got bikes, I really wanted a Raleigh Twenty, but got a Raleigh Safari. This was very uncool and not only that... It was also orange! My brother, Rex, got a full-sized Raleigh Cruiser and my buddy, David, got a Chopper! The Chopper was *the* kids cycle of the 70s and is still talked about today with envy if you never had one.

I would cycle like mad to David's farm with my overnight bag on my carrier. The last few hills up Matanuku Road where he lived were a real killer so as I approached my Aunty Oriel's house on the same road, I knew that that was the stretch of road to get my speed up so I'd pedal like the clappers to get enough speed to make it to the top. I don't ever remember making it without getting off my rather small-wheeled bicycle. I'd push it to the point just before David would see me coming then I would quickly jump back on and fake that I had actually made it. He never believed me anyway.

Along with his hereditary condition, David also suffered from extreme asthma and would often land himself in hospital because of our antics. He was also incredibly thin, which was a side effect of his illness, unlike his bestie — me — who was still at my chubby, fish and chips with lashings of coca cola stage.

Now and again, we would pitch a tent way down the back of the farm and go survivor style for the weekend. We'd be set up with enough food, drink and our tape recorders to play the music we had recorded from the Top 40 the week before. Torches were always a must as it was so bloody dark in the back of beyond and we were still a teeny bit scared of the dark.

We'd light a fire and cook our dinner and usually David's younger brother, Michael, would have to come along as he'd seen us steal a bottle of David's father's beers and he'd tell if we didn't let him.

We would cook our tea, drink the beer, then retire into the darkness, listening to music, recording ourselves and telling ghost stories until we were too petrified to sleep. By the time Sunday rolled around and it was time to cycle home, we would be absolutely shattered. On Monday at school, we would argue who was the most terrified during our outback adventure. I still have some of the recordings we made and play them back every now and then, which is hilarious to listen to as we are all screaming like girls!

School time with my best mate David

David would come and stay at my house from time to time, but his farm was way more exciting. He arrived for a sleepover one weekend and brought with him the new album release of *War of the Worlds*, which we played loudly on Mum's record player with the speakers hooked up and hanging out our wash house window… The whole neighborhood must have heard it and we learnt the narration and sounds, word for word. I still think of David when I hear that soundtrack with Richard Burton's deep, velvet voice narrating on the original tracks. I think of it and all the fun we had as kids and teenagers every time I visit David's grave in the Tokoroa cemetery. He had a full Catholic Mass, followed by burial in 2018. I walked graveside to drop a flower into his final resting place and as I looked down at his casket to say goodbye, I noticed how unnecessarily deep they had put him and also that they had lowered him down crooked! I smirked as I bid him farewell because I knew he would've found that irritatingly funny. Rest in eternal peace, my bestest buddy.

Rock Me Gently — Andy Kim 1974

By the time I hit intermediate school, I started to change both physically and emotionally. My body was changing, and I was noticing the change in those around me also. My own sexuality was creeping in, but I was totally oblivious at first of what direction it was taking me. It was predetermined at birth and no matter what I did, it was always going to shape me accordingly.

I don't know if it's a "poof thing" or just an individual human thing however whatever it is , it affected not only my interest in sport or any outdoor activities but certainly my ability to want to compete in any of the pre-mentioned.

The myth around this is that as a Fergusson male, I would automatically be the first to stand up and be included in any sports team, hunting activities or the like but in reality I was horrified EVERY time I was confronted with the activities and felt so ashamed that I just couldn't grasp what was going on and how the others competing had so much passion and aggression around the happenings.

If I was forced to compete as I was regularly, I would pray that I would go un-noticed and overlooked by the rest of the 'team' and prayed that the ball would never come my way. When it did, I would gulp and try to participate but was regularly humiliated by the actions that followed and was the subject of ridicule from disappointed team members. I was the boy that no one picked for their side, I was the boy that never made any winning moves, I was the boy who was so ashamed that I couldn't perform or indeed had any idea how to.

I started to pay more attention to my appearance, therefore more time in front of the mirror at home to make sure I mastered the look just right. Mum and my sisters had started buying apple shampoo and conditioner which I was forbidden to use but I'd help myself anyway. Conditioner was like a miracle potion that made my shaggy cut, thick hair flow like a movie star, so I used it at every opportunity. 'Who's been bloody using my good shampoo!' I heard coming from the bathroom. I never said a word, but it was obviously me as my hair was as shiny as Liz Taylor's engagement ring.

It was at this time my body started to sprout hair in really embarrassing places. The kind of places that you could never discuss with your parents or even friends... The early 70s in small-town NZ seems quite prudish now, looking back, and there was no one I could ask about this rather weird occurrence. I initially tried shaving it all off but to no avail as it grew back twice as fast, so I just went with it. Phys Ed. and swimming classes were a bit of a challenge as I was always hiding from the other guys in the changing room, but they were obviously going through exactly the same dilemma.

The next obstacle — you guessed it — controlling random hard-ons. These would occur at the most inappropriate times and were hard to conceal (excuse the pun). The bed wetting was becoming less frequent; however, it was always so embarrassing when Mum had to call my teachers just before we headed off to school camp to let them know there could be an issue... Oh my God, I just wanted to fall in a hole in the ground and never be seen again.

Our dad, not only being a bushman, was still out pig-hunting and deer-stalking most weekends and would take anyone who wanted to go along. My brothers, of course, were always keen and even some cousins were first up on the list to head out in the early hours of a Saturday or Sunday morning. It wasn't my thing but some of my earliest memories are of being out in the bush, climbing trees, waiting for Dad to return with the dogs and any other hangers-on.

Now I had a choice to go or not, I would always opt to stay at home with Mum. If Dad returned with a massive boar or deer, we would all run outside to marvel at the result of a long day of hunting in the bush around Tokoroa. We would then all return inside to watch TV, Mum cooking and sisters sitting at the dining room table. Dad or my brothers would then drag in the catch-of-the-day carcass, hang it up on the hooks where the baby bouncer would usually go, and start to skin the pig or whatever it was. I still remember the sound of the skin and pieces of fat hitting the newspaper that was laid underneath to stop any blood or meat getting on the floor. None of us even blinked at this regular occurrence as it was part of our life and was how we could afford to eat.

One of these evenings marked the end of Mum's wedding dress as our bushman father, on another skinning and beheading session, couldn't find anything to catch the remnants of blood and meat so reached for anything out of the cupboard, throwing it down on the floor, then wrapping it all up afterwards and throwing it in the bin. Mum screamed as she realized her favorite memento had gone forever.

Dad, working in the bush with a chainsaw, would sometimes cut himself and these were not minor cuts but massive lacerations that needed stitches. We were always so excited when he would arrive home after work at night, running to see him and ask about his day. However, on the occasions that he was injured, he would drive up and just sit in the Land Rover. Mum knew that signal and she would drop everything and get into the vehicle with Dad and drive him to the hospital to have it cleaned up. We would always marvel at the number of stiches each time he returned. It was a hard job with many hazards, but our father was so stoic when it came to accidents or associated pain.

During this time, we had a new word to throw about. None but a privileged few even knew exactly what it meant. 'Wanker!' we would yell. As far as we were concerned, it was just another type of abuse... Never occurred to me that it described a certain type of self-abuse that almost certainly would send you blind if you were to take up this activity for a prolonged period of time. Yup, the penny dropped, and I was fascinated, eager to give it a whirl.

Not really knowing what I was doing. I took the opportunity at bath time, locked the door and soaped up as I knew nothing about personal lubricant and don't even think it was even readily available at that time, so away I went.

Well, I remember the sensation was so intense and mind-blowing that I thought, *well, this can't be good?* So I stopped immediately before anything else happened or, heaven forbid, I damaged something. It wasn't long before I was in there again, giving it another go... Boom! I got to the end and had an orgasm. I was horrified that I had gone too far and what was produced was more likely the result of some hideous disease or affliction, but just to make sure, I did it again and again. I loved it, it was like my own secret toy that I wanted to play with again and again. I did it at every opportunity, at every place I could! The secrecy and guilt that is attached to masturbation is immense, but totally unnecessary…

I also wondered if any of my mates had discovered it and how it worked and felt. It was at that time that the thought of some of the hot guys at school doing this as well got me a little excited but I sort of pushed those thoughts and fantasies to one side. It was just too foreign to deal with and I certainly couldn't accommodate the thought that I was a bit of a funny boy, surely not. Was I going to be *the* Fergusson who let the side down…? The one who brought shame on the family? My parents? No, no, no, this just was not an option I could even remotely consider. Nope.

It was in early '75 that "Ern", my grandfather (Fergusson), was diagnosed with terminal cancer, which had spread through his entire body. The whole family was in total shock that our family's Rangatira was destined to depart. We were totally ill-prepared for such an event and, to top it off, we were told that it wouldn't be far away.

I remember a few months before, when arriving for a visit with him and our nana, that he looked different and I just couldn't work out what it was. He had lost a lot of weight and he was always a solid 5ft 11 ¾ inches tall, with bronzed skin due to his Māori heritage that he was oh so proud of.

He started to look frail and was in and out of hospital. After he was operated on for the final time, he was sent home and told he wouldn't last past three months. I walked into the bedroom and he was propped up on his bed, reading the newspaper with his pajama shirt open, so as not to rub on his stiches. He was cut and sewn from under his chest to below his belly button. 'Gidday, boy,' he said and prompted me to come closer, so I did. I remember the sight of the large stitches and inflammation around the cut made me cringe. 'I won't bite,' he said softly to me, so I went closer. He must've seen me staring inquisitively at the rather large area. 'Doesn't hurt,' he promised, as I got closer. I don't remember much else about what we talked about and I was asked to leave as Mum, Dad and Dad's sisters fussed around making him comfortable and trying their best to make him eat.

He died on a Tuesday after being admitted back into Rotorua Hospital to manage his pain and, beforehand, all of us kids were ushered back home to Tokoroa. That's where we waited for that dreaded phone call. When it came, my brother, Ray, answered and we all rushed to be within listening distance. 'So, is he gone?' we heard Ray say. 'OK,' he said, 'I'll let them know.' He hung up the phone and told us our dear Ern had passed away. We all took off to different parts of the house to process the news.

I was in the middle of playing Mum's records so went back into the lounge. The next song on the album was a Kris Kristofferson song, *why me*, and it seemed appropriate, so I cranked up the volume. We knew he was in so much pain and wanted to go but he just didn't want to leave us — his family — and our nana. Our hearts were broken and from that day, Dad's family were never the same, or even as close as they had been in the past. He was our glue and he was gone.

We were taken to view his body when it was laid out. We walked in and up to the highly polished box. 'Here he is!' our mum exclaimed in her best smiley, calming voice. As I peered into the coffin, I saw an olive-skinned, thin man who looked nothing like my grandfather but then I saw the thin strip of grey hair on the sides of his head, which was pressed into a shiny, satin pillow. I realized that it was him, he really was dead, but how could he look so different? This was my first introduction — looking straight into the face of death and the grief that followed was so real. We supported our nana, Effie (Eppie), who was quite lost without her husband but eventually the acceptance of his death got us all through and we kept living, including Nana.

Returning to school, everyone was very sympathetic to my loss and I remember being one of the first people in my class to actually lose my grandad. Such a weird feeling, as death was the last thing you wanted to think about when you just turned thirteen.

Girlfriends — yup, no problems here getting them, swapping them for the next, hanging out with them. The only problem that I had was that they all became my good mates and then I hit a barrier. Sure, I went through the motions and dated — or, as we called it in those days, "to go around with", which meant that you were an item — but it never really sat right with me. But the alternative was definitely not an option so I kept any sign of it locked away so deep down that it would be impossible to find out or uncover.

I can actually pinpoint the two occasions that I had the self-realization that I was definitely a poof, funny boy, homo, queer, fag — all the names that I had heard over many years but just managed to duck.

The first was when I was changing around the posters on my bedroom wall, much to my mother's disapproval as it meant more drawing pin holes in her new wallpaper which she would change out every year or so. I was a huge Donny and Marie Osmond fan and would eagerly await the latest *Tiger Beat* magazine, which featured them regularly along with free posters that I would rip out and hang on my wall or ceiling, as all teenagers did with their favorite pop stars of the day. So, here I am, placing this latest pic of my adored duo when I caught a glimpse of Donny's partially open shirt and I noticed he had hair on his chest. I was drawn to this image like a magnet and fascinated — what he was like totally naked and what he would smell like, taste like… Oh my God… Stop!

This needed to *stop* and go away. Maybe it was just a phase and it would just correct itself, or so I hoped. I felt so much shame that I was so attracted to another guy, but the feeling was so strong, and I actually fell in love with not only the poster but the man himself, which made me so moody and miserable. One of my close cousins, Bronny, was also a huge fan and would write to me with all the latest gossip on our favorite singers and declare her undying love for Donny, *my* Donny, and she just naturally assumed I adored Marie Osmond. I was so jealous that she could openly proclaim her love and attraction for this man and mine was locked away — it was total torture.

The second "fairy dust" moment came when I was in form 2 at intermediate school. I was moved to a different class that year, away from my regular mates, and my new teacher was a guy in his mid-twenties, I guess — Mr R. He was an attractive guy for his time, with longish, styled hair and a full beard. I thought he was kind of nice but never really took too much notice... Until the 1976 gala day.

Our class was in charge of the sausage sizzle fundraiser and we all turned up on the day to help. It was a beautiful, sunny, warm day and the crowds that attended school gala days in the 1970s were full-on and very supportive as it was truly a major social event. Our teacher, Mr R, complete with short shorts and a rather tight tee, was in charge of the BBQ and the rest of us handed out bread and sauces, etc.

The temperature soared and we were all feeling the effects of the stifling heat, then, all of a sudden, my teacher slowly started to take off his top to relieve the heat. I remember the moment as if it was in slow motion... As I turned to look, his T-shirt was slowly being peeled off... Over his tight, flat stomach, revealing a snail trail of hair from his navel that disappeared down to his shorts. Then up, up, the T-shirt went, over his manly chest and then his head, and to finish, he shook his head to readjust his hair.

This moment was to stick in my mind for decades as the moment that I realized that there was no doubt that I was attracted to men. It wasn't really about the teacher, Mr R, but more about me noticing every part of a man's body and responding with an inner, deep arousal that I had never experienced up until that time. The fantasy pop star feelings had been replaced with an underlying urge to know more about what it would be like to touch and be touched by another guy.

My attendance at class was never a problem as it felt good to be close to the teacher and it was so important that he liked me. I guess it was like a crush on a real man that I could spend all day, five days a week, with. I worked really hard that year and my grades were better than usual, receiving a certificate of excellence for art that same year. I loved it and it made me get more and more into sketching and photography rather than any sport activity at all. My parents were still pushing me to do at least some sport, so I weakened and took up hockey. I never understood the rules but went hard until the bloody hard hockey ball bounced up off an opposition stick and smacked me right in the gob... I never went back.

By the time I hit high school, I had become a little more careful about who might find out my dark, evil secret and I clutched the truth — my truth — close to my chest. The thought of anyone finding out consumed my every thought, the horror and realization of what my life would be like was overwhelming… More ridicule, more guilt, more shame and self-disgust, resulting in an overwhelming feeling of loneliness. Bang! I kept it all locked away, deep, deep inside me where no one could see it.

Girls followed me around and again, as at intermediate school, I had no lack of girlfriends who either got my mum's approval or not. She always had an opinion of who was more suited and the reasons why. It was as if she needed to ensure I was on the right track and she definitely wanted to keep me on the "straight" and narrow. Looking back, it was if she knew the unthinkable even then.

My top lip sprouted a dark fuzz that kind of resembled a soft moustache around this time and I contemplated a trial shave with Dad's extremely sharp Gillette hand razor, complete with Old Spice shaving foam… In walks Myrna, questioning what I was doing as my brother, Rex, had shaved his entire face, including his eyebrows, a few months before. I explained that I thought it was time I started shaving and I was intrigued by her response. 'You need something to show that you're a man, so best you keep the mo,' she stated. My own mother thought I was either too pretty or too camp and I needed the so called "mo" to rough me up? I shaved it anyway as a mark of protest about that comment.

In the late 1970s, there was no queer information or reading material at all that I could access so I was stumbling around, picking up snippets of material as I knew nothing about homosexuals other that they were to be ridiculed or ignored. I was watching TV one night when a promo came on to highlight an upcoming movie. *The Naked Civil Servant* — The story of Quentin Crisp, an openly gay man in the UK. My ears pricked up and I made a mental note of when it was scheduled to play. By that stage, we had a second television in my brother's bedroom so I planned to watch it in there as he wouldn't be home. My parents were in the main lounge, catching up on their regular programmes, when I excused myself, saying that I wanted to watch the TV in the bedroom so I could lie down.

The movie started and I had one ear on the TV set in front of me and one ear focused on anyone walking towards the bedroom door. My heart was pounding, and I quickly changed the channel if I heard footsteps heading up the hallway. The movie was fascinating, albeit interrupted, but I totally understood the story and was amazed that some men could actually live a "normal" life full of normal things, except they were homos. It depicted gay bars, gay relationships and even gay bashings and homophobia, depicting it in a way that was all quite before its time.

At the end of the movie I thought, *well, it's good that I'm not that gay*, and that I would probably just grow out of it as I was totally different to those depicted. I was reasonably "straight-acting", or so I thought, which in my mind meant that I could go on and live a "normal" life without being subjected to the horror of exposure and ridicule.

Armed with this information, I cruised on with life whilst keeping myself in check, nurturing my friendships and dating different girls at school. Every now and again, there was someone, either friend or foe, who questioned my façade. Of course, I would fly into damage control, which meant total shock and denial, which was not only external — I started to believe my own bullshit. I never even contemplated that I could come out… I never even knew what the phrase "coming out" meant.

Mum and Dad had a tight set of friends and one couple that they had recently befriended were regularly included in group gatherings. This couple had a son, Michael, who seemed to take a liking to me as we had a lot in common. He was a couple of years older than me, kind of geeky, with glasses, and he was really keen on tropical fish. He had a massive tank in his house with all the set-up of heaters, lights and filtering equipment, which I thought was very cool and a far cry from my fish tank that sat on our kitchen bench at home.

I would drag Mum along to Michael's house to show her how very flash we would look if we upgraded to tropical fish but, alas, the answer was a flat "no" — p a very cruel thing to do when you had already pictured it in your mind and how happy it made you. To compensate for this terrible disappointment, I began to spend more and more time at Michael's house, setting off on my bike at every opportunity and as he lived just down the road, I could be there in a matter of minutes. We started having sleepovers and camping out in his backyard... Great fun!

It was during this time that Michael brought up the subject of sex and of course my ears pricked up (so to speak). We discussed penis size and the growth of hair that started to happen around our nether regions. We were both so curious, but I definitely remember knowing which way this information-gathering was going. At no time were there discussions about girls or their bodies, as it was all about us and ours, so the time came to "put your money where your mouth is" and front up.

I can't really remember if it happened while camping or in his bedroom, but happen, it did! We started to experiment by showing each other our dicks which was always a little embarrassing as mine was rock-hard before I even got it out and his was quite a bit bigger than mine but, not one to hold back, out it came. Eventually we started to fondle and play with each other to the point of total arousal but never orgasm and if that had happened, I think we both would have got the fright of our lives and probably would have thought we'd broken it!

By this time, I had totally forgotten about his fabulous display of tropical fish because what we were doing was far more entertaining and it felt so bloody good, so we continued on for quite some time. Matt told me about anal sex and mentioned that it was something we should try, and I was so far into the whole experiment that I was totally up for it. I was amazed and infatuated with how much he knew about all the "ins and outs" of gay sex and I wanted to know more and more. We tried on a couple of occasions to penetrate each other, but we were both way too scared of the "poo" consequences that we ended up just toying with it and both laughing about how "yuck" it really was and probably not for us anyway.

We hung out for quite a while and continued with our body explorations; however, other people were starting to question our closeness and I was also getting a reputation at school for being a bit of a poof for hanging out with the slightly effeminate Michael. This criticism, not surprisingly, also came from my brother, Rex, as he looked for every opportunity for "Terry humiliation". So, because of this being a little too close for comfort, I started to distance myself from this friendship with benefits.

Because of my absence from the friendship, Michael came to see me. I freaked out and stupidly asked Rex to lie for me. 'Tell him I've gone out,' I pleaded, and he agreed he would go along with it. I flew down the passage to my parents' bedroom and slid under the bed and waited for the all-clear.

I heard muffled talking and then footsteps toward me, then Rex's voice, stating loudly, 'He's under the bed!'

Horrified, I flew out of the darkness to see Rex smirking, with a rather puzzled Michael at his side. 'Oh, I was just looking for the cat,' I explained and with that, my brother gave me a last grin and left the room.

Eventually, I lost touch with my friend due to me purposely staying away. I did hear sometime later that he moved away with his family when his dad got a transfer, but I never heard from him again. Looking back, I must have gone into self-protection mode to avoid the "big secret" being exposed and I thought that I had way too much to lose, so Michael was a consequence of that.

Pop Muzik — M 1979

"We can't be everything to everyone and still be totally true to ourselves"

High school meant a big change as I was definitely on the way to being a real grown up. It meant I went straight into being a "turd", which is Kiwi slang for someone in the third form at high school... Third equals turd.

It was so degrading but at least I wasn't in it alone. My friends, including David, were also thrown onto the "turd" wagon, which made you fair game for the seniors. Fortunately, it would only last for twelve months and even the seniors would lose interest eventually if you didn't bite back too much.

Halfway through that first year, I was cornered by a group of male fifth formers, who thought they would become a little cooler if they picked on a "turd" so I was surrounded and picked up off the ground and commanded to dance a jig. When I flatly refused, I was roughed up a bit and reinstructed to dance and make it snappy. Just at the moment, I heard a voice say, 'Drop him!' I was dropped at speed and turned around to see my brother, Rex, standing in front of us. With his words still fresh, the fifth formers scurried off, leaving me to thank my brother for saving me. However, all I got in response was a look of disappointment and annoyance as he walked off with his mates. He had defused the situation but still wanted nothing to do with me publicly. We never really spoke of it again.

Homophobia and the bullying that seemed to go hand in hand with it raised its ugly head about this time in my life. I didn't even know that such a thing even existed, but I was soon to be faced with it for the first time. I was hanging out with my school friends (which were mainly girls) on a Friday night in town as late-night shopping was such a cool thing at this stage. We would walk around and around the block, darting into the Disc Inn — our local record shop that had all the latest LPs on display and blaring out of speakers in and out of the shop.

We were stopped as we walked by a group of Polynesian guys who obviously wanted to impress my girlfriends and come across as big, strong men. Targeting me, they asked the girls who their *poofy* mate was and started to push me around between them whilst constantly calling me "poof", "pansy", "homo".

Eventually, I was pushed up against a wall and punched so hard in the mouth that I must have been knocked out for a few minutes. I remember my friends screaming at the guys to leave me alone and when I eventually stood up, they had scarpered. They inside of my mouth had been cut by the impact of the punch against my teeth and my lip was blowing up like a balloon. I begged my friends not to ever talk about this event as I was so embarrassed and ashamed of why I had been targeted so just wanted it to go away. I even managed to hide it from my parents and family, telling them that I had smacked it on a steel bike stand, which kind of explained the injury, and bathing my lip in cold water or packs of ice when no one was looking.

Still wanting to find my place and be good at something other than art, I chose to look at languages and was trying to choose between French, German or Te Reo. Overall, Māori language and studies had not long been included into the school curriculum. Ern, my grandad Fergusson, was part Ngāpuhi and our family roots rest in the far north, more specifically, the Hokianga. But that was all we knew, and it wasn't really discussed at any great length as Dad wasn't really all that interested in family genealogy and my Grandad Ern was long gone.

I chose Te Reo as it was something that I could identify with as it was part of me, albeit a small part. The subject and course gave me a lot of NZ history, which wasn't really taught in our schools at that time. It was fascinating to me and the romantic side of the legends taught to us was right up my alley as I could picture in my mind my interpretation as it was taught. Māori language and the different dialects proved quite the challenge as it's a bloody hard one to learn but two of my teachers were so supportive and seemed to be genuinely interested in my progress. Mrs T and Mrs TE were fluent in the language and passionate about the culture and spiritual aspect of Te Māori, which I felt so drawn to, so it was only a matter of time before I found myself enrolled to be part of the associated performing culture group at Forest View High School.

Being a smaller, plumpish young man, with a voice that hadn't quite cracked, I had to try that little bit harder to be heard, especially during haka performances, as I was surrounded by huge post-pubescent guys whose voices bellowed over mine. But I didn't care, I loved it.

When we performed, I was constantly singled out by some in the audience. They'd say, 'Ko wai te pakeha nei?' Meaning, "who is the pakeha in the group". It annoyed the crap out of me as, when I was performing with the others, I felt totally engaged and "raceless", if there is such a word. Racism in some ways was apparent, but not to me. I was a descendant of a NZ Māori, but because my complexion was paler than my fellow group members, I was singled out. However, I refused to let it affect or upset me and I continued with the learnings.

In time, close friendships were formed between myself and other members of my class and culture group. Soon we were performing all over the north island and making the local news for winning competitions. We practiced on weeknights and over the weekends and I had a hard time convincing Mum that it was just about getting our performances right. She thought I was out "getting up to tricks" and really, I wasn't. I was simply so engrossed in the language and the cultural side of my classes that I wanted to know more and more. It was definitely a sense of belonging to something that made me happy and taught me about passion.

Mrs T would often have practices at her house in Tokoroa and we would all turn up to learn our parts. During this time, her mother, Maria Maniapoto, would be staying over and she would happily get involved with the teachings and enjoy the singing. Mrs T and her mum were related in a direct line to the great chief, Rewi Maniapoto, and we would listen to many accounts of his actions during the Māori land wars. We even got to perform at the great ariki memorial in the middle of small town, Kihikihi, in the Waikato which had locals pouring out of homes and shops to watch. We all felt so proud as a group and I felt a belonging and feeling of safety that I had be searching for.

Not long after these events, Mrs T's mother, Maria Maniapoto, was diagnosed with terminal cancer. Her passion for what we were doing and her being part of it was so strong that she based herself in her daughter's house, where we had been constantly practicing, during her final days. Eventually, she passed away and we were all rounded up to head to Mangatoatoa Marae, where she was to be buried. The experience of being part of this tangi, or funeral, was amazing. We watched this small but important woman laid to rest alongside her whānau. We heard and watched as elders talked about Maria and the importance of her bloodline, from the great chief, Rewi, and beyond. Although I only knew her for a short time, the impact of her being in my life lasts to this day, as she showed me how to *kia mau ki to Māoritanga* — hold fast to my Māori heritage. She wasn't my blood family but the messaging around being proud of who you are and the belief around this still holds strong with me today. Mrs T kept all the teaching going and used her mother's death and tangi as something we could learn from and I did.

The overall sense of belonging that was felt as being part of this group was so calming and really helped me concentrate on my lessons and kept me at school. The group moved on to more events and fundraising for our uniforms and travel for our trips, which meant more weekend activities and time away from home. Mum, again, was questioning my motives and also asking if I really was where I said I was. This, as a teenager, was so annoying as I was involved in something that really did make me happy so the consequences were that I was constantly uptight and making sure I checked in as often as possible to keep the peace.

A few of my group members became close friends and we started hanging out more and more in and out of school. Sometimes, Mum would make an effort and invite a select few of these mates to stay over, probably just to see what the dynamics were and who, if anyone, I was chasing or was sweet on. I gave nothing away as I really wasn't that interested in anyone at that time.

A group of us got together to show off our award-winning skills and performed at Dad's fiftieth birthday party, giving a stellar and touching performance to mark the occasion in front of family and friends. It was such a proud moment and was received with cheers and thunderous applause. That was a time that my interests crossed over to my family and I could prove that what I was passionate about really did matter.

It was about this time that I met Nyda through someone from the culture group. She would often show up at our practices and be at my mate Sharmane's house as she was best mates with her sister. She was of Māori descent but had no real interest in the culture or what we were doing as a group, just really up for the social side of things, which was totally fine with me as I was always up for making new friends. We started seeing more of each other, alone and with the group, but nothing happened as I was still a virgin. The thought of anything going a little bit too far was a bit spooky for me as I hadn't quite figured out what goes where and what happened after that, so I just avoided it.

My parents thought I was up to all sorts but I really wasn't, I was just enjoying the company of people that enjoyed being around me. The girls in my small group of friends kept trying to make moves on me, which was great for my overall image but I was more taken with the guys in the first XV rugby team of even some of Rex's mates or my sisters' boyfriends who frequented our house during the late seventies. I was really spoilt for choice but obviously had to keep all this admiration to myself… There was nobody at all that I could confide in.

Phys Ed was a real challenge for me as it took me back to those old feelings of being totally worthless and useless at sport. The teacher of this dreaded subject picked this up, along with another couple of kids in my class, and rode us to the point of ridicule. It was as if he got off on humiliating the underachievers in sport. I grew to hate him and begged Mum and Dad to get me out of his class but Rex piped up, stating that Mr Chambers was a great guy and I just needed to try harder in his class. So, I had to stay on his teaching pleasure. He was a total prick and so was my brother for making sure I took all that was served up.

The exams at school hit and a few of my friends started to drop out of school, including my mate, David, who went to work on his parents' farm, and also a few of the senior members of our performing group who got jobs and left. I tried hard to concentrate on my studying and sat the exams and as expected, doing extremely well in my favorite subjects and dismally in my not so hot ones, and, yes, Chambers flunked me in Phys Ed.

All of this meant that I would need to return and do the fifth form for a second time! This was a daunting prospect as I didn't want to be seen as a total loser by returning to repeat the previous year.

Everything was changing, even at home. Heather had more children with Joe, Gloria had married her boyfriend and left, Ray had bought his own house and left, Desma had gone flatting with a friend, which left just Rex and I with Mum and Dad at home.

I struggled with the loss of friends and struggled with the way that everyone seemed to be moving on or away. I definitely thought that I should be making a more positive move and going back to school in 1980 was not an option in my mind. I needed to convince my parents to let me leave Forest View High School and get on with my fabulous life… I had no idea at all what would make it fab but I wanted to pursue it regardless.

I chose my moment carefully, waiting until my parents retired to their bedroom, then I jumped up and stood at the end of their bed, pleading with them to let me leave. I promised that I would hunt every day for the right job and if I didn't get one, I would sign up for the dole until I got one so, no matter what, I could pay my way. The answer was, 'Don't be ridiculous! You are too young!' But I pleaded and cried and stomped my feet until I got a 'We'll think about it and talk in the morning, OK?' I agreed and went to bed.

In the morning, Dad had already left for the bush by the time I got up and Mum was sitting at the kitchen table, drinking tea and smoking a cigarette. 'OK,' she said as I came into the room, 'you can leave school at the end of the term but you must sign up for the dole straight away and manage your own money.' I squealed and thanked her repeatedly.

I made the appropriate enquires and completed all the right paperwork to leave my school life behind me. There was a major feeling of loss as I said goodbye to members of my performing group and class and also the two teachers who taught me so much about who I really was and how to express it.

I walked away from the school gates with mixed emotions, leaving my remaining friends and the history we had created within those grey concrete block buildings. But I was so happy that I could finally be free from the noose around my neck called "education" and all the rules that went along with it. How silly I was, looking back, as your school years are some of the best years of your life.

Forest View High School Culture Club

Do that to me one more time — Captain & Tenille, 1979

My freedom was short lived as I applied and was accepted as an apprentice glazier at a local firm in Tokoroa and started work almost immediately. I was hurled into working life and struggled with how grown-up it was and how I had to comply to more rules than I had at school, or at least it felt that way. My boss was a short, irritating man who demanded I made the tea at every break; I became an expert tea-maker except I was actually there to learn the craft of glazing.

There were two other older guys working in the same building who helped show me as much as possible within a busy work schedule, which helped me pick up the basics but there was nothing that gave me the feeling that I was actually being trained. Yup, I bloody hated it and found it difficult to be anything but sullen when I carried out my duties of tea-making or running to catch the truck on the way to a job that had been driven off just enough to make me run after it, much to the boss' entertainment. I was trapped, once again, with people I just didn't like or understand and I struggled to find any happy time during the long days.

Nyda, the girl I had met through school friends, would regularly meet me for lunch and we would catch up some nights and catch a movie. I knew she fancied me but I was being very aloof, kind of amazed that she persevered.

The local funeral director was located in the same block where I worked and one day at morning tea (yes, of course I was making the bloody tea!), I was asked to make an extra cup for the funeral director himself, who appeared just in time for me to ask how he took it. He was a tall, good-looking Māori guy, dressed in a three-piece suit with dark, silky hair and a dark, bushy moustache, and extremely shining shoes. As I looked at him to ask if he would like any sugar, he smiled at me but it wasn't just an ordinary friendly smile, it was a knowing smile that made me feel an overwhelming sexual attraction.

It took me totally by surprise as I was had just turned seventeen and was in a totally "straight" environment, but there it was and he knew at a glance that I was interested. Well, put it this way, gay men have a certain knowing and can spot another queer at one hundred meters, or it certainly seems that way. His name was Paul; he was an extremely successful undertaker and an openly gay man. He oozed sex appeal and I remember that he always smelt so good as he obviously had a huge selection of all the latest fragrances, excluding Brut or Old Spice, of course!

'And who do we have here?' he asked as I handed him his tea.

"I'm Terry," I said as I cleared my throat nervously.

Here I was, face to face with someone that knew who I was with one glance, and I liked it, and I certainly liked him! From that day, he frequented our premises. This was especially exciting if I was on my own as he would stay longer and we would chat for what seemed like hours about all sorts, but at no time did he ever try anything, although I was praying nervously that he would. He did, however, invite me down to the funeral parlour to take a look around but I always refused as:

1. Funeral parlors scare the shit out of me.
2. I was shit scared of Paul, as I was a virgin.

How would I know what to do? Although there was no doubt in my mind that Paul would show me the way, so in my mind I would run through all sorts of scenarios and nearly wanked myself to death and rubbed the skin off it a few times thinking about him. Mum couldn't understand why the curtains next to my bed were going moldy. Well… What can I say? It was the only thing within arm's reach that could be used to clean myself up as I didn't want her to spot it on the sheets! My poor mum — I think she clicked in the end and washed my drapes on a regular basis.

The flirting between Paul and I went on the entire time I worked at the glaziers and I found myself looking for him at every opportunity and making sure I was within sight as he wandered past. My parents often talked about Paul as he was known in the community but I always commented that I only bumped into him irregularly during my working day as I didn't want them to know that we had any sort of connection.

My working environment started to crumble, as did my relationship with my boss and coworkers. I was frustrated that I was learning bugger all and I felt like a square peg in a round hole. We all, including my parents, agreed that a career in glazing wasn't for me and I left quickly after that and so my regular meet-ups and long conversations with Paul came to an abrupt halt.

I spent a few weeks collecting the unemployment benefit before Dad organized a job for me at Hutt timber sawmill and you can only imagine how keen I was on that! It was as if nothing that I wanted to do for a living was available to me and I was beginning to think that my dreams for a fun, entertaining and glamourous life were beginning to fade. The absolute last thing I wanted to do is work in a sawmill! But it was part of the promise I made to my parents — that I would take any job if I could leave school — so I was backed into a corner.

I showed up on the first day and was given my "issue", which consisted of a couple of pairs of overalls, steel-capped work boots, a hardhat and multiple pairs of the thickest work socks I'd ever seen. Dad's mate, Terry, aka "Duke", was the foreman and what he said was gospel so I stuck alongside him and he taught me the ropes.

It was really physical work and I was put on an area called the resaw, which meant I had to inspect timber that needed to be sawn again and send it to the right area. The equipment was old and would constantly fail, with me in the middle, trying to unclog the areas that failed. Often, some of the other workers would take pity on me and help out, which I appreciated because I really didn't know what the hell I was doing. I became more and more stressed and more and more hopeless at what I was being paid to do. Duke realized that I wasn't a great fit on the resaw so I was given every second day under the mill, clearing out all the huge piles of sawdust that fell from the massive saws above. A thing I learnt is that if you leave fresh sawdust for a few days too long, it will start to smell, and smell it did! It stank and it just kept coming and coming so I kept shoveling and clearing. I liked the job down there so much more as I was away from all the other really hard-ass guys upstairs on the saws.

My weekends were my savior and I would head to Rotorua to stay with my cousins at every opportunity. There I would confide about how unhappy I was once again and how I needed to get the hell out. I stayed with my cousin, Val, and her hubby, Brian, a lot as her kids were about my age. Val was the oldest daughter of Mum's sister, Joan, so the family connection was strong and I always felt at home when I was with them. It really was my home away from home and we always had so much fun when we were together and Val would tell stories about my mum and dad when they were younger and living in Mamaku. She would also share info about my grandparents, George and Gert, as she was very close with them growing up and I, of course, had totally missed out on meeting them at all. It all made me feel so included and relaxed but the reality was that I had to return to a job that I felt so inept doing and also a town that I really didn't want to be in any more. The feeling of being dislodged and not fitting had really started to fuck me up...

I felt the only way I could survive was to make a drastic change.

Maybe — Sharon O'Neill, 1981

It was Easter 1980 and I had been in Rotorua until the Monday when I was picked up by Dad, who took me back to Tokoroa as I had a day shift at the mill starting at seven a.m., Tuesday. The ride home was quiet as I was thinking and planning my next move, so rather than telling my parents that this job gave me the absolute shits and disappointing them yet again, I planned my departure in a way so as not to make a massive scene.

At dinner, Mum asked if I enjoyed my stay and I replied, saying, 'It was bloody great and I really didn't want to come back.'

She replied, 'Don't be ridiculous, you've got work in the morning!"

I thought to myself, *have I really?*

The morning alarm (Dad) woke me up as always, yelling, 'C'mon, you'll be late!' He dropped me off at the mill gates every day as I still had no license or car. I had a bag that belonged to my grandfather, Ern, that I would pack my lunch and drinks in, but this time it was filled with a selection of my clothes, my toiletries and cash. The bag was bulging and was heavy but nobody seemed to notice as I waved Mum goodbye and jumped into Dad's Land Rover.

We chatted all the way to the Hutt timber gates and I jumped out quickly so he could carry on to where he was working further out of town. I went through the motions of walking through the gates, dragging my feet just long enough for him to disappear out of sight, and as soon as he did, I spun around and headed to the red public phone box on the main road. I had planned this phone call and had a pocketful of coins stashed from the night before.

The ring tone was loud in my ear and the woman on the end of the line said, 'Taxis. Where to?' I instructed her that I wanted to be taken back into town and the taxi was there within minutes. I was dropped off centrally and made my way down to the local park where I dumped my overalls in bushes and changed into jeans and T-shirt.

With a not so full and much lighter bag, I wandered up over State Highway 1 and into the nearest taxi rank and made eye contact with the driver at the front of the line. He jumped out and opened the back door for my bag. 'Where to, mate?' he asked.

I handed him a $20 note and said, 'How far will this get me out of town?'

We both agreed that he would take me as far as the Rotorua/Taupo turn-off. That, in my calculations, was about halfway to where I was heading. My heart was racing as no one knew that I was about to go AWOL and I knew the backlash would be huge but this was my window of opportunity and I was taking it.

Soon I found myself sitting on the side of the road at the turn-off and as I was gathering my thoughts about my next move, a car stopped alongside me. 'Terry!' she yelled. There was a girl that I went to school with and her father was taking her to Rotorua. 'Wanna ride?'

Well, I was in that car before she even finished the sentence. I told her a huge pack of lies that I was going to live with my nana who wasn't well — my nana was completely fine and I really didn't have *any* idea where I was going to live but I knew that I was never going back home.

We arrived in Rotorua and they graciously dropped me in the central city so I started with the next part of my plan. It felt like a scene from a movie and I was a fugitive on the run, going undercover. How dramatic!

The next part of the plan was to get a haircut and change my image. My hair was longish and I walked into the barbershop and asked them to cut it as short as possible (with a little bit of style, of course). The next step was to buy some new clothes and to get changed, also splashing out on a stylish pair of sunglasses to complete the outfit. I changed into my new clothes and then stashed my work bag with my other belongings behind trees in the government gardens.

It was early afternoon and I wondered if I had been reported missing from work yet or if anyone had spotted me leaving, but either way, I felt free and I was lapping this time up before the big storm of "who, what and where" hit.

I can't really remember how I managed to fill that day but whatever I did, I remember having one eye on the clock, wondering if anyone had noticed that I was gone yet, as it got closer and closer to the time that my father would be at the mill gates to pick me up.

That time came and went, the sun started to disappear, and I was still wandering around the streets of Rotorua, knowing the chaos that must be going on back home. I started to get frantic so, remembering that there was a phone box on a corner between the lake and Pizza Hut, I decided it was time to fess up and take the fallout. I didn't call home but instead phoned my cousin Val. To my relief, my cousin Louise answered and when she heard my voice, she squealed, 'It's him!' The phone was quickly handed over to Val, who calmly explained that my mother was frantic but not to worry as she would phone them and organize me to be picked up and brought to her.

So there it was, I had left and was determined to stay that way.

This day was a turning point in the relationship with my parents and by the time I was handed the phone to speak with them, I was totally prepared to stand my ground and, for the first time in my life, they listened. Mum cried and Dad just grumbled in the background.

It was decided that I would stay on with Val and Brian for the time being until everything settled down and after that we would make a plan to move forward. Well, there was no bloody way I was budging and I became a permanent resident in my cousin's house, along with her four other kids. With me, it meant that she had four teenagers on the go — Gary, Ray, Louise, and Eden, who was younger than us.

It was a new environment with a new set of rules to be adhered to but these people had saved me and I so appreciated that and I still do, to this day. I knew there was more and I had to take these steps to find it.

Life with Val and co. was fun and lively and I loved interacting on a daily basis with people I only really saw when we were on holiday together. I met new friends through them, found a series of jobs so I could pay board, purchased a ten-speed bike so I could get to work, sat my license and bought my first car — a 1965 Ford Anglia, rego plate CU3525. It was the most beautiful thing I had ever seen and I polished it twice a week until I was legally able to drive. In actual fact, it was a total shit heap that burned and leaked oil and constantly broke down, but I reckoned that it was shit-hot and it was all mine.

I was on the road and mobile and I drove it around so much that I was constantly running out of gas. I must have pushed that car to the nearest service station more than I ever drove it! With Gary, Ray, and Lou being close to my age, we became more and more like siblings and especially Ray and I as we were constantly in trouble.

Daring each other to do this seemed to be the way we broke any kind of boredom. Our ten-speed bikes were our life and Ray was the only person I had ever known who would pull the entire bike apart, polish all the pieces (including the ball bearings) then put it back together, nice and clean. He would also insist on vacuuming seconds before any guests we had invited over were due to arrive. We shared a room at the back of the garage that was affectionately known as "the batch".

This room became the central point of our social life and was the room where we promised not to be too loud, not to have mates over too often, not to smuggle in alcohol and not to piss out the back French doors, as it made the whole place smell like a public urinal. Of course, we failed on all counts, including streaking up and down the street when we thought everyone was in bed. Riding around the suburb in the wee small hours was also a *very* cool thing to do in our youth...

Sometimes, in the dead of night, we would cycle around the car yards, trying all the car doors, and if some were unlocked, we would help ourselves to anything within that wouldn't make a noise to remove — cigarette lighters, etc. On such a night, we had to hide at the back of one of the yards to avoid the police search lights and as soon as the "pigs" were gone we broke the speed of light home, never to do it again, as we got such a fright that we could've actually been caught! That would've taken a hell of a lot of explaining to both sets of parents. Eventually, Val ordered Raymond out of the batch and back into his room inside the main house and Gary in with me. Well, I really don't know if it solved anything, in fact, I know it didn't.

One night, Gary and I decided that we would go on an outing in my Anglia with my cousin, Bronwyn, who he was kind of seeing, much to my delight, as I was playing matchmaker and it was so far so good. It was getting late and time to drop Bronny off at home. Her and Gary were in the back seat canoodling and I was driving. We were all laughing and joking and playing the music as loud as it would go and as I turned right into her street, I failed to see an oncoming car… The impact was massive — the sound of crunching metal was deafening and unforgettable. We were flung around inside the car and showered with broken glass. The impact had pushed us right across the other side of the main road with the other vehicle more or less on top of us. The silence that immediately followed was eerie, then came the shouting of voices from the other car, asking if we were OK. We were shaken but OK and luckily so was everyone in the other car.

Bronny and Gary ran down to where she lived to call Val and Brian, but they were out on date night having a well-earned break away from all of us noisy teenagers. It just so happened that they went zooming passed us on the way home so were pursued by Ray, who had come to pick us up in Brian's new work ute and were made to stop and were informed of our latest drama. This poor couple, who had a house full of kids plus me, couldn't even have a night away without being run off the road by one of their own vehicles and ordered to turn around to sort out another mess.

We were all fine, the car was fixed, so Gary and I thought we would head over to Tokoroa for a party night at the local rugby club. Ray mentioned to us that we were pasty white and should have a session under Val's latest purchase, a "sun ray" lamp, to give us a healthy glow. He set it up in the batch and we each had a few minutes under this extremely high-powered ultraviolet light.

'Get closer,' Ray said, and insisted we do it for longer as he couldn't see any immediate change. We agreed as we wanted to look like Mediterranean gods. After a while, we stopped, as nothing was really changing, but little did we know, we had practically cooked ourselves. A few hours later, we were dressed and on our way to the rugby club in Tokoroa. The band was great, the drinks were flowing, and we had some nibbles to soak up all the booze we were pouring down our necks.

Somebody at our table commented, 'Geezus, Terry, your face is red!' I put it down to my antics on the dancefloor but after looking at

Gary's rather red, swollen face across the table, I realized that something was up. As we sat there, we got hotter and hotter to the point that we opted to leave and head home before our heads exploded.

'I'll bloody kill Raymond when we get home,' Gary grumbled but when we got home, we crawled into the caravan so as not to wake anyone inside the house.

The last thing I said to Gary was, 'Fuck, I feel sick and sore.' He felt exactly the same.

We were woken my knocks on the caravan window. It was Louise yelling, 'Get up, breakfast is ready.' We opened the blinds to tell her where to stick her brekkie and she gasped and just stood there, looking at us. 'What the hell is wrong with your faces!'

We ran to a mirror and we both looked like two big, red Mr Potato Heads, with slits for eyes. Well, the entire household erupted with laughter as we showed ourselves and after a very stern ticking off from Val, which included the dos and don'ts around the use of sun ray lamps, we both submerged our blisteringly hot faces into a basin full of cold water. The swelling eventually went down but was followed by scabbing and peeling — not the best look when you're trying to be cool teenagers, huh!

Still struggling with my sexuality but keeping it well hidden (or so I thought), I decided to reach out to the dashing undertaker that had given me a taste of what it was like to be actually fancied by another man, especially someone as grown up and successful as him. I wrote him a letter and he responded a while later with a phone call. I was out and he left a message with my cousin. I was horrified as he left his name and number to call him back. I snatched the note as soon as I saw it sitting by the phone in case anyone made a connection between us. My nerves were in tatters as those old tensions around my inner truth came back. I don't really know what I was expecting... I reached out, he responded, I ignored it and hoped it would go away and it did. I lied, of course. Paul gave up and once again I was safe.

Hanging out with my cousins and new mates was all important at this age and so was the right image so Ray and I always made sure we looked good and were always with the right crowd but having fun was always top of the agenda. We went roller skating at Skate World in Rotorua, which was always such a hilarious time as we would all fall arse-over-head, smack into walls or take each other out unintentionally, all while fueled by the odd bottle of Chardon that we downed in the car beforehand. This made everything even more funny than it should've been, but it became a regular occurrence.

One night, after our skating antics, we were driving home when Nicola — one of the group, whose Dad had been in the police force — commented that we should take a detour through the local park or lakefront to spot where the homos cruised around at night to make out, etc. My face dropped and I felt sick to my stomach, trying to change the subject to something else so it wouldn't happen, but off we went to go "gay-spotting", as everyone else thought it was a great idea. As we drove through the dark park, I went along with the jokes and the fun that was pointed at these people who were apparently skulking about in the darkness. We saw nothing and nobody but learnt that it was common knowledge that this went on down here on a regular basis. I was so relieved when we turned out of the park and headed home.

So guys would actually meet in public places to have sex and then return to their "normal" lives afterward and no one was the wiser. A lot of these guys were married men, I was told, and a few had been caught in the act over the years, dragged out, openly humiliated and prosecuted. The conversation around this faded but my curiosity didn't and I found it became all-consuming and even though I knew it was unlawful and dangerous, I knew that there was somewhere that I could go to possibly gain sexual satisfaction with another guy.

Wanting to relieve myself of my virgin status, I made plans to be absent from home and "out being busy" one evening. I drove myself down to where we had been during that humiliating drive a few weeks earlier and sat in my car, waiting, not sure what for. Some movement? An invitation? I didn't even know what to expect and my heart was pounding so hard I thought it was about to pop! I was so incredibly nervous that I bailed and went home where no one was any the wiser that I had been out, thank God.

Did I go back? Did I try again? Fuck, yes, and I became a regular cruiser of "the beat", seeing other local guys that shouldn't have been there. One night I was propositioned by a man older than me who looked as though he was a traveler for some company. Well- dressed and well-spoken, we chatted in the park and eventually he asked me back to his motel — I nervously agreed.

I followed him into the room, we had a drink and then he made his move. Up to this point, the odd fumble and blow job was all I had experienced but by the time I left that room, I felt different, having experienced what it was like to actually have sex and feel fulfilled. It wasn't just a quick tug and go and I learnt so much about what it was that I liked and needed and although I had no feelings for the guy, it was completely satisfying. I had lost my virginity to a man but obviously couldn't boast about it, so it remained my secret along with everything else.

I made regular trips home to Tokoroa to see my family and stay with my parents. While there, I tried to see old friends as well and one night I arranged to see Nyda. I picked her up and headed to the movies along with my old mate, David. It was obvious to me that the movie was the last thing on her mind, and it all got a bit heated during the movie, so we left, leaving David looking a bit miffed at the theatre.

Here we were, zooming about in my clunky old Anglia and we eventually ended up driving to the lookout point on Colson's Hill, where we parked up and made out. I expected this, but didn't, if that makes any sense at all. We had sex on the very tiny back seat, and it was good, albeit kind of awkward, as I saw her as more of a mate than a girlfriend or sexual partner. I dropped her off and said we'd catch up next time I was in town, and she seemed totally fine with that.

I was back in town a month or so later, visiting my mum, and I had dropped her off for a swim in her friend Faye's new heated pool. I took the opportunity to excuse myself from the swim and call Nyda. She answered and informed me that she had been in a bit of a state and when I asked why, she said, 'Well, it's all your fault.'

What! Yup, she was pregnant! What you need to remember here it that I had just finally broken my virgin bubble by having sex with a man and the first time I have sex with a woman I knock her up! I was completely gob smacked so ended the call and went to pick Mum up from Faye's. 'Get in the pool with us!' they both yelled like a couple of giggling schoolgirls, which was always the case when these two were together. I agreed and went through the motions of having fun and trying my best to distract my mind from the life-altering news I had just received from Nyda, who Mum despised and resented. *Fuck my life!*

I drove back to Rotorua the next day, not knowing what to do, what to say or who to tell. This was another massive blow that I had to deal with and I really didn't know if I had any more room for it, on top of everything else I had to face, but it was real and it wasn't going away. Nyda and I spoke again a few days later and she absolutely insisted that she was keeping the baby and her family would be helping her raise it...

OK, so not yet eighteen and I was going to be a dad. She was calm and knew what she wanted and I was struggling to get my head around it. I needed to talk to someone, so I called a "youth line" that was confidential and it helped to discuss options from my end and it helped me think more clearly about becoming a parent. I couldn't tell my parents as, once again, I would have let them down and so I decided to do nothing and tell no one until it would eventually bite me in the arse, and so it did.

My head was spinning and around this time, my anxiety took on a life of its own, resulting in my world resembling a dark hole that I was constantly trying to crawl out of. The anger and rage within me about not knowing what I was doing and why, and also how the hell I got myself in this situation where I was hiding my attraction to men and had managed to get a girlfriend pregnant. I was called "highly strung" and would flip out over the smallest things but, looking back, it was no wonder I was an on-edge kind of guy.

This point was the beginning of my slide in and out of the darkness of depression, anxiety and anger, which would plague me until society gave it a name and some coping mechanisms, but it's been a long journey.

Unable to cope at this time and adding this to the folder of secrets I was carrying under my arm, I reached out but not to friends or family. I had heard of a new service at that time called Life link youth line, so, in a phone box in the central post office, I called them, looking for the answer on how to cope with the situation I found myself in. The person on the other end of the phone was understanding and calming, telling me that there were services that could help me. Counselling was one of those options that I could use to help cope with some of these issues and getting my head around it. I remember hanging up the phone and thinking, *bugger that!* So, in good old adolescent style, I decided to do nothing… Ignore it and maybe, just maybe, it would go away.

It didn't, of course, and one evening I was taken aside by a concerned cousin Val and told that my mum had received a call about a certain pregnancy with my name all over it! With no choice but to discuss, it I spilled the info to her and then to my parents. My mum, not accepting of this news, said that I had to be sure it was mine and just to wait.

Baby Arron was born and as we had all kept our silence. Nyda's family took action and arrived on my parent's doorstep in Tokoroa holding a rather large, red-headed baby. 'This is your grandson,' they explained to my mother, who slammed the door in their face. I got the call from Mother screaming down the phone at me about the shock and shame she felt being confronted by "these people". I mean, it shouldn't have been such a shock as she knew the baby was mine and living in the same town but there it was!

Soon enough, I was confronted with letters from the social welfare, naming me as the father and demanding payments for maintenance so I pushed back and was advised to get blood tests to prove paternity. The day came and I was standing alone in a ward in Rotorua Hospital, waiting to be called for the test and at the end of the same hallway stood Nyda holding Arron, with a couple of family members for support. I felt like such a fraud as I knew I was wasting everyone's time and the outcome was obvious, but I continued with the fraud, not making eye contact with anyone and scarpering as soon as I could.

It was confirmed a few weeks later that I was 99% Arron's father. From that point, it was out in the open and he was no longer a secret. I paid the regular maintenance but kept my distance as he was surrounded by a close, loving family, and I was still so young I couldn't really see how showing up would add value to his life. I did manage a visit when he was around eleven years old and spent a few hours with him, leaving him the jacket I was wearing as he had admired it throughout our time together. The contact continued sporadically over the years and eventually social media made it easier to stay in touch and be in each other's lives and so we did.

Sweet Dreams" (Are Made of This) — The Eurythmics, 1983

Still hiding behind the guise of a straight man, I continued with my life, dating girls but satisfying my sexual appetite for men at every opportunity, by any means possible. I soon became old enough to hit the pubs and clubs, which I did with friends and cousins on a regular basis... Thursdays, Fridays, Saturdays, and even Sundays, if the club was open over a long weekend. This meant my cousin, Ray, and I were spending every cent we earned on our social lives and were constantly pushing the car to the petrol station as it was more or less running on fumes. '$5 should do it,' we would often say at the pump, so no wonder we ended up walking home on a regular basis!

Having no cash but not wanting to miss out on a night at the Towers nightclub, we came up with a plan that would get us in and bladdered. We emptied a large plastic bottle of cooking oil and rinsed it out to the point we both confirmed it was clean and then we emptied a cask bladder of the cheapest, nastiest wine we could buy into said bottle. We fronted up to the club with our contraband hidden under my right arm and out of view from any security guys on the door. Swanning in, we found a great seat and started to consume our secret stash from under the table. Drunk, yes, however, we both started to feel a little queasy as the night went on. Pulling out the plastic bottle for the last dregs, we noticed a rather large slick of cooking oil floating on the top of our wine! As we started to turn green, we fled the scene and headed home, not knowing whether to laugh or cry. Our hair and nails were great that month.

It was around the time of my twenty-first birthday and I landed a job behind the bar at the local Cobb & Co., which meant I was in the thick of it when it came to socializing as it was the most popular bar in town. I started on the floor, emptying ash trays and collecting the glasses to be washed and restocked. I soon graduated to bar work and found myself in my element — I was sociable and worked hard to be the slickest and fastest barperson on the shift… I loved it and found myself working every shift that was offered to me. I clicked at something and couldn't wait to get to work each day.

Along with other permanent staff, there was an older openly, and rather effeminate, gay guy named Marty with whom I joked and laughed with on a regular basis. I had seen Marty get picked on and abused at work by rather drunk, homophobic customers and it was heartbreaking having to watch him defend himself against this sort of regular abuse… I hated it but knew that I would be guilty by association if I jumped to his defense. I feel sick to my stomach now knowing that I just stood back and let him take it.

He was a hilarious man to work with and I liked him a lot. I also felt he could see right through my façade and, sure enough, at a "lock-in" after work one night, he signaled me to join him and a couple of his gay friends, so I did. We all had a great time and became great mates.

Seeing that I just really needed to chill the fuck out and "come out", Marty's friend, Patrick, convinced me and a couple of friends from work to accompany him to Auckland to hit the town. We all agreed and picked a date to head north.

I hadn't spent any time in Auckland since those holidays with Mum and Dad with our cousins in Mangere so this was unchartered territory for me, especially with a couple of gay guys in tow. I was nervous but so bloody excited about having a raw look at what potentially my life could look like if I had the balls to do it. Patrick was a tall, older man with a bushy moustache and gentle demeanor with whom I felt a certain brotherhood and compatibility. I could feel that he knew the real me but was comfortable with me not saying it out loud. He was also well-connected and one of the first stops was to see an old friend of his from hotel days and this turned out to be Rachel Hunter's mother, Janeen, who was so welcoming and warm. I liked the feeling of getting to know new people and, surprising myself, I found that I could really hold my own in the company of just about anyone.

Not wanting to waste any time, I was whisked away to Patrick's old flat in Parnell where his flat mates still lived. This was my first experience being in a "homo" only environment, with each of them going about their business, laughing, joking and making obscene remarks about how good I would look naked. Not denying anything, I lapped it up and joined in with the hilarity. What you need to remember is that this was pre-homosexual law reform and the act of sodomy between two males was still an offence punishable by a prison sentence but here they all were living their best life and loving it.

So, it was organized that we would all meet at a bar in the city and go from there. At this age, I was quite a pretty, young man, if that makes sense, so I knew that the "fresh meat" neon sign would be blinking over my head. We arrived at a rooftop bar where Patrick worked a few years before so were given the royal treatment, which meant free drinks and food along with access to amazing areas with an amazing view — I was in heaven!

I liked the feeling of being made a fuss of and sampling the "better" things in life, it was definitely something I could get used to. In the company of these great men, I felt no anxiety, no frustration or anger, for not being the true me and Patrick could see it written all over me.

We soon left the classy rooftop bar and headed into Fort Street, which was the site of one of the first all-inclusive gay bars in NZ and there I was, walking in the front door with my entourage, not quite knowing what I was about to encounter. My heart was pounding through my chest as I stepped down into the dark, smoky bar and the heat hit me at the same time as the loud disco music the DJ was playing. The dancefloor was busy with all kinds of couples — straight, lesbian and gay. This was the first time in my life I had ever seen two men dancing together, touching each other and kissing.

I took it all in as I was ushered to the bar by my new mates, and I was introduced to another group of people that were all connected in some way to Patrick. I must say that they were all so kind and protective of this young man from the regions, making sure I had a drink and was comfortable enough to stay… Of course, I wanted to stay, I was soaking it all in like a very dry sponge!

I was standing watching the people on the dancefloor when a rather tall and very handsome guy caught my eye. He was looking straight at me and smiling as he danced and, not knowing what to do, I kept looking away so as not to look too interested. The next time I glanced back, I was shocked to see him talking to guys in our group and I could hear him asking who I was. Within a few seconds, he was next to me, introducing himself. 'Hi, I'm Adrian,' he said. With a rather dry throat, I introduced myself to him and we started chatting. He took me over to the bar and he brought me a drink so we could get away from the rather loud, vibrating speakers and continue talking. Turned out he flew for Air NZ but was also a model and had just finished a magazine shoot for Seiko watches, which were hot property at that time.

All of a sudden, he grabbed by hand and lead me onto the dancefloor and as we walked, I started to freak out… *How do I dance with another guy? Where do I look? How do I move? What if somebody recognizes me?* The music was loud and he turned to me, grabbed me by the waist and pulled me close, yes, I liked it and started to move slowly in unison with him to the beat of the music and I must say it felt like the most natural thing in the world. However, in the back of my mind was my life back home and my parents and how absolutely horrified they would be by this image. The phrase "what the hell do you think you're doing!" kept running through my head… However, I just kept dancing.

I felt the feeling of freedom, even total abandon, surrounded me as I moved to the music and all the way through it, Adrian kept looking and smiling at me which encouraged me more. Eventually we joined the others who insisted on heading to another bar and, as I was in the middle of the city with no idea which way was north, I needed to leave with them. I said goodbye to my rather tall, spunky, dance partner and walked towards the door, only to be stopped by him handing me some paper with his number written on it, so, again, I blushed and then left.

The night after that got wilder, with lots of cocktails and shots of Galliano, which was very popular in the 1980s. Even now, the taste of it takes me back to that weekend.

Love Action(I Believe in Love) — The Human League, 1985

By the time I got back to Rotorua, I had decided that the city was my best bet to live the life I needed to life without discovery. The regular phone calls from Adrian made me nervous but excited. Nervous when the phone rang and flat mates or cousins answered and questioned who this guy was and excited that I could escape to a better, larger, more glamourous life where I could be myself and dance all night with any man I wanted, in particular Adrian.

Still working at the Cobb & Co., I applied for a transfer to the Auckland central hotel and was accepted so I packed up and headed to Auckland on my next big adventure. Adrian was sharing a flat in Royal Oak and invited me to stay with him so of course I jumped at the chance, leaving all my friends and family completely unaware of what was really going on. I arrived at the hotel and was shown around and was given a choice of bar work and also concierge work in the main foyer… I signed up for both and then headed to Adrian's flat, meeting his flatmate first and then waiting for the man himself to arrive home.

I was so excited to see him and spend some more time together. I didn't really have any expectations about our relationship as I really didn't know what to expect so I just rolled with the punches. Adrian, within a few days, informed me that he was moving to his own flat further out in New Lynn and said it was organized long before he met me. I was a bit taken aback and a little hurt, which seemed to piss him off to the point I found myself lying alone in his bed as he stayed out for nights on end.

I knew that he was a bit of a party boy but soon found out that he was also vain, self-indulgent and not very caring once he had got what he wanted. I felt so let down and lost and eventually I came to realize that he wasn't ready for any kind of relationship especially not with someone as green as me.

His flatmate was furious at the way he was acting, however, I was probably coming on a little strong being a first-timer, so accepted that he was going, and he did. I stayed on in the flat for a while before flatting with some girls from Rotorua in various suburbs around central Auckland. We partied hard at various gay clubs and pubs.

I remember the actual day that the Homosexual Law Reform Act was passed into law in 1986. I was in the Alexandra Tavern in central Auckland, which was a fantastic little gay pub for all queers and friends. There were cheers and lots of loud music, singing and celebration. The age of nuclear ships in our harbors had ended, apartheid was recognized as evil and the end of these and other issues created a significant level of controversy and reflected a general move towards a more post-modernist society.

The homosexual law reform bill was, in many ways, a part of this general societal change and I was there, right in the middle of it, celebrating something that I couldn't even discuss with my family or old friends. Did that make me a hypocrite? Smiling, laughing and drinking to something that I couldn't even accept myself and share?

Deep inside, that's how I felt, but I went along for the ride as it was a historical moment and I wanted to own a piece of it.

I was determined to make a go of my city life so carried on my bar work and socializing with gay and straight friends who also worked in bars around the city so we would attend a myriad of "lock-ins" up and down queen street.

Money was short and sometimes we would hit the bars on a Sunday by catching the "bendy bus" into the city with no cash for drinks but end up staggering home absolutely off our faces. It was at this time that I started experimenting with drugs. I can't even remember what we were taking but we would get a few hours of dancing out of them and afterwards home for a joint to help us come down and relax. Getting pills or tabs in the 80s was never a problem as people would hand them to us on the dancefloor at various clubs and we would throw them down out necks and then ask what it was we had just taken.

The whole Adrian episode really did damage me as I felt small and not good enough so wanted to change my image to make myself feel better. I thought I was fat so I started binge eating and then making myself vomit in the shower where nobody could hear me retching and, along with that, I would drink vinegar as it was said that it would dissolve fat.

I was about ten kilos lighter before some friends asked me if I was OK… I wasn't, I was sad and so disappointed in this "gay" life that I had been seeking, full of glamour, celebrations, great friends and a loyal man at my side. Instead, I was thin, exhausted and constantly let down and used by guys I had met at bars and clubs. It seemed that the scene was just about looking good at any cost and shagging as many men as you could without any kind of emotional connection.

It was the age of HIV and with no cure or preventative at that time, a lot of people were getting infected, sick and eventually dying because of the lack of information and a huge amount of the scene being majorly promiscuous. It was a bullet that I managed to dodge and even though I was very sexually active, my common sense seemed to keep me on track and scared enough to keep me safe.

I was tired and broke and sick of performing like a trained seal at work and socially. Maybe it was because I was brought up in a small town and from a big family that I expected more. I really did need to get out.

Meanwhile at home, my parents thought everything was fine and I had a good, steady job in Auckland and a couple of female flat mates and that's exactly what I reassured them was going on with every phone call home.

Gay life was hard and soulless and it left me feeling empty and hurt and I wanted to remove myself from it, so I started to plan my exit.

I felt that my only way out was to go back to what I knew, to return to the quieter life back in the regions, back to acting and back to pleasing everyone but myself. A quick phone call to Mum and Dad and the decision was made that I would pack up my things ASAP and head south to Tokoroa initially so I could lick my wounds and have some quiet time to understand what had happened and why I felt I had failed at a life I should be living. The way I saw it was that if that was "gay" life… I wasn't interested… I tried it and it wasn't what I wanted or expected.

Driving away from the big city I once felt could offer me a certain release and protection, I felt a kind of relief and a sense of clarity that this was just "my lot" and I would just have to find a way to adjust and live with it and find a strategy to move forward and leave that hard, thankless, amoral life behind, and that is exactly what I did.

How will I know — Whitney Houston, 1986

Boom! I was back in Rotorua, looking for work, and working in a bar was the only thing I knew and I did it well so I started there.

I was told that the local RSA was looking for a bar person to fill a vacancy left by a long-term employee. If you worked in a bar in these days, the uniform across the country was black pants and white shirt so through the washing machine they went and were then ironed to within an inch of their life!

I walked through the CBD as I was early, of course (a trait I got from my mother). Ugh! And eventually made my way to the club, right on time for my interview.

I met with the bar manager who was a stumbly, gruff, tall, older guy called Brian and he put me through my paces about the dos and don'ts of working in a chartered club — I was terrified and totally overwhelmed. It was around that time that I dropped in that my grandfather, Arnie (Ern), used to be a regular at this very club… Everything changed at that moment as if he — grumpy Brian — was looking for a way to connect me, a young guy, with his old man's club. I was in and was then taken to meet the CEO and office staff who squealed that they had seen me walking through town prior to my interview in my very clean and sharply ironed bar uniform and said to each other, 'That's what we need… A nice young barman like that!' There I was, at the right place at the right time.

My time at the club was so enjoyable and I made great friends with a lot of the old punters and their wives. The hubby's liked me as I was fast, efficient and polite… In other words, I poured their drinks before they even got to the bar and gave the right change with little cheek. The women and wives wanted to look after me, often flirted and showered me with baking and dinner treats when I was pulling a late shift.

During summer, I would often wear shorts behind the bar as it was cooler and easier to crawl in and out of the massive beer tanks that I would often have to scrub and rinse by hand before that beer tanker was due. To be fair, my shorts were as short as George Michael's in his latest video and seem to upset a few of the older gentlemen in the club. I remember being pulled into Brian's rather messy, stuffy office and told that my shorts were just too bloody short! How is that even possible? I was so pissed off as I rocked those pants and the inner poof loved the attention they attracted, alas, they were banned from being worn at work.

Even now, writing about this "incident" makes me smile as I must've subconsciously been looking to stir the musty old place up whilst letting a little piece of the real me come to the surface.

There was never a dull moment during shifts as sometimes (often) a punter would disappear from sight as you were serving or drop down flat on the dancefloor. They were very old guys and one by one, they would die, which saddened me as I became quite attached to a favorite few. Others would just be so pissed that they would fall arse over tit, knock themselves out and bleed everywhere or just refuse to leave at closing time as they insisted on one more roadie. Needless to say, I had ambulance and police on speed dial and I took no shit. I would usher the stragglers out, yelling, 'Get outta here now, as I wanna go to the Towers!'

That was a local night club and I was often on a mission to get there to meet up with mates ASAP and these old pricks weren't gonna stand in my way. Most of them would laugh and comment on how they would be coming with me if they were a few years younger.

My relationship with these customers was so precious when I look back at it now. Here I was, a spritely and cheeky twenty-something young guy but I got on with the majority of them better than I did with people my own age, which was reflective of my childhood and the connections I felt with my older relative or some of my parents' friends.

On one occasion, I contracted the flu and was so ill at home that I couldn't get out of bed. One of the RSA women, Celia, came with soups and lemonade to help aid my recovery, but not only that… She would also bring her knitting and sit with me during the day to make sure I was doing as I was told and well on the way to recovery. The odd bar patron would even come along to any home party I was having and bring along a few mates from the club. After closing time, of course!

I loved my time there and even though most of these people have now passed away, I remember each and every one of them with a smile — even the grumpy ones who complained about my shorty shorts or just really didn't know how to take me but accepted me at face value, which meant a lot as I couldn't even do that for myself.

During this period, I still had my secrets and even though I was an incredibly sociable and a friend- and family-focused person, I still managed to spend a lot of time alone. This gave me the opportunities to satisfy my secret sexual appetite and try to deal with my inner battle. It never went away; it just went into hibernation at times.

"Are secrets designed to hurt or protect?"

I had no shortage of takers when it came to sex and especially the kind of sex I was interested in, remembering that this as before we had any access to computer dating, Tinder, Grindr, etc. Therefore, the only way to meet men was "the beats" and they consisted of parks or toilets or even the pub at the odd time. There was a certain look or feeling that you gave or received from someone who was interested. Today it is commonly known as your "gaydar" and it would ping in your mind whenever you met someone who saw you as something more than just another guy in the pub.

I had some regulars who would frequent the RSA club and they were loosely linked to a friend that I had flatted with in Auckland. This was terrifying for me as they obviously knew that I was gay but very closeted so would bounce up and treat me as an openly gay man just to make me cringe, and cringe I did. Deep inside I was a little excited that I could totally be myself with them. However, I was forever on edge that someone within my close circle of friends and family would click to what was going on.

One of the people in the know was a lady called Sonia and she constantly invited me out with her and her crew, along with Mary, my ex-flattie from Auckland. I finally accepted and rocked on up at a party they were at. Little did I know that they had hatched a plan to drag me out of the closet by introducing me to a close friend of theirs who was gay but a little more relaxed than I was about coming out. I was instantly attracted to him; Jamie had the look of a cross between a member of the green party and a surfer, complete with long, straggly blondish hair tied up in a man bun, with a longish beard and spectacles. He was tall and very well spoken...

As the night went on and we were pushed together, I started to relax and he asked if I would like to see him again. I said yes but wondered how the hell I was gonna do this without getting caught out by anyone. The bunch of people I was hanging with were encouraging the match and organized the next gathering that we could be together at, but the only problem was that Jamie would drink and drink until he fell over. Maybe this was his way of coping with his homosexuality, I'm not sure, but after a couple of catch-ups with his friends at parties, I realized that this guy was just too far gone... I mean, the only time we were kind of intimate, he was so pissed that he would pass out. So I gave it all a wide birth, only to have him arrive at my house in the early hours of the morning, having driven from wherever he had been hauled up drinking. I would put him into bed and usher him out early before anyone in the house woke up.

This was my first sneak peek at what it would've been like to be with another gay guy in a sort of relationship. I liked him a lot but we never even got past first base as his alcoholism had him tight in its clutches and wasn't going to let go anytime soon. He took the news badly and still showed up a few times before I said no more, and he left me alone after that. Looking back, I think I was quietly relived as there was no way I could've juggled him without being exposed so, once again, I was alone.

During my time at the club, my nana, the only grandmother I had ever known, had tripped over while staying at Mum and Dad's in Tokoroa. She had broken her hip but was sent home from the A & E, saying she was fine. The poor thing was in so much agony that Mum insisted they look again and then they picked up the fact that it was severely broken and, at eighty-five, the bones were so brittle that they wouldn't mend and she was too frail to survive an operation. The pain was so horrendous that her mind slowly slipped into the dark cloud of dementia. This quirky, funny lady, who used to hold my hand in town, take us for the holidays, bake scones and Chelsea buns, and made the most incredible stew and dumplings was slipping away, day by day.

She was eventually placed in a geriatric ward in Rotorua Hospital that was the old-style open ward with huge rooms full of beds with people who would scream out to you as you walked past to find Nana. She would be there in amongst the smell of stale urine and mold, chatting away to herself and trying to fold all her bed sheets up as she thought it was washing that needed to be put away. She wouldn't even notice I had arrived as I sat on the chair next to her bed with fresh flowers that I took with me every day. She would glance at me and carry on so I would just sit quietly trying not to disturb her too much or lean on the bed as she would whimper in pain from any pressure on her hip. The days of her remembering my face or name had also disappeared but it was enough to just be with her, watch her fall asleep and smile at the odd nurse who would turn up to fill the water jugs. It was a kind of death row or a waiting room for death and you could feel it every time you walked in.

It was the day that I chose to hang out with mates instead of my regular "pop in on Nana" time that she slipped away to be with Ern, and because I was at a friend's place and there were no mobile phones, I didn't find out until later that evening. I know that it was a merciful release for my dearest Effie Fergusson and it meant no more pain or humiliation in death row.

However, I was completely devastated and once again I was standing in the same undertakers, in the exact same room where I had seen my dead grandfather, with Mum saying, 'Come on in, doesn't she look lovely.' She pulled back the lace cover that was draped over her coffin. She looked so tiny and pale but her hair was perfect and she laid there in her organza pink dress, complete with her favorite pearls to match. Her lips were thin and I could see slight bloodied cracks in them due to the lack of water and food that had led to her death. She was gone and now would exist only in my memories.

After a few days of bereavement leave, I was back in the thick of bar life, serving all the old boozers at the club but something had changed and I wanted out, I wanted more than to smell of booze and cigarettes and the end of every day. I guess it was my grief for Nana that helped me look at myself and what I wanted out of life more than I had ever done in the past, but, interestingly enough, "coming out" was never part of those plans. I couldn't ever imagine, telling that particular truth, so it continued to be my dark secret.

I landed a new job in a fashion store in town that was *the* place to buy if you were cool and chic. Keesings was an old family business that had moved with the times and had moved from a funny old menswear store to a funky men's and woman's fashion Mecca. I liked the way it made me feel and look as, of course, I had to buy and wear all the cool gear we sold. It made me one of the "cool" guys in town virtually overnight and opened lots of doors to a lot of the elite in Rotorua.

I started to be invited to posh events and parties and found that I fitted in immediately with ease and became very body- and fashion-conscious but never lost my raw charm, which only coming from Tokoroa could provide. The upper sect found that part of me rather charming and endearing so I went with it.

Still keeping my original mates and drinking with my cousins, Ray and Louise, we would frequent the local Cobb bar as we always had until the wee small hours. It was on one such night that we had had more than a skinful of rum and were refused any further service, much to our horror, so before giving up altogether, I spotted a young girl at the bar about to order for her group of mates. I ushered over to her and mentioned how very thirsty we were and that the stupid barmaid had blocked us from ordering. She agreed to buy our drinks — I gave her the cash, but she always says I didn't — and then she and her friend joined us for the rest of the evening.

Her name was Lisa and she was a dark-haired, pretty, eighteen-year-old hairdresser who turned out to have her own car and insisted that she would be able to drop us home as taxis were few and far between. Oh, and I think we had spent every last cent we had on booze so a lift back to the flat was very welcome.

Lisa stayed the night and we quickly became an item, which, at the time, I was very happy about and encouraged. We had an electric sex life and I could feel that I was developing more and more feelings for her with each passing day and I knew she felt the same. She had noticed me working in the coolest store in town before we even met so was thrilled when we eventually hooked up. My dark secret seemed to fade into the background and I was over the moon that I could feel this way with her, which meant maybe I had moved on from the whole "gay thing" and I could look forward to a normal… Normal?

Head to Toe — Lisa and Cult Jam, 1987

It was rather quickly that Lisa moved into the flat with me and I met her parents. Her mother, Barbara, affectionately known as Barbs, was a sweet woman but was very matter-of-fact and I took an instant liking to her and our friendship was incredibly important to me. She would always tell the story of the first time Lisa took me to meet her and the family and how she was amazed that I could get my jeans *that* tight! I rocked those bloody jeans.

I fitted into the family rather effortlessly and even managed to befriend Lisa's four brothers to a point, however, it was so evident that I was incredibly different to these rough and ready rally-driving and road-marking men, but we all managed to keep the peace.

My parents adored Lisa, especially my mum, as a hairdresser in Mums' eyes was more majestic than being the queen of England and therefore would pop over regularly for a perm, colour or blow wave. Myrna was in heaven!

The pace stepped up a notch and after a few more months together, Lisa and I decided to buy a house together instead of paying rent, which looked great on paper as an investment but locked us in together in such a short period of time. We moved in and became a new, young couple moving forward in life, saving money, and doing the regular thing when you buy a new house — renovate.

Lisa fell pregnant almost immediately. We were both thrilled with the news and couldn't wait to share it with everyone. It was the late 80s so it was still thought that marriage should've been on the cards and we both decided that we would tie the knot before Lisa was showing. Could we afford this baby and a wedding? No, but what the hell, it was all coming regardless. Family and friends rallied around, donating nappies, cots, bedding and in no time, we were set up. Lisa rented her dress and I borrowed some nice grey shoes from my cousin Louise's boyfriend at the time and within about a month we had tied the knot at a small church in the middle of town.

Did I have cold feet beforehand? *Yes.* Did I ask a close friend what the hell I was doing? *Yes.* Was it all too late to turn and run? *Absolutely.* And what about my former life and the urge to have sex with men?

Having a family was always so important to me and I felt that it would definitely happen as I knew deep inside I would be a dad again after Arron was born. I never kept my first born a secret from Lisa and she knew that a certain amount of my pay went out as maintenance every single week.

Benjamin was born in early 1988 right in the middle of Cyclone Bola which devasted the east coast of New Zealand, wiping out small communities and trapping people for days on end. I remember driving through the horrific weather, dodging pieces of trees and other debris to get Lisa to the delivery suite. I adored this wee man and loved watching him grow and teaching him that it's not OK to eat dirt, cat shit or anything else that he found in the backyard.

I started my first job in media at the local Rotorua newspaper — *The Daily Post* — and absolutely loved what I did and the people I worked alongside. The *Post* had a very active social club that we paid into every week, giving us regular parties, drinkies at work and even ownership of two baches on the beach at Ohope. It was as if we were drunk most of our working lives... Well, us youngers ones were and the older employees would look disapprovingly at us if we were too rude or crude or hungover at work. Although most of the management at the time would be some of the worst behaved.

A lot of my workmates had been working there for years, coming straight from school, and one in particular was my mate, Chrissie. She was a delightful girl, younger than me but we got on like a house on fire as I had known her and a few others before I started work there through my cousin, Louise, who had also been on the payroll. Chrissie was an identical twin and whenever I would see her outside of the office I would scream at her, 'Chrissie, aye!'

But her sister would turn around and say, 'No, wrong again.'

I decided to only talk to her in the office so as not to embarrass myself every time I got them mixed up. I didn't know it at the time but my friendship would continue for decades, even giving us the chance to work together in the future in the same building.

I remember the other office girls, computer girls, reporters and more, all sitting at their desks, cigarette in hand and coffee in the other. If you were lucky enough, Betty the tea lady made one for you at ten a.m. and three p.m.

For most of our regular parties we would need to find a new venue each time as we were never allowed back, which paints the picture of how loose we became when hitting the booze. We were all young and even though we were young parents, we were in, boots and all!

Lisa and I slowly built our small empire, buying and selling homes and getting better paid jobs and even second jobs to get ahead. At this time, I had moved from retail and into media, selling advertising for the local newspaper and then into radio, which set us up financially before our second son, Daniel, arrived in late 1990.

He was an adorable baby who smiled continuously through his dribble and was incredibly sociable from a very young age compared to his older brother, Ben, who seemed to have the weight of the world on his shoulders and just wanted to be at my side at all times, which I secretly loved. These two little boys looked at me in a way that no one had ever done, they relied on me, needed me and loved me... The feeling was mutual and unconditional — I felt complete.

However, my relationship with my wife was not so great. We had a volatile relationship that went into safe mode on a regular basis. We were very young parents with big plans to move forward in life to build a better environment for ourselves and our family.

It's so hard to write about this period of my life as I feel like such a fraud reliving it and capturing it all on these pages... Here I am living a life in a kind of bubble, a life that I always imagined. The perfect couple with two beautiful boys, a lovely home and garden and careers that were on the move. I wanted to be perfect in every way but my darkness and the secret within continued to haunt me daily, reminding me of my true human self that was bubbling just under the surface, scratching at me, taunting me, and reminding me that this bubble could easily pop.

This would cause conflict, not only within myself but also within my marriage and friendships. The result of this inner turmoil was inner rage which quickly turned to depression and even worse anxiety than I had experienced when younger. I would lash out and my wife would lash back and because we were both so competitive, neither of us would back down, which caused long periods of silence. She would retreat to bed for hours on end and I would head out to the garden, sometimes until dark, as it was the place, I found solace.

Without even knowing it at the time, we were starting to look away from each other and compensate for the lack of intimacy with "things" — the best appliances, the best address, the best schools, the best set of friends and social groupings.

However, there was one person who continuously grounded me and that was Karen, a client from my advertising days who quickly became a great mate and confidant. She herself had been through a broken relationship and the ups and downs of rebuilding her life. I can still see her walking down our driveway in tears with her six-week-old baby, Ryan, in a carry cot. She had come to inform us that her husband at the time had been having an affair and now she was alone and extremely traumatized by the entire experience. Karen was a salt of the earth woman with a wicked and filthy sense of humour, which always brought me out of the dark cloud surrounding me. Although she was friends with both of us, it was her and I that had an amazing friendship bond that would last decades and survive all the turmoil that life brings.

The only actual period of time that we didn't speak was years later when she was in a mentally abusive relationship with a new guy who showed traits of severe narcissism and isolated her from most of friends and family, resulting in her and her young son fleeing the house in the wee small hours while he was working out of town. Upon finding her gone, he pleaded with her to return that turned to anger when she refused. She was ready to do what she did and put herself and her son's life to the fore and I admired her strength and was envious that she had broken away from something that was killing her slowly inside.

I remember thinking to myself that it took so much guts and determination to make that change and follow her truth. I wish I could've looked and made a change during these years of my life, but I guess I felt that I had too much to lose and was inwardly so ashamed of myself being the way I was that I refused to even believe that I could ever make it happen. I was too far gone and had too many people relying on me to get it right.

My parents and Lisa's mum, Barbs, were embedded in our family life, along with most of mum's family (the Jolleys). My Aunty Joan and husband, Andy, would welcome us and our kids on a regular basis and we adored them both so much. Uncle Andy would pick Benjamin up from our front gate every Wednesday to go to the dump. He would be taking orders from Joan that the rubbish had to go on that day each week and he would always oblige. Ben loved it and I was so thrilled that this big family had embraced my new young family.

The Sign — Ace of Base, 1994

My media career was gaining more and more traction and I accepted a management role at the local radio station I had been working at. During this time a new overall manager was appointed and came bursting through the doors of the station, promising a tidy up and refresh of the entire operation, which was desperately overdue. Tony was married with two daughters and gave a better impression of the perfect marriage than I did. His reputation preceded him for being a tough operator within the industry and also had the reputation of cheating on his rather insipid wife, so I braced for impact.

Quite the opposite happened and he befriended me in a way that I see now was not only manipulative but also extremely despicable. He had encouraged us to meet up as friends outside of work and seemed to support my vision to learn and grow in my role. Our families were introduced shortly afterwards, with meetings outside the office environment and we all became great mates and shared a lot of common interests through our kids. However, Tony could see the cracks in our marriage and he, right from the start, had his eye on a certain prize, regardless of his wife and young family, and he wasn't going to stop until he got it.

He mentored me at work and introduced me to the right people I needed to know so I could grow as a media specialist and I, in return, worked my ass off to show him I was good for it and worthy of the help. But he also was steering me in a way that I would open up about the troubles in my marriage. The "advice" he gave me was to not put up with the behaviors and be strong and decisive about what I wanted but he was also grooming my wife with the same action. Did he know my secret and saw an opportunity too good to miss out on? Was it easy picking? I don't think I will ever know but as a result of having this man and his family in our lives, our relationship started to fall apart.

He started to show up at our house at odd times for a catch-up and even sometimes in his running gear, which I thought was rather weird but, let's face it, the entire situation was totally weird but, at the time, I just couldn't see it.

Christmas came and went and we welcomed in the summer, which meant lots of BBQs and work events that Tony insisted that I attend, which kept me away from home.

In the meantime, my mate, Karen, started to become suspicious when a rather brazen Tony brought Lisa into her jewelry shop, giggling and cooing in front of her. She instantly picked up the vibe as she had done years before in her own marriage. 'They're fucking,' she said to her co-worker. The word quickly spread about town because of these rather public outings and I slowly became aware that there had been a shift in Lisa's behavior and the way we were treating each other.

The arguments grew more fiery and bitter between us and my very caring boss' advice to me was to leave and he offered me time off to sort my head out and take a break from all the hostility before it started to affect my work. As I was so career-focused, I agreed and thought for the first time that my marriage and family were about to fall apart. Had I created this entire situation I found myself in? Had I subconsciously created it as a way out or was my dark secret dragging me back to that once lonely but free place. I was confused but it was developing at a rate of knots, and I felt powerless to stop it.

After agreeing with him to take time out and head away on leave for a while, Tony left for an appointment and I decided leave the office to take a walk to grab some food and take in some sun. So along the old familiar path I went to the local park, which doubled as my old "beat". Quite ironic with what was about to happen…

I was walking through the carpark, sandwich in hand, when I saw the radio station vehicle, which was hard to miss as it had the station log on the side. I thought this was strange as I thought my boss man had gone on a client appointment, so I looked around to see where he was.

Coming around a corner, I saw the Honda that Lisa and I had owned for a number of years. It was parked away from the carpark and I could tell it was ours as it had Ben and Daniel's car seats strapped in the back seat. I was confused until I saw them both together, sitting on my beach towel, kissing and caressing each other. My heart sank and I sat and watched to make sure what I was seeing was actually happening. Yup, happening it was!

I felt quite stunned and numb and made my way into town where my cousin, Val, had a small rug shop. As I walked in the door, she looked at me and instantly knew something was up and through the shock, anger and tears, I managed to get it out and tell her what I had just witnessed. I felt so humiliated that these two people had double-crossed not just me but also Tony's wife and kids, who were sitting at home.

I composed myself and after organizing that I would once again stay with my amazing cousin, I made my way back to work to find Tony in his office. I stood at the door and calmly told him that I had seen him with my wife and everything that had happened over the last months had fallen into place. His face turned white and he was silent. As I turned to walk away, I heard him mutter something under his breath, so I turned and rushed back to his office door in a blind rage, yelling something I can't even remember… But I can tell you that I can't imagine it would've been very suitable for an office environment. He rushed to the door before I got to it and locked it, which left me pounding and kicking it and screaming, 'Let me in, you gutless prick!'

Other staff members were standing around, stunned, not knowing what to do or say until a couple of them pulled me away before I kicked the bloody thing in.

On that day, I lost my job, my family and my mana. I felt so humiliated… But was this my opportunity to exit gracefully and start a new life being who I really was, living the kind of life I should've been living, and being the person I was born to be? I messed up being with a woman so maybe I should've been with a guy after all. So many things in my head and it just wouldn't stop spinning. All I could think of was my kids and how close we were and that I would absolutely lose them long term because of this ginormous clusterfuck.

Looking back, I can hardly blame my wife for this as she was as manipulated by this guy as I was. However, my masculine pride was severely dented and I couldn't shake the feeling of being wronged so I needed time to lick my wounds and time away from everything. After confronting Lisa about what had come to light, we argued when she denied the whole thing, which made me angrier, so I pack my bags and left.

Our parents, friends, family and extended family were all reeling from this exposé surrounding our marriage and again the humiliation and anxiety took over, sending me into a dark place that I found hard to emerge from. It was only the love of my kids that kept me from retracting into the darkness completely.

After finally admitting her part in this affair with my employer, Lisa wore the brunt of criticism from everyone and I backed that as part of the whole wounded party thing I had going on. However, I slowly started to see that we were both to blame and that I obviously wasn't giving her what she needed out of our relationship. We started to talk about what had happened and took some counselling around how to move on alone or together. I felt drawn back to my family bubble that we had created and the window of opportunity to leave started to close in front of me.

Could I totally leave this marriage and my kids? Could I come out to everyone as a gay man? Was I totally sure that any love for my wife had gone?

So many decisions to make and we all needed to move on and I kept looking at how all this turmoil and fighting had affected my sons. I couldn't bear the thought of leaving, losing them, or breaking up their family and stable life. My parents were adamant that I should take my wife back and had no problem telling me that on a regular basis. Most of their anxiety about the whole event was around their two precious grandsons and I totally get that now so we reconciled and we, as a unit, moved away for a bit so I could work and earn.

It wasn't long before I was offered a job back in Rotorua with a rival media company and I jumped at the chance because if I couldn't knock Tony's block off… I would take him down professionally, which made him squirm. He then tried to take me to court for breach of contract. That was all I needed for motivation to keep the pressure on against this opposition and crush any opportunities for revenue by getting in there sooner with better service and better deals for those particular clients. It felt so good and definitely muffled the remnants of total humiliation. The case was eventually dropped and I continued my work with the same gusto I had before.

My new work environment was great and filled with the most amazing people, a lot of them becoming lifelong friends. My relationship at home was steady, we were happy enough and the boys were doing well at school and looked after by Barbs when we were both at work.

After my thirtieth birthday party in the basement of our garage, which rocked the posh streets of Kawaha Point, we decided to buy a bigger house and start new memories through renovating it to our own taste and doing lots of entertaining. I loved it as it was an older Tudor house with a grand staircase, lots of room and even an in-ground swimming pool.

My garden became my life and I enjoyed the challenge of creating something from nothing as the backyard really was a blank canvas. Along with my sons, and the way they played, I created different areas and spaces. Our family was complete with two cats, and our collie dog, Lass. We had great friends, neighbours and family support around us at all times and we would entertain a lot around the pool and socialize with our work colleagues on a regular basis. Mum and Dad where regular visitors and Barbs was still our sons' after-school caregiver, so life was good.

My wife and I still had a volatile relationship and old patterns started to emerge and we again were concentrating on other things, such as our individual careers and our place in society, making the right contacts and as much money as possible. Sound shallow? Well, we were young and wanted and needed to get ahead as fast as possible. Some of our friends started to drop off and new ones entered our lives.

But... My secret urges? Within my workplace, there were a multitude of personalities and I had a lot of fun working with this colorful group of people. A lot of them went on to become top broadcasters, highly successful media managers, reporters and sales magnates. I lost couple of these mates, buddies, colleagues to shock suicide and sudden death, which brought us all together again as a lot of us stayed in touch throughout our media careers and beyond.

One of these people was a guy I became extremely close to and I felt an overwhelming attraction to and I knew that he was as far back in the closet as much as I was… So far back that we were both just about in bloody Narnia!

We would see each other every day and there was always a laugh, a comfortable feeling, and a spark which quickly turned into a sexual attraction that we both wanted to act on and did!

We were thrown together through work and, without going into too much detail… Here I was having a sexual relationship with a man that I worked with while trying to make my marriage work and recover from all the trauma my former employer had put us through. Not an ideal situation, as this only made me feel as if I was paying my wife back, for all the hurt we had endured as a family, or at least that was the way I looked at it at that time so I could live with myself.

This newfound relationship quickly evaporated for me when my workmate started to call me randomly and ask to see me more often. I was petrified that someone would click and all hell would break loose so I pulled away, leaving him quite distraught and myself feeling hugely guilty and flat. "No one was the wiser and no one got hurt" — a pretty selfish statement. No one except for my college, who took a while to even speak to me again but, because of his own situation working in the public eye as a respected broadcaster, he eventually came around and our friendship continues to this day, spanning nearly three decades.

I had a big love for my little family and always needed it to be perfect and my still undiagnosed anxiety made life hell at times for those closest to me. Eventually, I realized that inside I was normal and anxiety is something that a lot of people manage and live with, but this realization and diagnosis wouldn't happen for me for many years. So I carried it around, which meant I would continue to overact, spin out of control and be on edge and angry, which gave me a bit of a reputation even with my own larger family.

Oh yes, I was still the hilarious Terry at parties and with mates but that was my persona I used regularly to get by and suffocate my inner rage and hurt. What the hell did I do in a previous life to have this stowed on me! I just couldn't understand why I was chosen to be like this and not someone else. Sometimes, with my everyday life, I would feel like I was suffocating and my secret was just too big to hold down where it needed to stay, and these days would consist of retreating into a dark hole that took ages for me to climb out of. The faces of my boys and my close friends would always help but Lisa understood less and less, and I know that she was simply losing interest in coping with it.

I would look at other couple's relationships and wonder what it would be like to just live happily without having to carry the burden of another life deep inside that was scratching to get out and be lived and be true and be healed. This feeling was getting closer and closer to the surface and harder to live with and I knew that the end was near. I contemplated suicide at times, leaving a note that explained everything to my family, but I couldn't do that to my kids and it seemed a massive sacrifice to make just because I was too scared to tell the truth.

A couple of Lisa's brothers during this time had left for the UK and were working and managing pubs in London, so Lisa and I took the opportunity to plan a trip while they were there to take in some sights and catch up with them and some other friends that were on that side of the planet. It was arranged that, between them, my parents and Barbs would look after our boys as well as the house and pets. It was the first time either of us had been that far abroad, so our close mates threw a soiree for us beforehand and then took us to Auckland to fly out. Saying goodbye to the boys was incredibly hard but we both knew that they were in good hands, so we tried to relax and keep looking forward to this massive trip.

Not knowing what to expect when it came to long-haul travel, both of us had packed way too much to the point our cases were overweight even before we left! We also had bum belts full of traveler's cheques etc., matching neck rests, with matching tracksuits in hideous 90s colours, which made us look like we had escaped from a really bad sitcom on its third repeat! We were told that we needed to be comfortable as it was a long flight but we looked stupid!

We settled in and waited for our flight and boarded. It was at this time I realized that we didn't have a lot to talk about now that we were on our own as usually, we were surrounded by friends, etc. It was so obvious that we needed other people to make our relationship work and this was proof of that so, as to not feel too awkward, I knocked down a few massive rum and cokes (the chosen tipple at that time) and also knocked back a sleeping pill (or two) to knock me out for a good part of the journey.

I woke hours later to a feeling of intense nausea and signaled Lisa to hand me the sick bag, like now! I vomited to the point of total dehydration and found it hard to stay awake but only had myself to blame as a cocktail of rum and pills wasn't such a great idea — I felt like such a dick. Before we landed in Heathrow, I was given oxygen which started to bring me back to life a bit and I don't know if you have ever had it before but it's like a thousand virgins are blowing breath into you with the cleanest air you have ever tasted.

We had fun escaping from everyday life and took in all the sights and saw all the people we wanted to see, all along with hauling around these massive suitcases full of shit that we didn't really need to take with us, but as newbies to long-haul travel we had absolutely no idea. By the time we got home to NZ, we were totally up with the play when it came to how much to take with you — Fuck all! The flight back was so tight and uncomfortable as I was hiding so much shopping in carry-on luggage so, again, we looked like a couple of muppets.

This trip away made me realize that Lisa and I were no longer compatible and that my days of hiding were nearly over but I just needed to think about all that was about to come and what the aftermath would look like. My thoughts were always around my sons and how I would lose my day-to-day life with them as I loved being their dad. I would even have to get used to not being Lisa's husband but, in my head, I had no other choice. I had a lot to lose and the shame was too much to take on… But…

It was at this time that the media sales team I worked in achieved a milestone and the prize was a trip for all of us to Sydney as a team. We were all so stoked and were counting down to the big, all-expenses-paid trip and when they day came, we all rocked up to the airport with our specially printed T-shirts on and rushed onto the plane so we could start drinking. It was a great trip and we were very spoilt, with the best of everything and lots of shopping and opportunities for giggles all round.

During the trip, there was some downtime and I took advantage of this by disappearing into the known "gay" areas of the city. There were lots of sex-on-site venues and saunas for gay guys, but being absolutely petrified of those at that time, I opted for a drink or two in the odd gay bar on Oxford Street and the surrounding area. I felt so comfortable for the first time in a long time, being with people who didn't care what society thought about them and dared to be judged. There were gay, transgender, and lesbian people, and anything in between, all coming together in a safe environment. This helped me imagine what living in truth must be like without preparing a multitude of lies or cover-ups — just being you.

The events of that night rewrote the future for me as no longer did I want to feel sorry for myself or be unhappy or deceitful to those I loved. I stayed out to the wee small hours, which were full of laughter dancing and fun.

I met up with the other team members and we had our last outing before returning to the airport. During this time, I started to feel ill after eating a hearty breakfast and quickly went downhill from there. I started to turn green, along with my friend, Lyndal. By the time we checked in, I was so sick that we had to pretend to feel OK as best we could otherwise the airline would hold us back. Arriving in NZ, we were both shuttled back to Rotorua in a hire car and delivered home. Lisa opened the front door and as I stumbled in, looking a lighter shade of emerald. She commented, 'What's wrong with you now?'

The decision came that I would leave my relationship as soon as possible after that, and the day I confronted my wife to say I thought our marriage was over was one of the most traumatic to date. She was calm at first and then fell apart, telling all who would listen, before we had even sorted out any details, that I was leaving her and the kids. I was instantly branded an asshole by the wider audience and I felt totally hideous that my kids had to endure my eminent departure.

The day I left I had packed a bag and explained calmly to the kids that Daddy was leaving because Mummy and I weren't able to live together happily any more… It was horrific and my heart felt like it had been ripped out. I grabbed my bag and made my way to the old Volkswagen I had parked in the garage, praying that it would start, but it wouldn't at first. I just wanted to get the hell out of there before there was more shouting and crying in front of my boys. Vroom! The Beetle roared into life and I backed out of the driveway to leave my beloved family behind me, but then I saw Lisa usher Ben and Daniel onto the front step to see me off. There they stood, so young and confused, waving goodbye. It was the cruelest thing for those boys but I get why she did it — anger, frustration, grief, or all of the above. I drove off in tears, watching them in the rear-view mirror, still waving goodbye until the last glimpse. What the hell had I done?

Aunty Joan, who had always been a support for me, ushered me into her little unit where she had lived since losing Andy to cancer a year before. She was still quick-witted and cheeky and now just about to turn eighty years young. 'Get in here, you little mongrel!' she chuckled. That was one of the first places I stayed as I was totally at a loss as to where to go.

Not used to entertaining at all, she would always insist that we go to Aunty Velma's unit, which was practically next door, so she wouldn't have to do anything or use her own tea bags. The jug would be on and we would sit for ages, chatting about all sorts, which helped me relieve some of the anxiety about finally leaving my marriage. These aunties became my "guard of honour" to some degree and continued to support and make sure I knew I was loved right until they left me.

Search for the Hero — M People, 1994

The days and weeks following our separation were tedious with both of us taking swipes at each other and screaming arguments that sorted nothing between us and actually made the entire situation worse. My mum and dad were totally broken and couldn't understand why I left as I still hadn't given a legitimate reason to anyone, other than that our marriage was totally beyond repair, and I certainly wasn't lying about that.

My parents, Myrna and Stubb, continued to go to the house and visit Lisa and the boys and never came near me because of the anger they felt toward me. I still had friends and other close family to lean on and work was a saving grace.

As part of the separation, we both attended counselling again, as Lisa said it would help both of us communicate without anger and she was right as my anxiety of off the Richter scale. There was a point during the counselling when the counselor wanted to speak to us separately and he said, quite unprofessionally, that I would definitely have regrets for what I had done to this family unit. 'Regrets!' I yelled. 'Of course I have fucking regrets and of course I feel responsible but isn't it your job not to judge me on that and to counsel!' With that, I stormed out and that was the end of the so-called help.

At this stage, I was kind of sofa-surfing and staying with friends and colleagues, such as my old friend, Eileen, who made me laugh and had a knack of making me feel so at home in her little princess house. We would drink wine, walk the dogs and smoke weed almost every night, putting the world to rights. This kind of unconditional friendship kept me going and enabled me to cope.

To add to all of the confusion and change, I was offered a job with TV3, based in Hamilton. This was everything I had wanted and had been working toward and I was so tempted to grab the opportunity with both hands. So, after a conversation with Lisa about ongoing access to my boys, I accepted!

I felt good about that decision and Lisa had calmed to the idea of our separation so all was well and I moved to the Tron, finding a flat and furnishing it with what little I had accumulated since I had moved out of the big house. Being from our massive family, I have relations in most places, it's true! So I had a few cousins to hang out with on the weekends, with or without my sons, but I must say the "withouts", were so hard and I soon started pining for their company.

My soon-to-be ex-wife had moved on and was rumored to be seeing someone rather quickly, which made me totally freak out about the space I left being filled and my sons looking up to someone else in my absence. I was trying to concentrate on my new role at the network but I was falling deeper and deeper into a depressive state. Lisa and I would end every conversation with an argument and that made the situation deteriorate more and more. I was angry but why was I angry... I couldn't eat, I couldn't sleep and eventually I couldn't work. The counselor's words kept ringing in my ears... *Regrets, regrets, regrets.*

I definitely didn't want to be in my marriage any more but I had lost my family by walking away and I was starting to freak out at this loss and my anxiety (still undiagnosed) took over.

Eventually I was rescued from my new prestigious work office by my friends, Max and Lynare, from Rotorua, who had called me continuously and had been monitoring my mental decline. They both walked into my office to find me looking blankly at the screen and I remember them both talking to me calmly as if to keep me in the right headspace to get in the car with them. It worked and I was driven back to Rotorua to their house and set up in a room off their garage, where I just sat and slept and tried to pull myself together so I could see the boys. Again, I was on the phone to my ex-wife, yelling and screaming, but not even knowing what the hell I was doing, as I wanted out, and out I was!

Max had recently joined the police force and Lynare had a muffin shop and café with her mum, so they were busy people and bloody good friends to take the time to support and help me through this massive fuck-up. They would include me in all the social events at home and away to keep me occupied and I did my bit to earn my keep.

One morning, Lynare called me from work asking me to bring in the dry washing. I agreed but she phoned back moments later coyly asking me to not look at her old "period knickers", which she unknowingly had left on the line. I didn't even know that was a thing! The things you learn.

They went on to marry and start a family, with both careers going well, when suddenly their young daughter was diagnosed with a rare form of cancer, which left everyone reeling. But these two parents rocked up and did everything that needed to be done to get her through to a full recovery. Just when the treatment had a grip on their little girl and hit a crucial period, I had a phone call from Karen telling me that Lynare had died suddenly at home with her kids and husband present. The news was so shocking. She had hit the floor and couldn't be resuscitated as it turned out she had inherited a gene that gave her Long QT syndrome and from that, there was no coming back. She was thirty-seven.

The hurt was all-consuming and I just wanted it to stop. I had been to see my doctor to get some medication to help me sleep and afterwards I was in town, walking around aimlessly, not knowing what to do next. I had lost my home, my boys, my parents wouldn't communicate with me, and I was about to lose my new job as I couldn't function. I honestly felt that I had fucked up majorly and I should've just lived with that dark secret and kept my life as it was.

At that moment, my legs stopped working and I dropped to my knees on the footpath by a busy intersection and ended up leaning against a concrete power box as if I was trying to hide from the busy traffic whizzing by just meters away. I was completely overwhelmed and I could feel my entire body shutting down, my mind felt as though it was being shrouded in what felt like a dark grey fog. I was sobbing and had my head in my hands as I thought it was about to explode. I can only imagine what people in their cars driving by must have thought.

I heard a voice. 'Terry, Terry, what's going on?' Looking up, I saw the practice nurse from my doctor's surgery. She was driving back to the clinic after her lunch break and had spotted me huddled up on the roadside... What are the odds of that happening?

She helped me up and into her car, strapping me in so she could take me to the medical centre to see my doctor and get some urgent help. The details are fuzzy but I remember that I wasn't having a bar of it when I got inside, and I reacted violently when my doctor, who is a softly spoken man with fantastic manners, tried to make me sit and talk about what was going on. Within minutes, I had been sectioned, straight-jacketed and pushed into the back of an ambulance destined for the psychiatric ward on hospital hill. I was yelling and kicking the poor ushers whose sole job was to get me inside in one piece and then I was medicated to calm me right down.

I was awoken by a familiar voice; it was Cousin Val calling my name as she knelt over me, holding my head in her hands. I could feel her tears hitting my face. Looking up, I saw that I was in a white padded cell and I was lying on the soft floor with hospital issued clothing on.

'It's time, Terry,' she said. 'No more lies. It's time to tell the truth.' She knew what was at the core of my trauma and wanted me to say my secret out loud so it would set me free, but when I clicked that she actually knew my truth, I looked away, saying nothing in return. For some reason, I still couldn't admit who I really was as the shame, on top of blowing my life to smithereens, was still so real and unbelievably terrifying. My inner rage was still bubbling just under the surface and for some reason I just couldn't do it… I couldn't say the words that would finally set me free.

The nights in the ward were the most terrifying, with people screaming out, calling names, crying and the odd one trying to escape. The staff were always in and out to check on you and top up your meds to keep us all in a calm state, which sometimes didn't work and there would be a huge punch-up and food would go flying and the culprits would be dragged off and locked away. I ended up in a shared room as the place was really full, bulging with different people — different ages, genders, from different walks of life.

The counseling was intense and regular, and helped me realize what had been going on and why I found myself in this predicament. With each passing day, I started to feel stronger and stronger, making friends and entertaining some of the more colourful "inmates", who understood my style of humour. I had a steady stream of visitors, which became a bit of a joke with the door staff and some patients as it seemed that every announcement that a visitor was at reception, was for me!

My close friends and family would show up and spend hours with me, chatting about what was happening "out there" and it felt nice to see them on a regular basis. My parents, who had never been exposed to anything like this in their lives, also fronted up to see me, which blew me away as I thought it would be just too hard for them. Mum cried when she came in and cried again when she left, but Dad was quite silent through the entire visit and I could see he was struggling being there and seeing me locked away.

When they were leaving, I walked with them to the front door, where Mum kissed me and walked out. Then my dad, that old bushman, turned back to look at me before he walked through the exit and said out loud, 'Love you.'

I stood there in total shock, thinking, *did I hear right?* I had never heard Dad ever say that to me before — ever! But there it was and I was going with that.

Soon I was allowed to roam around the facility freely and was able to go outside and sit in the sun, which felt so amazing after weeks in confinement. One afternoon, I walked up the track from the ward to a spot on the hill that looked over the city. I could see the traffic and people busy rushing around, going about their business. In the distance, I could hear the squeals of kids from the nearby school. I wanted back into that life and I was feeling stronger and calmer than I ever had. It was as though I just needed to check out of this life for a while to gather my thoughts and heal and the healing felt great. Soon I was free to go out on day visits and Val would pick me up and we would go to Aunty Velma's unit where Mum and Joan would be sitting waiting for me and after lots of chatting and a thousand cups of tea, I was dropped back to the ward.

The nights seemed to get easier as I got to know more and more of the other patients, or "inmates", as we affectionately called each other, and we would take our sleeping pills last thing at night and then wait to see who could stay in the lounge the longest before the meds kicked in and turned your legs to jelly and who had to have help to get to their room. It was hilarious.

As my head cleared, my courage grew and I felt in control of my future for the first time I can ever remember. I was sitting at Val's house on a day release and while she was painting her lounge and I was redesigning her mirror frame… I said the words…

'You know I'm gay, don't you?'

'Oh yes,' she replied, 'of course I do.' She then played it down to prove to me that it really wasn't that big of a deal. My next breath felt like I had exhaled for the very first time in my life.

Out of the shadows and into the sunshine

Speaking the truth was a foreign concept to me after decades of secrecy, denial and lies, as shame likes to keep itself hidden very well. But no more — this became a turning point in my life.

My therapy sessions were becoming more and more helpful as we were now discussing everything out loud and the frankness was very liberating. Within a week, I was released from the ward and it was time to say goodbye to my newfound friends and peers on all levels. These people, who had some major problems in their lives, had become part of my recovery and I hope that I became part of theirs in some way, even if it was only the odd rude joke that made them cry with laughter. My medication was key to me keeping well and even though we were only really discovering mental health and medication in those days, it really did keep me level, even if it was a bit monotone at times.

I was out and free and was looking forward to planning my next steps but continued with therapy long enough to feel that my recovery was complete.

Slowly I started to deconstruct the life we had built through our rather turbulent marriage by selling our investment properties and settling who got what and why. I was in a good place mentally and wanted to stay on that path by cleaning up all that wasn't needed and rebuilding with what I had left. Coming out of the closet was still something I was doing bit by bit with the people I could trust to come with me on the healing highway. My ex-wife was not on the list at this stage, as there was still so much negativity between us and I didn't want anything to keep me from my now regular contact with my sons. I felt that there was a chance she may use it against me in some way so I was taking no bloody chances. Eventually, it was all done and dusted…

I went back to work in radio, Lisa moved away to Papamoa, and I bought the big house, which came complete with our two cats and Lass the collie dog, but not much besides that. I think I counted two towels, the odd stick of furniture and bugger all else, but I accepted this as she had the boys and needed that stuff to set up home as a single mum.

I decided to get a flatmate for company and to help with the bills, which opened up new opportunities to meet new friends and I was totally into my new job so life was coming back together well.

The network that I was now working for had some of my old media buddies employed there as well, so I felt completely at home and back to my old self — focused and driven. I clicked with one special person and we soon found ourselves constantly in trouble for skiving off work, drinking too much at client functions, arriving home late and generally misbehaving. Denise revived me and it felt so good to have a new mate who was exclusively mine since the separation. She was sweetly spoken (until she had a few wines in her) and loads of fun. Being part Māori, she was blessed with the most amazing hair — a mass of ringlets — and she would always have it piled up on top of her head with a banana clip that they stopped making decades ago but she had stockpiled in case she ran out. Her personalized plate on her car was "FUZZY1", which looked awesome when you would see her driving along with this massive hairdo, but it suited her so well.

Her partner at the time tolerated me and her young daughter, Casey, thought I was a bit of a laugh, albeit a bit of a piss-head, who kept her mother out late. She soon inherited the nickname "Kaka", as she would mention how much Kaka she would be in when she got home after a night out with me!

Our friendship grew into a special bond and no matter where we worked, where we lived, we were always in contact, however, it was more me as she was so bloody hopeless at picking up the phone. They say it's men that have trouble with multitasking, but I beg to differ!

I'm sure our boss use to cringe when we had social events as "Kaka" and I would always completely write ourselves off, however, it was totally accidental — "honestly" — as we always had such a good time, we would forget to pace ourselves.

Our Christmas parties were usually a dress-up, which we always got so excited about and would spend weeks sorting out our outfits. Denise was Scary Spice, complete with leopard print and teased up curls. I was the devil wearing only undies, a cape and horns, which was rather revealing, but I thought, *what the hell… it's only us at the venue*, so I went with it.

We all boarded the bus and I felt okay about being seminude around my work mates when suddenly the bus pulled into the Novotel bar as pre-drinks were set up there, as a surprise for us before going on to the actual party… Surprise was right. I was practically naked and I had no choice but to get out of the bus and go into one of Rotorua's poshest bars at the time. Mortified would be an understatement as I tried to slip off the bus and into the bar unnoticed, using my colleagues as a shield.

The hotel was packed and so was the small bar and as we ordered the drinks, the crowd split and there I was for all to see, trying to cover everything up with a rather small cape. After a couple of rums, I didn't give a shit and started to enjoy the night. Kaka thought it was hilarious but there were more hilarious moments to come between us.

Like the time we attended the radio awards in Auckland which was *the* social event of the year and always ended in everyone getting trashed at the after-party. It was a formal occasion so I was suited up and Denise had her hair done on the day, which could only be described as resembling a massive beehive. It was like concrete as it took cans and cans of hair spray to hold it up.

It was this night that I decided to "come out" to my new buddy and because she already knew inside, she was so gracious and reassuring. We were on the dancefloor when I leaned into her and said, 'You know I'm gay, don't cha?'

She replied, 'Oh, hell yes! Shall we get outta here and piss off to a gay bar?' And that we did.

We ended up sitting on a bench on Auckland's infamous K'Road at four a.m., waiting for a cab. Denise's money had been stolen out of her purse earlier by some drag queens who insisted on sitting with us, there was vomit all over the footpath from some juveniles who couldn't handle their booze, and Denise's beehive had started to lean like the Tower of Pisa after a bad storm. Thank God no photographs exist of that night!

So, I had told another person close to me my dark secret and it seemed to get easier and easier, and *not* the massive deal I thought it would be. People who loved, liked or cared for me totally supported me and accepted me for who and what I was. After that, I came out at work and slowly the word spread which I was totally OK with.

My family were next and I set a time for my sister, Gloria, to come to Tokoroa after work for dinner and a chat and to make sure my other sister, Desma, was also present. I arrived and they both sat there looking rather sheepish and making small talk, when I piped up and said that all my life I have been so different and struggled with my mental health, and a lot of the reason was that I was gay.

They both sighed in relief as they thought I was either going to tell them that I had cancer or that I was going back to my ex-wife, and neither scenario was preferred. Once again, I was told that they always knew and it wasn't such a surprise — well, they could've bloody well told me!

By this stage, I felt like it was all I was talking about, which is kind of ironic as it was not a topic for discussing for most of my life to that point and I was now thirty-six years old.

Mum and Dad and the rest of my immediate family needed to know and it was agreed that Gloria and Desma would sit them down and tell them collectively. They had a couple of attempts to do the dreaded deed but every time they tried to do so, someone would turn up and interrupt. Finally, they were alone with Myrna and Stubb and out if came. Mum cried and said she also always knew but hoped when I got married and had a family that it would all just disappear. Dad just shrugged his shoulders and said that he had no idea, which isn't surprising as I flew under his radar for most of my childhood as we had bugger all in common. Not a criticism of his fathering but more about us not having a lot in common and, to be honest, I was a bit of a "skirt holder" and never left Mum's side very often as a child.

I'll give my parents their dues as, instead of a phone call, crying and asking me to explain, they instead insisted that I meet them at Aunty Velma's unit (not Joan's, of course) for a catch-up, so I did. Again, there was small talk and a thousand cuppas. I said that we should head out for a coffee and morning tea and with that the three of us began walking up the long driveway to the car.

Mum and Dad were walking behind me, not saying a word, so I thought I should break the silence, but with what? Out it came. I spun around as we walked and said, 'I know that you've been told my news and I just want to say that I didn't ask to be here... You both made me so we are all in this together!' A bit shocked by my comments, they agreed and we had a great talk and they both said that I had their support to be my true self as I was born to be. I could see in my Bushman father's face that he now understood why I was in that psych ward and why I had struggled so much to tell the truth. However, my mum wasn't so keen on the whole idea and it would take years for her to be totally comfortable with it, but, hey, I was so happy that the deed was done, no matter the final outcome!

My ex-wife was next but the bush telegraph got to her first and she called me on another matter to disguise her main question. 'So, I hear you have some news for me? How did your parents react? Is your dad OK with this?' We discussed the issue and she also mentioned that in her heart she actually knew the truth but then went on to say that I had to tell our kids or she would.

This last conversation put a full stop when it came to hiding or defending so even though I knew she right, I felt pressured to get it right and struggled to find the words to tell my babies that Daddy was a poof. In my mind, she wanted me to faulter with this next step, maybe to teach me lesson for not telling her first?

The boys were with me at home, playing outside, when I called them in. 'C'mon... Family meeting time!' This was always the way I got their attention. They groaned about the interruption but managed to slowly arrive in the lounge.

After explaining that I wanted to share something with them...

I asked them both to look at me.

Listen to the sound of my voice.

Touch my hand...

Now.

'Dad's gay.'

Pause.

Daniel was the first to break the silence. 'Gay? Who with?' he questioned, which made me laugh.

'With no one at the moment,' I replied, trying to not crack up too much at his rather awkward but funny response.

And again, I said…

Look at me.

Listen to the sound of my voice.

Touch my hand…

'Now, am I any different from before I told you?'

'No,' they replied, 'can we go back outside and play?'

I agreed and they were off.

Sure, there were lots of other questions and chats over time, which made it easier for all of us to come to terms with this newly exposed truth.

I lost a few friends through the breakup of my marriage, but also when I came out of the closet, which amazed me as some were really close mates from my younger years, but they obviously couldn't cope with the revelation or me so I had to let it be and move on. Homophobia is alive and well in society and pops up its ugly head when you least expect it. Like the time a few of us walked into a local bar and, with the news being still quite fresh, I heard a voice yell out over the crowd, 'Oh look, it's a homosexual!' And, to my surprise, it was someone that I actually knew and not only that, but I had also worked with years before, so after their sniggering and whispering waned I continued with my night.

Everyone is entitled to their own opinion but to do it so publicly was really childish and uncalled for, but because I had heard it all before, I chose to ignore it. I didn't need to defend myself; I knew who I was and such an outburst could only mean that there was nothing else to discuss in their sad little world.

Another example of this sort of behavior happened as I was coming out of work and I crossed paths with one of my ex's friends who, in her own mind, doubled as one of Lisa's many counselors. She was walking with another female and, upon seeing me, said, loud enough for me to hear, 'That's him.' They disappeared, muttering and laughing together. Again, that's fine, as I knew that there would be fallout from all sides surrounding the event, however, it exposed how bitchy it could become. Years later, I was at a reunion of sorts when this self-proclaimed counselor tapped me on the shoulder and said, 'Hey, Terry, remember me?' I'm sure you can fill in the blanks of what happened next.

Denise and I laughed it off over a KFC lunch and once again stressed that nothing else must be happening in their small, grey lives.

Work was busy as all hell and it was "beginning to look a lot like Christmas" again and our company Christmas party was coming up. Once again, we were all ushered onto a bus and D and I had a plan to drink as much free booze as possible. Afterwards, we landed back at my place with a few of the stragglers to end the night in style.

Missing my boys was still quite raw, and I felt so sad and low about them not being home with me so I got a crazy idea in my mind that I would drive to Papamoa in the middle of the night to see them. I made an excuse to those staying that I was off (walking) to the service station to get milk so they wouldn't stop me leaving. I strapped Lass into the passenger seat of my car and we were off on the forty-five-minute trek to the coast. I hadn't even thought about what I would say when I got there, but nothing was going to stop me.

It had been a long, dry summer and that night it started drizzling, which made the road slippery and quite treacherous, but I carried on at normal speed to my destination.

I remember as the car slid out of control and, as if in slow motion, it flipped on its roof, still sliding across the road. It came to rest after a loud thud against a large dirt bank on the roadside.

Hanging upside down in my seatbelt, I looked immediately for my dog and there she was, looking straight at me, also hanging upside down, still strapped in. I managed to loosen her free and she scrambled quickly out of the wreck below me. I quickly followed. My hands were cut from the broken windscreen, but other than a rather big lump on my forehead, I was OK. How the hell we had survived such a massive crash, I will never know.

I stood in the dark next to what was left of my car, not knowing what the hell to do next as my phone was AWOL and I was starting to feel rather woozy. Next minute, there were headlights shining on us from an approaching car, which slowed down and stopped to see if we were OK. My rescuers were a car full of local gang members who, out of concern, checked us out and also managed to look over the car for any leaking petrol, etc. Lass and I got into their car and were sandwiched on either side by these really friendly, concerned and big mountainous guys. This scene must have looked hilarious from the outside looking in.

After they dropped us home, I woke Denise with my news and we had coffee and food while getting ready to call the cops to report the crash. Before I could even dial the number, there was a knock at the door. Yup, it was the police, as they had found my car without me and had plenty of questions to ask. I was breathalyzed and was just under the limit at the time, but because I had been out at a function that night, the insurance company insisted on talking to everyone I was with leading up to the accident. I had passed the breath test but they certainly put me through the wringer before paying out.

I spent one night in hospital for observation but was released the next day. My beloved car was a complete write-off.

Fergusson vs Fergusson

So here I was, working to get on the brink of exploding into gay life with no fear or anything to hold me back, when everything halted with a simple phone call.

It was my soon-to-be ex-wife on the phone, wanting to talk about our eldest son, Ben, as he wasn't coping with the fact that she had more or less moved in her new boyfriend. Ben was causing a few problems for them both, adjusting to this massive change. 'No shit,' I replied, 'I mean, really? Of course, he is going to play up when you push him in a direction he just doesn't want to go!' *Not exactly rocket science, huh?*

The relationship between Ben and his mother was in tatters and he was behaving really badly at home and faltering at school. Daniel was still very young so nothing really affected him and he was not a problem. She insisted that Benjamin come to stay with me long-term.

Let me set the scene. Here I was living in this big house, a flatmate, all the same pets. The boys' room was still set up as they left it to make them feel comfy when they came every second weekend, so one of them returning wasn't a problem, space-wise.

The next day there was a knock at the front door and as I opened it, wine in hand, there was Ben standing there with two PAK'n SAVE bags full of clothes and his favourite toys. He was ten years old…

'I'm home, Dad!' he exclaimed as his mother zoomed off with not even a wave. I ushered him in to put his things back in his room and then come downstairs for a celebration takeaway dinner.

Ben wanted nothing to do with his mother and even *if* I had encouraged him more than I did to talk to her, it still wouldn't have worked. He wouldn't go to any event that she was at and he begged me not to make him go to see her every second weekend, to the point he would go hysterical and hide. Not ideal as, sure enough, I got the blame from his mother, accusing me of poisoning him against her when actually she had done a great job of that herself.

What followed was a balancing act between son, home, work and my newfound social life. Ben settled back into his home routine as if he had never left but was missing his little brother enormously. Daniel was still with Lisa in Papamoa, commuting every day to get him to school in Rotorua where Ben would see him at lunchtimes and after school. During this time, I applied for sole custody of my son to make sure there was no toing and froing between parents and he would then know where his home was. I served Lisa with the papers through my solicitor and she signed it without question — phew!

After putting him into bed one night, I heard him softly sobbing as I left the room, so asked him what had upset him. He said, 'I miss Daniel being here.'

Those words broke my heart…

It was ridiculous that, as parents, we had not only separated from each other but also separated our kids. What the hell were we doing? I felt so responsible and knew I had to make a stand and put this right.

In the meantime, Lisa had mentioned that she and Daniel would like to move to Auckland for work reasons and to be closer to her new man so, as you can imagine, I hit the roof as that kind of separation for these boys would be damaging in the long term…

You learn — Alanis Morrissette, 1995

What followed was like pouring petrol onto a fire that was slowly becoming controllable... Boom!

I started off with a chat to the ex about letting Daniel come home to live with Ben and I but was laughed at and then shut down completely. So I realized I really had no choice but go down the legal road to bring these two brothers back together under the one roof. Can I just say that this entire scenario was so damaging to all involved, but especially, the kids.

There was fighting, yelling, letters to other lawyers and finally a date for court as I had applied for sole custody, as I had done with Ben. I read these court papers every now and again and the horrific things that were said from either side. It really was a shit fight and the ones that were suffering the most were Ben and Daniel.

As part of the case that was being built for custody, we were all referred to an independent counselling service who would release their findings to the court for consideration. The meetings were intense and included in-home interviews at both houses and interviews with any caregivers, including Barbs, and us together, alone and with and without the kids... Wow... it was so intense.

I was now an openly gay man and, apart from the label, I don't think I had changed in any way, and by that I mean I certainly hadn't got any more "camp" but that was about to be challenged. No doubt it was part of my ex's defense and she said to the counselor that she had real concerns around Daniel living with me full time because of my sexuality (um, what about Ben?) and that she thought that Dan would or had been acting more feminine after his stays with me. Even the counselor's mouth dropped open in shock at this comment. Homophobia reared its ugly head right there in that room.

That was the start of the character assassination that was to come. I was accused of being insanely jealous and stating that no other man could ever have her (hmm) and also that I was trawling around public toilets and could have infected her with the AIDs virus and that I was also influencing our youngest son to camp it up. I had smoke coming out my ears but stayed focused and no matter what was said about me, my end goal was to reunite my kids and rebuild their lives.

It was court day and we arrived early so we sat outside the family court waiting for our time to be called in. Mum, Dad and Aunty Joan were there as my support people as I was shitting myself. I looked to the end of the building and I could see puffs of smoke coming from around the corner so I walked over and there was Barbs, my ex-mother-in-law, who I adored, smoking like a chimney, nervously and waiting for her daughter. I felt sick as I really didn't know what to say or do so we hugged it out and I returned to my stony-faced support team.

Lisa showed up being physically supported by two friends and stopped to talk to us... My mother stood up and blocked any communication by putting her hand up to her and saying, 'Go away, Lisa!' I was gob smacked, as Mum had obviously had enough of all the hurt and bullshit that had been going on from her favourite daughter-in-law and made a stand on my behalf. Go Myrna! I was incredibly proud of her and it felt good to walk into the courtroom with these staunch people at my side... My family.

The entire performance of the broken, wounded woman and mother on show didn't make sense to me at all and, sure enough, as the proceedings kicked off, her lawyer stood up and announced she was dropping the case and awarding sole custody of Daniel to me, as she wanted to move to Auckland!

However, she had also included in the statement that I wouldn't ask her for any maintenance... What? News to me. I now have two kids to support on my own and I had paid my share when the boys were with her?

It all fell into place and the act was maybe to make her feel and look better in public about what was about to be revealed and the way she would be seen or judged for giving up custody of her kids without a fight — who knows?

Barbs was devastated and took a lot of talking to from Lisa's side to accept her daughter's decision but I kept her in the boys' life regardless and she eventually became their afterschool care again, which kept her close to all of us.

Within a week, Max and I went to Papamoa to pick up Daniel and his belongings. He was quite happy to jump in the truck with us and head home along with a broken chest of draws and not much else, but who cares, my sons were finally back together and overnight I became a solo dad.

The boys and I managed to get ourselves into normality reasonably quickly. A lot of that was down to their living environment, being back at the house they called home, and schools and sports clubs actually helped that along. I would hear them giggling at night and chatting when they were meant to be sleeping. All was good…

Lisa had reasonable access but it took time for Ben to really get into it again, however, eventually he relented and spent weekends with his mother and her partner in Auckland, via bus if she was too busy to pick them up.

The question of maintenance was raised again but the ex's answer to this was that if I tried to push for it and through inland revenue, she and her boyfriend would simply cry poverty through their company. Frustratingly, her take on it was that she would buy them things as needed. As a solo dad, I was questioned by any income support agency about me having the boys as a solo and not their mother. I was constantly called by them, with the details all ass about face, as they really didn't know how to treat a dad that ended up with the kids as it's usually the mother… But not in this case. Obviously. She soon married her partner, divorced him and then married again.

Lass, our collie dog, got sick and was diagnosed with cancer. The boys were devastated when I told them that she had to be put to sleep so we all spent her last night kissing her and cuddling her, making her comfy in her favourite spot in the laundry. The next day, the vet came over to do the deed and as she laid on my lap looking at me talking to her, I could see the unconditional love in her eyes that doggies have for their owners. I was still telling her what a special lovely girl she was when her eyes, which were still fixed on me, went still and she was gone without a flinch or whimper. Ben and Daniel, who had been taken out so as not to witness the injection, returned and sat with me still cradling out sweet girl until it was time to wrap her up in her blanket and bury her in the back yard. We planted a tree on her so, if we moved, no one would ever accidentally dig her up and there she remains to this day.

Te Hokianga Mai. At this time, I decided that my boys and I would take some time out and go on a trip of self-discovery to find out who we were as "Fergussons", where we came from, and why. Family, and our history, were always important to me and I wanted me and my offspring to know more about all of the above. My grandfather, Ern, always talked about the far north and his connection to the *tangata whenua* in the Hokianga, so I thought that was a good place to start.

I thought of speaking to Stubb, but as he wasn't really into the "need to know this" stuff so I decided that I would do all the digging and research on my own so as not to taint any valuable information with misinformation or opinions. We didn't know stuff about our *whakapapa* (family history) outside of the Jolleys (Mum's family) so I wanted my two boys to know all there was to know about who we were as a family.

I researched through records to find out as much as I could, based on the scraps of info that Ern had left us, and found some cemetery records in a place called Kohukohu on the Hokianga Harbour, and then some Fergussons that were still living in the surrounding area. Bingo!

I packed the boys and a pup tent into the car and, after a night in Auckland at my niece's flat, we heading north. To get the boys excited, we nicknamed the trip "Our Big Adventure" and we still fondly remember it as that to this day. I decided we would head up along the east coast, through the Bay of Islands, Waitangi and then Cape Reinga, then down to the west coast and the Hokianga, where I hoped that everything I needed to know, was waiting for me.

It was the week of New Year's Eve, 1998, and our first stop for the night was at Waitangi and because it was midsummer and post-Christmas, it seemed as though the world was on holiday, including us!

All the camping grounds were full and I was starting to panic as the boys were tired and grumpy and just wanted to stop and get out of the car. I was directed by a local to Te Tiriti O Waitangi Marae, where the *tangata whenua* had opened their land for camping for a small fee. We all lined up and were shown to a tiny space where we pitched our tent.

Dinner was takeaways and we settled in for the night, with the boys playing on their new handheld Nintendos, which took up most of their attention. I had been narrating on historical points of interest for the past few hours, which obviously fell on deaf ears.

The so-called campground was absolutely chock-a-block full of teens and mid-twenties partiers, and our wee tent was not far from the toilet and shower block. The number of idiots who tripped over our tent pegs and ropes all throughout the night was infuriating, as I had to get up each time it happened as I didn't want our shelter to fully collapse on us. By the time morning broke, I was tired and ropable at these bloody idiots who continuously kept us awake, so we packed up early and hit the road.

We came to a small village called Kaeo, which Ern would always talk about as he was born there. His parents, Hudson and Emma, owned a farm. My nana told me that every time he ventured back here to his hometown, he would get off the bus by the bridge and walk a few minutes to the cemetery where his mother was laid to rest at only fifty-four.

Emma, apparently, was a strong woman who looked after her family when "Papa" (Hudson) would venture into the bush for months on end to find work and she would run the farm. Being a crack shot, she would always have a pot of wild pigeon stew on the stove to feed her nine children and was also one of the first women in the north to sign the petition to parliament to give women the vote in New Zealand.

As we drove into the village, we stopped at the bridge by the store but there was no sign of a cemetery so I parked the car and walked up the main street. I chatted to a few of the locals who gave me directions to the local cemetery but it all seemed a bit new to be housing Emma's remain. Just as I was about to load the boys back in the car and continue north, I was approached by a local store owner, who told me of an old settlers' cemetery that was quite hard to find and close to the bridge at the southern entrance of town. 'That's it!' I exclaimed.

My boys and I retraced Ern's footsteps from the bridge on the main road and came across a small church in an overgrown paddock, wedged between some new housing, so no wonder we couldn't see it.

Walking up to the gate, I saw the cemetery entrance to the right-hand side. It was on a small hill underneath some massive older trees and the old broken headstones were dotted and visible through the long, unkempt grass.

Wandering about in between the crumbling reminders of lives long ended and forgotten, we saw a small, neglected headstone and grave that was facing the opposite way and covered by moss and scrub.

In Memory of Our Dear Mother — EMMA FERGUSSON.

We found her! My great-grandmother — my boys' great-great-grandmother. So we sat there... All us Fergussons together and cleaned up the overgrowth to perhaps make her feel that she wasn't forgotten. Ben's tooth had fallen out that day in the car so he decided to leave it under a stone by Emma's headstone.

We continued on as far north as possible and eventually arrived at Cape Reinga, where the Tasman Sea meets the South Pacific Ocean at the northernmost tip of New Zealand. It was breathtaking and even Ben and Dan loved being at the "end of the world", watching the surge of the two water masses meet. It was a gravel road to reach this point in the 1990s, so rather than heading back on it that night, we decided to pitch our tent at a DOC site in the next bay, which had a small concrete utility block and was surrounded by a stony estuary and surf beach.

On that beach, I gathered the three of us up, put our faces together, turned my old camera around and tried to take a picture of us. It wasn't a digital and our phones didn't have cameras at that time, so I didn't know if it actually worked until I had the film developed weeks later. However, it was a great shot, which we all have a copy of today, that captured our close relationship... A snapshot in time... A *selfie* before we even knew what a selfie was!

Our accidental selfie. Daniel, Ben and me.

As we continued, getting closer to the Hokianga, I felt a sense of excitement and anticipation about what I would find out about our whānau (family) and who I might meet.

Arriving in Kohukohu, I was soon directed up a small gravel, dusty road to another old settlers' cemetery, and to talk to long-time resident, Vic Gurney. We were given directions to his house on the same road and told to ask him for details on who was in that old cemetery and where.

I was nervous but drove up and made my way along the broken path to the front door, which was wide open. I knocked a couple of times then finally a rather gravelly and grumpy sounding man's voice responded, 'Who's there?' I gingerly I stated my name and business.

He appeared out of the darkness of his run-down villa's hallway. He was a small man with a weathered face, some random teeth, loosely fitting clothes and a walking stick. 'What did you say your name was, boy?' he grumbled. 'Oh yes, OK,' he responded, seeming rather annoyed at me for interrupting his busy day. But then, rather abruptly, he signaled me to help him down the path and into our car. My sons were bloody horrified that this old man was now sitting in the passenger seat.

My rather bored and hungry sons' eyes rolled as soon as the next boneyard came into sight as they were totally over old dead people, headstones and long grass. They just wanted to sit in the car and play on their handheld consoles, but, of course, I insisted on another walkabout.

Old Mr Gurney gave us the entire rundown on the region and the occupants of that *urupa* (cemetery). It was because of him that we located Papa Hudson's parents, who were at the top of the hillside cemetery, surrounded by Fergusson after Fergusson. They were obviously very loved to have so many family, wanting to rest alongside them. The headstone had long gone, due to slips and age but there was no mistaking their importance and connections to the area.

James and Elizabeth Fergusson had nine children; Papa Hudson was their eldest boy. Elizabeth had met and married the Scotsman, James Fergusson, whilst in Australia, having been sent to Sydney and Bendigo to be educated by her parents, John Leaf and Te Rangahau Terewhare, whose father was paramount chief, Taku Terewhare.

How amazing is this! Travelling by ship to be educated for a better life in those days seems mind-blowing as, at that time, travel was more a luxury than necessity.

There's not a lot known about James, as he was as elusive as the ship he said that he arrived in Australia on. It's thought he may have been a convict or deserter and used the name "Fergusson" as a *nom de plume* to avoid detection, so the truth behind it is lost in the pages of time where no doubt he wanted it to stay. They married and came to live in New Zealand in 1853, settling on Opara, our ancestral land, on the banks of the Hokianga Harbour

All these fascinating stories came at me like a machine gun from all the people I met next. It was like a domino effect and it just kept coming after that fateful meeting with the old man, Vic. I just wish my sons were old enough to appreciate all this history about our family that was unfolding but, at this young age, they really didn't care too much.

A huge amount of this information was recorded by James himself, as he was a writer, scribe and poet, who had obviously been well educated in his youth before his venture from the old country to the new world. He had married into Māori aristocracy and recorded all the happenings and history that surrounded him and his wife's colorful family. He wrote about Te Rangahau, his new mother-in-law, capturing her and her husband's stories about Great Chief Taku and how he was murdered by rival tribes that were constantly trying to take him down and grab his ancestral land, Opara, as the grand prize. He was written to be nearly seven-foot tall, good looking and extremely popular with the Victorian settler women at the time. When he was taken down by his rivals, James wrote of the huge amount of grief and mourning and cutting of skin, which was tradition at the time.

Te Rangahau, he great Taku's daughter, made her own mark in Hokianga's history when she reportedly swam out to a ship that was anchored at the mouth of the treacherous entrance to the Hokianga Harbour to warn those aboard about an impending ambush by some local warriors. She saved many lives and subsequently married Mr John Leaf, who was on board.

All of these writings were captured by James and stored in handsewn books that are now housed in the Alexander Turnbull Library in the National Library of New Zealand. How lucky are we as a family to have all this recorded history and *whakapapa,* which documents our lineage right back to Kupe and the arrival of the Māori to Aotearoa — New Zealand.

Ngaru Nui

Ngaru Roa

Ngaru Paewhenua

"Big waves, long waves, waves landing on the shore".

Elizabeth (Leaf) Fergusson (My Great Grandmother)

I had finally found my very own *whakapapa* that deep inside I had been searching for but never new actually existed. I would be envious of people with those strong family connections and yearned to know more about Fergusson for the longest time. I had the calling to my *Māoritanga* during my high school years participating in *kapa haka* and the learning of *te reo*, the Māori language, but here it was on paper, the real me and something that I could pass on to my own family as direct descendants. Wow!

Opara, being our ancestral land and home, had long been sold by the last Fergussons who lived there, but was still known as our land. It was now uninhabited and rather overgrown where the houses of James and Elizabeth once stood but being on a mission to take my boys there, we drove slowly to the end of the road and then to the end of a dirt track that led to Opara. It must have looked like the townies had come to the country as there was my BMW parked awkwardly in a paddock in the middle of bloody nowhere.

The wind was howling around us as we started to walk along the roughly cut track to the gate with a sign saying "Opara". The boys went running ahead of me as we could see peeks of the harbor. I ran to keep up. It felt as though a thousand eyes were watching us even though these was no one around this deserted piece of land. I thought about the generations of my family that had lived and cared for this land and felt their energy surrounding us as we made our way down to the water and remnants of houses long since gone.

We took photos and I explained to my sons the importance of this land to our whanau (family). Ern had told the story of when his grandmother, Elizabeth, was dying and he rode his horse from Kaeo to Opara to be with her before she passed. Even though he was a great one for stretching the truth, the dates lined up — he would've been sixteen when she died, which meant that he was definitely there on our land on her last days.

However, he had also told us that he had jumped off a cliff on horseback, into the Whangaroa Harbour, and outswam many sharks that were snapping at his heels. Never let the truth get in the way of a good story, huh?

It was a hard trek back to the car, which was mostly uphill, when halfway there we bumped into two women on horseback who said that they had had a quiet chuckle at this abandoned BMW further up the road. Again, they reiterated that this was still known as the Fergusson land and I felt a certain pride as I told them that we were indeed the descendants from this whenua. The boys, at this stage, were completely over it — tired and grumpy — so I halted any further history lessons for the time being and we headed back to civilization.

I was then directed to the town of Kaikohe and the home of Pick and Anita Fergusson, who were distant cousins of Dad. The boys and I walked into their home and were greeted with hugs, handshakes and the smell of fresh baking. One look at Pick's face and I could see my grandfather, Ern, smiling back at me with those twinkly Fergusson eyes.

We were made to feel so welcome and were shown into the lounge where another cousin, who was called over to meet us, was sitting.

Wilma leapt to her feet and grabbed me with both hands, looking at my face. 'You're a bloody Fergusson, all right! Just look at those eyes!' she yelled. Apparently, I had the same twinkly blue eyes we all inherited from James, along with the olive skin from Elizabeth's whānau.

Boom! Yup, I was definitely in the right place with the right people and even though I had been through hell in the recent past, I felt such a sense of belonging to a family that I shared a surname with but was never told anything about. I'm sure Ern would have loved to see this reconnection playing out.

The boys and I were so over camping that we had booked into a motel with hot and cold running water and a TV — bloody luxury, much! Exhausted after all the chatting and catching up, we made our way back to the unit for a well-deserved rest and early night, but not before Wilma invited us to her home the next day and then onto the family baches, owned by her two daughters, back on the Hokianga Harbour.

We arrived at their baches on New Year's Eve and were asked to stay with Wilma, her husband, Maurice, their daughters and extended family. It was a time filled with food, great stories, great company and sharing of information on all our connections.

Ben and Daniel lapped up all the fun with their distant relatives of the same age, foraging and discovering gems along the rugged shoreline, swimming, collecting shells, etc. And here's me even oystering in knee-deep mud under mangroves in my new flash sneakers, along with fishing in the wee small hours with Wilma's nets and riding around on the back of the truck to bring all our treasures back to base.

New Year's Eve came and went and we all enjoyed the food, music and great company and even though the three of us were so far from home, there was absolutely no anxiety about any kind of separation.

Elaine and Marie, Wilma's daughters, made us feel like kings and knew that I was searching for something at this time, knowing that my sexuality and the trauma of my family breakdown had played a significant part in getting me there to them. All this without uttering a word, which gave me a sense of belonging and closeness. Now that's unconditional love in its finest form and I felt so at home with these new cousins.

Home was something that I knew we had to return to, but in the meantime, we enjoyed the stillness of the historic place of our ancestors under the magical starry skies of the Hokianga.

Wilma and her family made regular trips to Rotorua to stay with us and also made time to see Dad and Mum in Tokoroa. Some of my siblings and kids now attend regular *huis* in Kohukohu to this day to make sure the next generation is aware of all that contributed to who we are today.

It was so cool that we all reconnected through one random trip to the Hokianga, which unlocked the unknown part of our family history that would most certainly have been lost in time.

During this period, it felt so good to learn more about where we came from by uncovering my past. Elizabeth (Leaf) Fergusson, 1835–1912, my great, great, grandmother. I am them and they are me… And I carry their spirit within my very being. Ever since this trip of self-discovery, which I can now hand over to my children, I like to talk about it at every opportunity so the full meaning of who we are as descendants is installed in our family and never to be once again lost.

However, as I write this, I am once again reminded that it's not that simple to be merged with a community where you have strong family ties and expect to be welcomed with open arms. The Ngāpuhi are a strong noble people and I get that, but as a direct descendant, I expected a little bit more from the local people and also surrounding area and not only on this trip but the ones that followed.

The rudeness and racist remakes that were spat at us as visitors were horrific and escalated when it was found out that I was gay. I was directly related to these locals but they judged me as just another honky. I struggled even to get served at the bar and when I did I, was treated like something they had stepped in. One woman, who owned a fish and chip shop, took one look at me and turned her back… Why? I was too white? It was so disappointing that I needed to explain who I was and that I was, in fact, related. I received a written apology from the owners of the pub and the employees were talked to about the incident, but this kind of behavior can leave a bitter taste in your mouth.

My first actual visit to my great grandmother's *marae, Matai Aranui,* was also tainted with disappointment. I arrived and found some people sitting out the back of the *wharekai* (cookhouse). I introduced myself and asked if there was anyone who knew of my great granny Leaf's family. The answer was a direct "no" and they also turned their back on me. A few years later, there was a Leaf and Fergusson *hui* (gathering) held on that very *marae* and when the invite came, asking me to be part of it, I declined. So hurt was I, that I decided that, as long as I live, I will never set foot on that *marae* with those who turned me away. Why would I?

Racism in the far north is alive and kicking and delivered extremely well by a hand full of these ignorant locals, however, their *whenua* is also mine and I won't be locked out just because the shade of my skin is lighter than theirs.

Colonization of New Zealand has a lot to answer for as it really did devastate the Māori as people and the confiscation of land left a lot of tribes displaced. A huge amount of us in NZ are mixed race and, like me, can prove their lineage right back to the arrival of Kupe. So where does that leave us, the slightly caramel-colored people, and where do we belong? Is it right to be pushed out and judged? This really never sat right with me and still doesn't to this day.

After a couple of years, it was time to move on and I sold the big house in Rotorua and we all moved out to Lake Okareka, on the outskirts of the cit. Here we enjoyed the "lakes lifestyle", with kayaking, cycling, tramping, swimming and great times overall.

During the time out there, it passed two years since the end of my marriage so I called the ex and asked her to sign the divorce papers. For some weird reason she said no and she would consider it in time. As I didn't even know her physical address in Auckland, I was well in my rights to divorce her anyway, by serving the papers to her next of kin. I apologized to Barbs as they were served to her and she gasped as she said, 'Oh my god, Terry, I'm going to be in so much shit with my daughter for signing these.' But as I saw it, her daughter had every opportunity to do the right thing, sign and move on, but because it was me that was asking, she was going to drag it out as long as possible. So, of course, I got the call from her screaming at me down the phone about how I dare involve her mother in this! I hung up.

My flatties at the time said we should mark the occasion with a divorce party. However, the lakes community was a little bit "nice and quiet" so I wondered how we could get away with having a massive piss-up at home…

We nailed it by coming up with the idea of disguising the party as a wedding and starting mid-afternoon, so we flew into action. The invites went out, bridesmaids were chosen, flowers ordered, along with white balloons and white ribbon for the cars. We also decided that there would be a ceremony of sorts, declaring my marriage to single life. With the boys being present, we made sure there was no reference to my ex or divorce and they were chuffed to be involved and dress up for the occasion.

The day came and all the guests showed up in wedding attire — men in suits and ladies wearing hats and fascinators, with me and the other members of the faux wedding group arriving in our pimped-out cars shortly after. The ceremony was hilarious and complete with Sheeba, our new collie, who founds us and insisted we were her forever family. After the formalities, we headed lakeside for photographs and then the party started and boy, did we rock that night. Our plan worked and no one complained about the noise, cars or people wandering everywhere. Well, it would be rude to complain about a wedding party at home, wouldn't it?

Halfway through the party, Lisa was phoning to speak to the boys and insisted they tell her what was going on and why Dad was having such an enormous party. It sounds silly but that function really did make me feel free of the past and her and also made me realize I was ready to meet someone special.

Y2K was almost upon us, along with the huge marketing campaign telling us that all our electronics would stop on the stroke of midnight, which had us all twitching with anxiety. A bigger dilemma with just as must importance was what to do on this rather historic New Year's Eve and everything that was suggested in our household just didn't seem appropriate to mark such a major event. I was lucky enough to have both of my boys at home over this time so my options were limited anyway. It was decided that the entire household, including flatties and cousins, would all attend the free concert at the lakefront soundshell.

The final day of 1999 was overcast and drizzly, with a forecast that showed it getting worse… Great! This meant limited options, but off we went with umbrellas in hand and a chilly bin full of food, juice and booze. We positioned ourselves dead center in the crowd to see all the entertainment and to keep as dry as possible. I sat Ben and Dan on either side of me as the rain started to really set in and, as the magic moment drew closer, and just as the last minute of the twentieth century was about to pass, I picked them both up in my arms and we all screamed at the top of our voices, 'Happy New Year!' The band started singing "Auld Lang Syne" and the crowd erupted with cheers followed by hugs and kisses all round. We had made it into the twenty-first century and the lights were still on!

The only thing really missing was the massive fireworks display, which had been cancelled due to the shocking weather. It was something that will always be etched in my memory as a special moment, not only in history but in my experience of being a dad.

Ready, set, go!

Life was good and the lake was awesome but my job wasn't paying what I needed to survive with my two dependents. My buddy, Denise, had moved away with her partner and daughters, which added to work being a little more drab than normal. I started to look around and almost immediately I was offered a transfer with the same network to Auckland, which really wasn't on my radar at all but the money was good and I would get more opportunities for progression in the big city. Being closer to the boys' mother *could* be a plus for them when it came to access, which would take the pressure of them having to travel to see her. It seemed like a no-brainer to me but my boys dug their heels in and didn't want to live in the big city at all, saying that they were happy living in the country, by the lake and not in a smothering, busy city, so I had to work on a compromise.

I had a friend, Julie, who was living in Pukekohe with her sons and she found a massive old house with enough room for all of us and, to top it all off, it was on a farm, being the original farmhouse. But this meant I would have to commute to the Radio Pacific studio in Ponsonby for work each day, but my boys liked that idea so it was all I had to work with. The moving truck was ordered and we were off, zooming up the motorway with two kids, two cats, and a dog. We were all so excited but a little unsure as well, because leaving all our friends and family behind was a massive call and here we were driving off from everything that was secure and familiar to all of us.

We arrived in Pukekohe and drove up to this massive old farmhouse where Julie was frantically trying to unpack and work around all our furniture and stuff that had arrived the day before. What a mess!

We soon got it sorted and the kids started at the local school on the Monday. I was so worried about them and how they would settle in as I hurtled north daily into Ponsonby for work. The pressure was on at work and it was difficult for me to navigate myself around the city at first, with the A to Z in one hand and steering wheel in the other. Again, I was incredibly lucky as I met and worked with some really cool people and had a lot of fun. It was a bit like "work hard, play hard" and that's exactly how we rolled.

However, the pressure was on to get back to Pukekohe straight after work and NOT stay for drinks or any functions, as I didn't want Julie to feel as though she was a glorified babysitter. But that's what was starting to happen.

Lisa would try to have the boys every second weekend, which gave me a break and a sleep-in or even a night out with my new colleagues, which was really refreshing and very welcomed. But after taking them on one Friday evening, I was woken (rather hungover) by a seven-a.m. phone call, on my mobile. It was Ben whispering for me to come and get him — actually, he was pleading for me to drive to Albany to bring him back home. He explained that, once again, he was clashing with the new stepfather and there were a couple of physical altercations between them. Ben wasn't quite twelve years old, still a kid. I know that kids can be hard work, believe me, but they only had to have them one weekend every now and again and they couldn't even get that right!

'Put your mother on the phone,' I growled and reluctantly he did. I was laughed at when I queried what the hell was going on and why the hell the situation couldn't have been diffused instead of scaring the shit of the kid. Of course, we disagreed and I said to pack up their things and I would drive the hour to pick both of them up. I asked Julie to come with me to make sure I didn't lose my shit and be the voice of reason, but when we arrived, I was absolutely fuming.

'One weekend!' I yelled. 'That's all I ask and you couldn't even make sure your kids felt comfortable enough to stay!' I ushered both of the boys into the car where Julie was waiting and then I went back in to face Lisa and her husband.

It was explained that the new stepfather ran a tight ship, very regimented, and felt that Ben and Daniel were just too naughty so he smacked and chased to enforce his laws. I lost it. What the hell? Ben had just got back to a place that he felt OK to stay with his mum and here are her and hubby being all hard-ass. 'You ought to be ashamed of yourself, letting this man hit your babies!' Then I pointed to the step-daddy. 'And you! You are *never* to touch my kids again!' Of course, they both shrugged it off as if I was overacting but I had had a bloody gutful of their crap and with that I left.

So, I was back in the same boat, with the boys' home every weekend, as their mother wasn't in touch much for a while. With this extra stress, I decided it would be easier to rent in the city so I was closer to work and closer to the boys and their schools. So we left Julie in Pukekohe and moved into the eastern suburbs of Auckland and enrolled the kids in a nearby school. Eventually, I sold the lake house in Rotorua and brought a unit in Kohimarama, so I guess that meant we were in the big city to stay.

Being a gay man in Auckland was certainly becoming interesting and I was becoming more and more aware of the options that were open to me. On one hand, I had all my new mates trying to set me up with guys at every opportunity, and I had the option of a multitude of bars and clubs to frequent, along with a selection of sex-on-site venues, including saunas, that were there if I just needed to get laid. The fact that I had two kids that were relying on me and I couldn't just disappear into a big rainbow fog whenever I wanted to definitely kept me grounded and aware of my responsibilities. Oh, I was no angel, but I always knew when my cut-off was and that I needed to head home.

I was lucky enough to be put onto an English language school who offered their students as au pairs in exchange for free board. Over the years, we had four Asian students stay with us and all of them became very special to us. They were great with the boys and freed up a lot of my time. We treated them as part of our family and had a lot of laughs and fun trying to teach them English. Each time one of our students would leave to go home, we would all get so upset and really miss them after they left.

My mate, Denise, had split with her partner and moved to Auckland with daughter, Casey. I was thrilled to have my buddy close to me again and soon we were working together at the same radio network. This time, we were actually trying to behave ourselves and not go out on benders too often as we were both solo parents now but we were always so excited on a Friday night to wind down after a long week and have a wine or ten.

It was coming up to my fortieth birthday and I didn't really want a party as such, so I compromised and booked a party bus which would pick us up, serve us drinks, play the music we wanted and drop us off home afterwards. It was a crazy night and shitloads of fun. All my sisters had come from Tokoroa, including Heather and husband, Joe, who insisted on taking his shirt off and parading around the top of Mount Eden, where the bus had made a pitstop. Joe was a cross between Billy T James and Prince Tui Teka, and adored both. He would always insist that Māoris don't get sick at all, just pākehās, however, a few years later, he succumbed to heart disease after a lifetime of smoking and bad habits that shortened his life, leaving Heather a reasonably young widow.

Also on the bus with us was my first attempt at dating — a guy from Yugoslavia. I had met him through mutual friends and found myself quite taken with him and his husky accent. On the outside, he was an intellect, coming across as squeaky clean and perfect in every way, apart from his sometimes-explosive temper and inability to communicate with my kids, which made things bloody hard at home. Again, my sons were always my priority so any relationship I entered into was bound to be a juggling act.

After a few years of ups and downs, break ups and reunions, with this guy, I found my anxiety levels were through the roof and I felt so vulnerable and exposed being in this relationship as I never really knew where I stood and my emotions were all over the place. Unfortunately for me, I had self-diagnosed and had come off my medication a few months before, as I thought life was great, and mentally, I was in such a great place. But this act of defiance left me living on my nerves most days.

Why do we do this to ourselves when it comes to medication? Well, there has always been a stigma around being on any drug for our mental health and it can be seen as a weakness, and that we don't really need them and should just harden up, But, unbeknown to me at this stage, I would need to be on some form of medication for the rest of my life.

My foreign partner's parents were so great and I grew quite attached to them both, although their English was hard to understand. My mum and sisters, and even brothers-in-law even met them and we were both so happy that our families got on famously. His parents were so sweet and accommodating in every way.

But all was not as it seemed and his regular fierce outbursts and sulky episodes, which lasted days on end, were a symptom of a really fucked up idea of being a faithful, loving partner. I know that there is a stigma around the gay lifestyle and that we are all promiscuous but I was in love and I wanted this to be the real thing and wanted to believe what I was experiencing was the real thing. Remember, that was my first real attempt at a male-to-male "gay" relationship and I was in, boots and all.

Looking back, I find it amazing that I allowed his verbally abusive behavior and controlling nature acceptable and my self-esteem began a downward slide. However, my new love spent more time arguing with me about the smallest things and, as I found out, spent more time on sex chat lines, internet dating, and hook-up sites. And more time in public toilets than council cleaners do. When I found out, I was so angry that I totally lost my shit and threw him out of the house, screaming at him never to come near me or my family again. I was humiliated beyond belief and totally disappointed that I wasted my time and trust on this guy who was a bit of a non-starter and not really boyfriend material.

My anxiety was off the scale and I fell into a deep depression and just couldn't manage to get out of it. It trapped me in the house and I felt such a failure that I put all my effort into a guy who bullshitted not only me but my family, who he had met as well. At times, I was curled up in the hallway of our house when I was alone, sobbing uncontrollably and tensing with frustration and fear.

I started drinking every night to dull the pain and the more I drank the more worthless I felt, but it really was the only way I could escape from all the voices in my head the shame and constant phone calls, asking me what the hell had happened.

I was still managing to play the part of a parent and, believe me, I should've been awarded an Oscar for my part in putting on a painted-on smile. To be honest, the parenting was the only thing that got me up in the morning and helped me stick to at least some kind of routine.

My buddy, Denise, saved my life, at this time, literately coming to my aid after a slurry, muffled phone call I made to her in the early hours. I had decided that I had just had enough of the hurt, bullshit and lies and wanted to check out for a while… I really had hit rock bottom for the second time in my life and I was only forty-two — surely, I should be able to manage by now! Maybe something's broken as it all seems to hit me too hard, affects me too much… Why can't I just deal with it like "normal" people do? Why can't I bloody cope with the "downs" in life?

I recovered with the help of my family who raced to Auckland to take me home to Tokoroa and into the arms of my parents so I could pull myself together. Mum and Dad were again really shaken by my actions and I felt so guilty to put them through stuff like this again as it seemed as though I was the only one giving them this level of stress.

My boss at the time was a woman called Sandie, who I always kept at arms-length as we kind of clashed over her ideas of leadership, as opposed to mine, and her gruff personality really rubbed me up the wrong way. Before my return to work after this latest "event" I had a knock at the door and there stood Sandie. I was shocked to see her in my home environment but could see that she was on a mission and wanted to talk to me.

Over coffee, she chatted about life and all the obstacles we're faced with each day. I was waiting for the punch line… It came in a positive form that made me really stop and think of the words she uttered on that particular day. She said to me, 'In this life, Terry, you can achieve anything you want, whether it be success in your personal life or success in your career. You personally have the potential to do anything you want; you just need to believe it yourself.'

I know that nowadays it sounds cheesy and textbook but these words became a turning point for me and I started to believe that I could change my life one day at a time. Sandie, as far as I know, left her media career and went on to set up her own life coaching business so maybe we both learnt something that day.

Returning to work was better for me than the next round of counselling that I was pushed into and I put my head down and went hard, concentrating on being the best I could within that environment. Denise and I fell into our regular routine, but this time we had discovered an old karaoke bar just up the road from the radio network we worked at. The booze was cheap and the surroundings matched the prices, so we hit it regularly and hit it hard. Celine Dion and Elvis Presley, we were not, but we had shitloads of fun trying our best to be as good as them.

I can't really remember why we stopped going there but it was about the time that we fell off our chairs and argued with the DJ about the songs we wanted to sing. As always, Casey, Denise's daughter, was at home waiting for her with a rather disapproving look on her face and my boys looked about the same if they were at home and not at their mother's for the weekend. 'Who are the kids and who are the parents here!' we would both exclaim! However, we were secretly scared of them.

It was another New Year's Eve and Denise and I were both single again the major topic of the buildup was where to go and what to do on the big night. All of our kids were away so we met a friend of D's at the Shakespeare Tavern in the central city. Her friend set us up with a little "something" that we added to our drinks and off we flew. We were at a private rooftop party overlooking Queen Street then decided, after a wee "top up" that we would hit the bars. We headed to Vulcan Lane and then on to Fort Street, where it was all happening. There were people everywhere and the streets were echoing with the thumping of bass coming from the different clubs.

We took a turn and ended up at the doors of a club etched deep in my memory. It was the old Alfie's Bar, where I had arrived in the 1980s and danced with a guy for the very first time. Now it was a big, glossy version of its former self and renamed G.A.Y. There was broken glass all over the floor of the entrance from a fight earlier and God knows what else. Denise had whipped her shoes off at the previous pit stop so I decided to piggyback her over the jagged, messy threshold for safety's sake. As I placed her down in front of a ginormous drag queen to pay our entrance fee, she (the drag queen) took one look at Denise's rather wayward bouffant hairdo and, with a bellowing voice, she shrieked, 'Nice wig, love!'

'Wig!' Denise replied, rather pissed off. 'This ain't no wig, it's real and I'm a real woman, unlike you!'

How we ended up getting admitted I will never know but in we were and hit the dancefloor immediately as we were both completely off our tits. The drinks were flowing and as I was on the dancefloor boogying in a crowd of mates who I had just introduced myself to, I looked up to see D dancing in the go-go cages instead of the gold painted go-go boys. 'Go, girl, go!'

The club closed and we were thrown out onto the street, which, by this time, was drenched in the morning light and the tweeting of birds. We hailed a taxi and headed home to my place still on a high from our antics during the night. We decided that we were too munted to sleep and six thirty a.m. was way too early to go to bed, so we poured ourselves a drink, put on some Kate Bush and danced ourselves to sleep mode. However, not before talking shit about how relationships were just too hard and how we were both sick of being sad when you come out the other end.

However, I decided to get back on the horse, so to speak, and cranked up my profile online with the best pic I could find and the best bio I could write, trying to attract the right guys that I wanted to shag. Fuck the whole "falling in love" crap, as I just continually got hurt when it went tits up. I was solely after hook-ups with no strings… Far less hassle.

Hooking up with guys on the net made me feel like I was in heaven!. All the fringe benefits with none of the hassle. no names , no chatter , just sex and a lot of it.

It may have been soulless sex with no commitment but it was exactly what I needed during this time. I had a steady stream of suiters that I would even go back to for seconds if they were any good. There was always someone online and getting laid was never a problem. On top of that, sometimes I would meet someone at a bar or club or sauna and set them up as a regular sex partner or fuck buddy. As far as I was concerned it was a win-win.

But after time, I realized that these fun, but brief encounters, do whet your sexual appetite, however, do little to gain and maintain self-esteem. Therefore, it tends to make us become very cynical about other long-term relationships and hard on the people within them.

Again, there was a certain *shame* around getting spotted at the sauna or online by other gay guys which is crazy as they are there for exactly the same reason. It tends to start the "chat" in the community — the poisonous conversations that happen to put you into certain categories, which then decides who you get to hang out with and what circles you get to move in.

The gay community can be so judging, which I find incredible as we are the ones that come out and say that we refuse to be judged or categorized in the straight world by straight people, however, we tend to eat our own and I hated that. I absolutely refused to be put in a box and labeled by anyone and I fought this by hanging out and doing whatever I bloody wanted.

This lifestyle suited me during this period of my life as my past relationships had been so intense, explosive and, for a lot of us in the same boat, they could be deeply wounding that left scars so deep that it would be too painful to try again with someone else.

Sex can become an addiction, along with alcohol and drugs, and I was dabbling in two out of three of these. I could feel myself getting dragged into an addictive cycle with sex especially and booze secondary... Drugs hadn't interested me up to that point and I had given them a wide berth since dabbling in the 1980s but I was definitely lacking direction and the darkness and soulless existence was making me feel worthless. My family life with my kids was the thing that kept me anchored from going any deeper into this messy, dark, angry, shameful existence.

As gay men, we are more likely to struggle with addiction, depression and even suicide, which are all symptoms of an individual who bears the pain and anguish of being unloved.

I was extremely lucky that I had them to keep me in the light along, with my mother's warnings about drugs and booze when we were kids, which put the fear of Christ into us! Thanks, Myrna!

Soon, Denise and I had new men in our lives, which was kind of nice but completely unexpected. She had met hers at work and I had bumped into mine at Urge, a gay bar on K'Road. There was only one major problem with D's man... He was married. The secret affair went unnoticed for a long period of time and they would only meet up at certain times of the day or night, when and where they wouldn't be noticed. As she was my good buddy, I would cover for her at work and wherever else so she could see her man. It was a rather traumatic time for her as she was falling in love with this guy and was becoming exhausted with late nights, early mornings and keeping it all as quiet as possible for everyone's sake. My biggest fear for her was that these kind of workplace affairs usually end with heartache and no job. I said to her that these guys never leave their wives and I was scared for her.

Manager Sandie saw Denise's work quality decline and because I seemed to be at the center of it, she pulled me to one side and asked me to leave D to do her work and not disrupt her. I even had a warning issued to me as she was deadly serious!

Not long after that, it all exploded into the open and, *yes*, he left his wife. I got an apology for being blamed and Denise got her man. She married him about nine years later, with myself and Casey being witnesses. The wedding was dry as she and her new man had given up drinking for a healthy, vegan lifestyle, shrouded with Buddhism and meditation.

And me and my new relationship? Well, I was about to enter into a partnership with someone I really wasn't sure of from the get-go. However, he was easy on the eye, tall, straight-acting (acting straight definitely doesn't make you straight), and kind. Being with a kind person was something totally alien to me up to this point and I kind of liked it. I felt safe for the first time in a long time and his smile was refreshing and new, if that makes any sense, but there was still something about this new guy that I just wasn't sure about. I even entered his name into my phone with a "HMMMMM" after it, but was I just being timid? The potential of a break-up was so bloody scary for me simply because my history of coping around this wasn't great so of course I was a bit scared and extra cautious.

He seemed to be genuine and had a lot of friends around him, which is always a good sign. He invited me to different gatherings and events as his plus one and I accepted gladly as I was meeting some great people who entertained me and made me laugh continuously — my weak point. Unbeknown to me, I was about to take the next step into the world of being a "big city" gay man and all it offered up.

We grew closer and eventually became a couple, which all our friends were excited about and the invitations came thick and fast. I was always a sociable guy but this took it to the next level and I had to be aware that I needed to have enough energy left for my kids and to juggle them through school, sports, and drop-offs here there and everywhere.

Their mother started to have the boys regularly on her weekends, which helped and gave me time alone with my new partner. She started to swoop in first to parent-teacher meetings and also school camps, which gave those present the idea that she was the primary caregiver and I was the absentee dad. This infuriated me as I was the full-time guy who cared for them every day.

'Whatever floats your boat!' I recalled saying to myself as I was losing interest in the game that she was always trying to win. Again, I was sure it was to make her feel better about her decision to walk away from her kids and continuously show the people around her that she was still "mother of the year".

My new love interest was boarding with friends on Mount Roskill and I would end up having the odd overnighter there if I was "childfree" and was able to party on.

In the early hours of one morning, after being at Urge on K'Road, we staggered into his house and crawled into bed. The room was spinning and I signaled rather hastily for the nearest vessel to be sick in. It became a bit of a joke from that point on that I vomited in his new rubbish bin on the second sleepover and he had to clean it all up, including wiping my mouth and putting me back to bed! I began to think that this *must* be love!

The next morning, I sneaked out of the bedroom to the shower as quietly as I could so as not to wake the flat mates. As soon as I placed my wet towel on the rather lavish rail, it totally collapsed and the many metal bars hit the polished, tiled floors with a loud echoing crash. Trying to escape back to the bedroom as fast as I could, I ran smack into John, who owned the house with his partner, Kim. 'Hello, darling!' he said. 'I know you!' We had actually met a few years before through other friends. I was taken to meet boyfriend, Kim, and we instantly became mates.

We became a foursome, always hanging out as two couples, out on the town and at parties and events. We always went together with hilarious results and some great stories that needed to stay in the vault but would surface every now and again if needed, to raucous laughter. The weekends I had off parenting I would head to their place where we would always have pre-drinks, which sometimes turned into the entire night as we were too drunk to go to any bars or clubs. Good times with great people.

My man and I decided to live together, and he moved in with me and my kids, as he was spending most of the time there anyway. I was excited when he finally arrived with his belongings and started to put his stuff away. However, he started to pick at the things I had in my cupboards and storage, cleaning out all the things he thought I really didn't need and also commented on how I could be a little pickier with my cleaning. What? I did my best with two sons in the house and, OK, I wasn't on my hands and knees scrubbing the floors everyday but our home was always tidy. I was taken back by his actions but put it down to us just being different with different expectations. My family, including my parents, fell in love with Stephen and I adored his family just as much. There was a lot of sarcastic banter between his father and I that I was always up for.

The categories within the gay community popped up again around this time as I slowly became immersed in "the scene", or becoming a "scene queen", as it was known. I have written earlier how much I hated being labeled or categorized, but it seemed as though I would be pushed to make a choice where I fitted. Twinks, bears, otters… The list went on. Also, "A Gays", "B Gays", and then everyone else.

166

Most of my new mates that I met through my new partner identified as "bears" — hairy men who like hairy men, so I went along with it — attending dance parties, random gatherings or private parties. There seemed to be little judgement within this particular group, which I liked, however, the A, B, and C categories, I just couldn't buy into. Just like I had been at school, I refused to only hang out with the popular kids, usually making friends with the underdogs and supporting each other.

There was an undertone of intense drug taking and sex addiction within all these groups and our group was no different. It was as if "gays" needed to escape ourselves, our minds and bodies, as often as we could at as many events as possible. We were "out" of the closet so what was it that wasn't enough or what the hell did we want to hide from? Anything? Nothing?

We were (mostly) accepted into society and now could legalize our partnerships through a civil union. There was still work to do around homophobia, I get that, but what I didn't get was why all the escapism?

I popped my first ecstasy at Kim's fiftieth birthday. My boyfriend and I were dressed in loincloths, and everyone there was on the same buzz, and it was a safe environment. I definitely liked what I felt from it but I expected to feel a lot more than I actually did, as it had been talked up so much. The actual feeling seemed a little underwhelming so I was keen to go again and I did.

Toxic — Britney Spears, 2004

Within this new-look life I had entered into, I could see a lot of different relationships between different couples I was meeting. A lot of these were "open" meaning that either party could have sex separately or together. I had dabbled with threesomes before and they were a lot of fun, especially if I was the third, as it was all about me. However, as a couple, we hadn't discussed this possibility so early in our relationship and Stephen definitely wasn't keen. He started to show signs of intense jealousy and mistrust, which made me incredibly uneasy. His relationship with my kids was on an OK level, however, as time went on, he started to pick on them for the smallest things, which made me, of course, come to their defense.

This caused ongoing problems between us all and it felt like I was walking on eggshells to keep everyone happy. My boys were the priority and that goes without saying, however, I had to consider my partner's feelings as well. *How do I balance it?*

Ben was faltering at school and begged me to let him leave but as a parent, I couldn't see a great future for him without basic qualifications at least, so, to his horror, I declined his request. He not only wanted to leave school but leave Auckland and live in Tokoroa. He had such a passion for hunting and wanted to be nearer to Stubb, his grandad... It was a definite "no" from me as I wanted more for him and that was more than a life in the town that I had escaped from decades before. Surely, it's not a crime to want more for your kids? He was relentless, though, and kept chipping away at me daily until I weakened and we agreed that, if he found a decent job, I would give him the green light.

Off he went on the weekends to Tokoroa, for hunting trips more than job hunting, but, bugger me, he came back with a decent job and I had to give him the green light as I had promised to do. I spoke to Mum and

Dad and it was agreed that he would stay with them initially and then see what happened after that.

As his dad, I felt that it was the worst decision of my life to let him go as I had the feeling that I had lost him into *that* life with no way of steering him in the right direction. My parents, being older now, couldn't really look for any signs that he may be heading off in the wrong direction.

Anyway, the day came that he would leave for Tokoroa — he packed up his room and everything else he wanted to take with him. We all walked to the end of the driveway to wave goodbye and when he drove away, Daniel and I ran alongside the car until he got up to speed and disappeared into the traffic. Daniel was stoked that his grumpy older brother had left home but my heart sank as I knew deep down inside our relationship would change from that moment on.

My man, Daniel, and I now had the run of the house and I personally, had a lot more free time, to do more things with my partner as Dan was spending a lot more weekends with his mum.

Ben started his job in Tokoroa and I would call him regularly to get updates on how he was doing but also because I missed him. Stephen and I thought that maybe a family holiday to the Gold Coast including the boys would be a good way for us to reconnect and have some fun, so it was all planned and even Ben was on board as I was paying. Leading up to the trip, it proved harder and harder to get hold of my eldest boy and I became so bloody frustrated with his lack of communication as I needed him to renew his passport and sign papers, etc.

Eventually, he showed up acting really casual about the whole thing, making me question that maybe I was just overreacting… We all headed off for the ten-day break — on time, with all documentation complete.

The Ben we had waved off that day he left home for Tokoroa was far from the Ben we had on holiday with us. He was distant, aloof and short tempered and I always had one eye on him to see if I could crack the code, so to speak. My anxiety was again growing, making me snappy and I was riding him constantly, demanding to know what was happening with him… Not a great move on my part. Even my partner was finding it so hard to have a conversation with him but we carried on with our holiday the best we could.

We returned home to NZ and Ben once again disappeared into the depths of his new life in Tokoroa. But this new life was something I knew nothing about and I became more and more concerned about his lack of communication.

It wasn't long after that I had a call from a very distressed Myrna. She told me that Ben had lost his job and had been disappearing for days on end, which was sending my parents into a tailspin. I felt so helpless and guilty for putting them in that position. I tried calling Ben on numerous occasions but he would never pick up. He finally made an appearance and Mum insisted he call me but again he didn't offer up any explanation and insisted that he had another job and to butt out. Nah! Not gonna happen!

I had random reports through my siblings that he had got involved with some really bad dudes and was using drugs randomly. I was at a loss as to how to help him so I decided to trust in his common sense and just keep in touch as much as he would let me.

Hung up — Madonna, 2005

I had just started a new job working at TV3 (again) and was settling into my role and bloody loving it. I was amazed and so bloody chuffed that they decided to hire me again after my breakdown in the 90s. The interview was casual but harsh and the director walked me to the lift afterwards and commented, 'You all good now, though, aye? No more crazy shit?' I looked at him with a bit of a puzzled look... 'All OK in the head department?' he added.

I laughed at how non-kosher that was but I loved the frankness. 'Yip, all good, Colin, I promise I won't lose my shit this time.' We both laughed and the job was mine — again!

This set the tone for my employment with the company and, for the first time in my entire working life, I loved it and really looked forward to going to work every day. It was so challenging initially, due to learning all the new systems, jargon and getting my head around the importance of daily ratings, which we lived by. The crew I worked with were an awesome group of halfwits that I quickly became one of. I managed a portfolio of agencies and their clients, which definitely kept me on my toes.

On my first day, my new GM, Linda, a tiny, slight, little lady with a severe black bob which would turn Cleopatra green with envy, took me to her dark office, situated in the underground part of the station building. The building itself was rather tatty and constantly leaked during storms. It was apparently a cheese factory in a previous life and had been transformed into a television studio and offices which, I always found quite amusing.

Linda made the call, summoning the person who would be my sales manager. The door swung open and in walked Sarah, a woman in her late forties, wearing small, framed glasses and had her greying hair pulled back very tight into a long, wavy ponytail that reached halfway down her back to the top of her long summer frock. She greeted me with a gravelly but friendly voice. 'So, you're my new "boy" rep?' I nodded nervously. I knew I had my work cut out for me with this one, however, there was definitely something endearing about her, but scary all at the same time. Sarah had been with the company for decades and it was her job to get me up to speed as soon as possible.

We meet a lot of cool people through work and I have mentioned very few previously, however, this working environment and especially the people within it are absolutely worth writing about.

Sarah asked me questions about what I knew about the industry and how different it was from the radio I had been involved with previously and, with a flick of that ponytail, she said, 'Follow me, darling.' We were off to meet the rest of our team and the others that worked around us. Being a woman of the world and very open minded, she was thrilled to know that I was gay as I knew a lot of her friends through the rainbow community.

My new boss lady introduced me to my planner and coordinator. Rosey was the planner *extraordinaire* and would teach me all the ins and outs of the ad booking system. The first time I sat down with her, she showed me about ten minutes of booking screens and how to set up new clients and pick the programmes for advertising. After that ten-minute window, we completely went off on tangents, discussing our kids, our families, telling jokes and discussing how, every now and again, you get shooting pains up your anus without warning! Work talk seemed to get in the way of our hilarious conversations but we seemed to get through our workload regardless.

Sarah was a tough operator and was tough on me when I just didn't get what she was trying to teach me. 'No, no, no,' she would say, pointing at my screen in frustration and then would push me out of the way to do it herself, which made me feel totally useless in a job that I really wanted to get right first time.

I would sneak across the office to Rosey and she would fix anything up that I needed done so grumpy old Sarah wouldn't rake me over the coals again. I was already doing long hours before and after the normal working day to learn all the systems, so it felt as though my eyeballs were hanging out on stalks.

When we were out visiting my portfolio of agencies, Sarah would take over as I obviously didn't have the knowledge to answer all the questions at that time and this was beginning to really grate on me, making me ask anyone else but her for the answers I needed. I get she was frustrated and just needed someone to do the job and get it right first time but training is an investment in your staff and patience is the mother of *all* the virtues, but not at TV3 it seemed.

This trouble between us seemed to get worse and she soon began to have zero patience with my pace of learning. The rudeness and grumpy behavior came to a head the day she hit me over the head and screamed, 'No! I taught you this already!'

It was obvious that I couldn't connect with her and things were getting worse so I needed to do something for my sanity before I completely lost my shit.

After talking to Colin and GM Linda, I decided that the best way forward was to take her out for coffee and drop some cyanide in it, but I thought better of it and decided to go with coffee and a chat instead. I called her over and asked her to walk with me to the café next door, she accepted and off we went.

I wasn't nervous as I was so over the constant confrontation and it just needed to end. I don't even think our drinks hit the table when I blurted out that I found her behavior and lack of empathy appalling and I just couldn't work with her any more, because I thought she was an absolute bitch. I remember seeing her face drop and the silence that followed before she leaned forward and grabbed my hand. 'Oh my God, darling!' she exclaimed with total shock and horror in her voice. 'I had no idea that I was doing that to you and I'm so fucking sorry!'

I felt like a total prick as I could see that she was absolutely genuine and shocked by these revelations. It turns out that she loved having me on her team and that, *yes*, she should have backed me up more. I was told by Linda and Colin at our previous meeting that Sarah wouldn't even know that she was treating me in a way that I found offensive and would be mortified when I brought it up. Yup, they were spot on.

This was a turning point in our working relationship and we became great friends outside of the office as well. Our teamwork became stronger and stronger and even though we had smaller portfolios than other teams within the network, we sure punched above our weight, hitting our budgets. We even qualified for a trip to Paris for the Rugby World Cup in 2007, which my partner and I attended, as the network was the sole broadcaster and our bosses used it as an incentive for sales. We nailed it.

One of the best sayings Sarah gave me was "you can never be too rich or too thin". Ain't that the truth!

Sarah received a Porsche for her fiftieth birthday from her hubby, Marty, and on quiet days in the office, she would take me cruising down Ponsonby Road with the top down so we could be seen out and about. I grew to love this woman and enjoyed her company so much in work and out, and we had so many laughs on so many occasions.

The Christmas season was so special in media as most agencies and networks would throw lavish parties. Cost was no issue so we would drink ourselves silly and all hell would break loose. One occasion, when Sarah and I, along with our coordinator, attended a large agency Christmas party and Sarah broke out her "posh frock", complete with tassels and pearls. The dancefloor was mirrored and every time we danced together; she would insist on confirming that she was wearing no knickers through the floor's reflection. I would scream at her, over the loud music, 'Oh no, the floor's got a crack in it!' We would all be bent over with laughter.

On the same night we decided to jump in the nearest cab as we were so full of booze and God knows what else and we wanted to go out for a couple more quiets to end the night. In those days, the network would give us taxi "chits", that were like cash to most cabs, to ensure we could get home after any work event. The cab we all jumped into obviously didn't hear us when we said we had a chit and when Sarah pulled it out her purse and waved it at him, he started to yell and scream at her that he was "cash only". I took exception to him yelling at my mate, so interrupted with a 'Don't you speak to her like that!' With that, he hit the brake and told us to fuck off out of his car. We did exactly that, stumbling out on a motorway overpass in the middle of the city.

Here we were dressed up, "posh as", on the side of the road, Sarah in that tasselly posh frock and the rest of us glittering in the dim streetlight. The taxi driver U-turned and came back past us again, hurtling more abuse, telling us to get fucked. We countered, yelling, 'Stick your cab up your arse!' This was followed by a few, well, quite a few, lewd gestures. It must have looked crazy and we couldn't quite believe it had actually happened. We were still laughing about it when the next taxi stopped and picked us up.

Rashika joined our team and I was so worried that this little Indo-Fijian girl would cramp our style but it was soon evident that it was to be quite the opposite, with us boozing, swallowing illicit substances, and partying until we could party no more. The three of us, plus Rosey, were inseparable and always had each other's back, like the time that Rosey took me to one side and told me she had found a large lump in her breast. I was so shocked but ensured that I kept my cool and tried to reassure her that it would all be just fine and that the doctor would tell her just that.

Later that week she was diagnosed with stage 4 breast cancer and had the operation to remove both breasts. Her kids were young and her husband seemed to be supportive through the horrendous effects of the chemo and other invasive treatments. Her lovely blonde hair started to fall out and she lost the plumpness out of her face and the sparkle out of her eyes.

She soldiered though, remaining at work even when she found it hard to function. Getting her first wig was a boost for her and, now and again, I would whip it off her head and wear it in the office to see it anyone would notice. The sight of me sitting at my desk in this short cropped blonde wig gave my dear Rose something to smile and laugh about and I made sure I gave her a reason to crack up every day to keep her with me. I was so afraid of losing her as she looked frailer with each passing day.

To ensure an even greater distraction, Rosey's husband organized a ceremony to renew their vows and booked a beautiful boutique hotel in Herne Bay for the special event. Rosey asked me to give her away and I agreed to do it for her. The day of the renewal, I walked into the area to collect her for the walk up the aisle. She looked so thin but beautiful and

I was so proud of her strength and determination to survive. I delivered her to her waiting husband and the deed was done. Champagne flowed and it was organized that Stephen and I would join the wedding party at a Thai restaurant just down the road, so we all walked together in unison with Rosey, still in her wedding dress.

The restaurant was extremely busy and we were sandwiched against another quite rowdy group, who continued to get more and more raucous the more they drank. Soon, the noise was so bad, that one of our group stood up and asked them to pipe down and have respect for others at the venue. That was it, tables and chairs went flying, punches were thrown, glasses broken, and Rosey was right in the middle.

I grabbed her around the waist to pull her out of the chaos and signaled to Stephen to clear a path to get her out of there. She was screaming and crying and swinging punches as I lifted her tiny frame off the floor to get her out. Her feet were scuffing as they made contact with the floor so I lifted her higher and ran. We made it out to the street just as the police arrived and I had to keep her clamped against me to stop her flying back into the chaotic scene. Stephen was still inside so, after handing Rosey over to someone else, I went back in to ensure he wasn't arrested or punched.

That night ended like Rosey's marriage — shockingly and abrupt. She found out that her hubby was actually seeing someone else throughout her treatment, even when they renewed those vows. She hit an all-time low and would arrive most days in tears, not being able to concentrate or eat or sleep. It was a draining time for all involved but we stood by her and eventually she got her groove back and years later, being cancer-free, remarried, meeting her soulmate and blending their two families. There's hope for us all after seeing her dark turn to light over this time.

Mum was quite famous in the TV3 office as I would call her on speaker a few times a week and those around me would love to hear our banter and arguments about the weather.

It happened one day that she was in Auckland to see her soon-to-be one-hundred-year-old brother, Ben Jolley. I convinced my brother-in-law, Bruce, to escort her and other brother, Alec, to call into the office to

176

see me before heading back to Tokoroa. They agreed and I informed the office that the famous Myrna was on her way for a meet and greet. I signaled that they were in the lift on the way up to our floor. She walked in and everyone in the office had lined up to meet her. As she walked through the line, she shook each hand and apologized out loud that her son was so rude and crude at work and how it was nothing to do with her at all. She was absolutely beaming and loved every minute of that welcoming committee.

Moving down the line, she came to teammate, Rashika, and not being able to pronounce her name right, she changed the subject immediately, and said, 'Oh, you're Indian! I have a nice Indian girl who lives next door to me in Tokoroa and they go back to India every year.'

'Mum!' I said in shock. 'She's Fijian!'

Without faltering, Myrna continued to the next person, changing the subject yet again without even flinching.

She was such a hit, using her natural wit, she threw out as many one-liners as she could to get a laugh, and entertain her captive audience. That's my mum!

The phone rang one night at home and my sister gave me the news that the situation with Ben in Tokoroa had reached crisis point and that intervention was needed. I talked to Sarah and organized a week off work to head down and snatch him out of the mess he had found himself in. I knew that this wouldn't be pretty but I couldn't help him if I wasn't in front of him.

Jobless and only spending odd nights with family is how I found him in Tokoroa. I asked him to come see me at Mum and Dad's when I arrived there, and to sit down and talk to me about what was going on. He denied that there was any problem with the situation and was aggressive as all hell. I spent a few days there, working on him. Finally, I tricked him into agreeing to return to Auckland with me for a short time, saying that I would then bring him back. He agreed but was determined that he would be back to whatever he was involved with. I never asked the question and he never shared what had lurched him off the tracks and the plans he initially had and, to be honest, as his dad, I really didn't want to know. Having him back under my roof was enough for me at this stage.

I had arranged some part-time work for him as soon as we arrived back and set him up with transport so he could get there. As the days went on, he became more and more aggressive and had stand-up fights with me and my partner almost every day. Daniel was also in the firing line and Ben would hurl abuse at him at every opportunity. I was on the receiving end of a swing at me when I tried to lock him in his room as it was the only way I felt I could keep him and the rest of us sane.

Slowly, he came out the other end and we had snippets of the old Ben coming to the surface. I was so torn as I loved him so much and the main thing that got me through was remembering his little face as a toddler, grabbing my hand as he crossed the road and playing with my hair as he fell asleep every night in a bed full of his toys. He had a good soul and I fought with him and against him to see that reemerge. He eventually realized that his place was back with us and landed himself a job and rebuilt his life, much to our relief. You're only as happy as your unhappiest child.

I acknowledge that Ben struggled as he got older having a gay dad and was happier if it didn't come up in conversation at school or work. I get that, but I always thought I had taught my kids to accept everyone for who they were and if anyone had a problem with it, it meant that they were just jealous or shallow and really not worth knowing.

If that wasn't challenging enough for him, there was more news to come. Daniel was such a delightful, easy-going child and was growing up to be a well-grounded individual who knew what he wanted. When he was little, my ex-wife and I always said that Ben would come home with his girlfriend and Dan would walk in with a guy named Steve. We knew that this little sugar plum showed gay traits and behaviors but maybe he was just a softer version of his older brother. I was afraid that my boys would end up like my brother, Rex, and I — not getting on, and the older/straighter sibling constantly humiliating the younger brother. I didn't want history to repeat.

All good things must come to an end and Sarah took Rashika and I aside, announcing to us that she was leaving TV3 and us after decades of service. We were absolutely devastated as it meant the end of our time in the dream team. She wanted to retire and spend more time travelling and hanging out with her elderly parents. We put on a huge leaving party and gave her the send-off she deserved. Sarah was eventually replaced by a woman who just wasn't up to scratch in my eyes and Rashika was moved to another team so it was a totally new ball game that I wasn't interested in playing.

After a few months, I decided that my passion for the role was diminishing and it was time to move on. Sarah, although meant to be enjoying retirement, popped up in a selling role at TVNZ — "The Mother Ship", as we called it.

My phone rang at my desk one day and there was that familiar gravel-like voice. 'Sarah!' I squealed.

'Shush!' the voice said. She continued with, 'If you were offered a job here at TVNZ, would you consider it… Yes, or no?'

'Fuck yes,' I replied, nearly biting the end of the phone off.

So that was it, I was offered a contract to be GM of direct sales at TVNZ and I was off, serving garden leave at home for a month, then into my new role.

The day I started, I remember walking up to the main entrance of the massive television centre in central Auckland and stopping to look up at the big TVNZ sign and huge satellite dishes. This represented everything I wanted to achieve in my media career and this was *the* moment I had waited for… I had arrived!

I wasn't really briefed, therefore, not really prepared, for the TVNZ way of conducting business so, for me, it wasn't an easy transition. My time at TV3, although very professional, was more casual and relaxed, and everything I had learnt was about to be spun on its head. I entered a world of the full suit, collar and tie, meeting after meeting, red tape, training, training and more training, and even more meetings, if it was decided by HR that we hadn't had enough meetings already.

It was my job to ease out some of the older team members and hire some new blood to take the "direct" team into the future.

The team I built was great and I even convinced my old buddy, Denise, to join us and learn the art of media sales in television land. I loved that we were once again working together and I always knew that she had my back, even though our karaoke days were over — thank

Christ! I played the game and went along with the TVNZ way of doing things but pushing back when I truly believed it was needed.

I think it was Daniel's eleventh or twelfth birthday and he asked if he could have a party at home. My partner, Stephen, and I agreed and the invitations were sent out. Not really knowing what to expect, we set up and put out the food and waited for Daniel's guests to arrive. I think that there were about eight girls and one boy. Stephen and I chuckled to ourselves as there was no doubt in our minds which team he was going to bat for.

It wasn't until around his eighteenth birthday that we knew his news was about to break. Lisa called me to say that he had come out to her and was on his way home. He walked into the kitchen where I was preparing veggies for dinner, and I asked him how the visit with his Mum was. 'Fine,' he replied and walked out. I stood there, not knowing what to say next, when he reappeared.

'Up to much tonight?' I muttered.

'Nope,' he replied and disappeared again.

By this stage, I'd had enough. When he appeared for the third time, I put the knife down, looked up at him and said, 'Bub, so, are you gay?'

'Yes, is that OK?'

I answered, 'Hell yes!' He bolted out the door yet again but this time I was right behind him, asking if he had a boyfriend, condoms or wanted any advice on safe sex.

'No thanks!' he yelled and then he was gone.

It was done and I was so proud that he came out at such a young age without having to hide or lie in life. He flourished from that moment and I would even bump into him out at the clubs with his friends, which we all found crazy but extremely funny.

Stephen and I got really involved in the local gay scene and also the scene in Sydney and Melbourne with our mates, John and Kim, at our side. It was a world that fascinated me to the max and I loved the excitement, bright lights and fun. It meant that I was constantly surrounded by like-minded people who accepted me and seemed to care. However, it was also a world with a dark side, full of criticism, drugs and rings of unsafe sex.

Regardless of all of the above, I was in, boots and all, because the "fun" aspect was a great escape from my being in a constant dad role.

The drugs side happened slowly with me as I was paranoid as all hell so my "no, no, no" turned eventually into a "OK, go on then!" I experienced a feeling of absolute escape — by that I mean that I felt so wonderfully removed from who I actually was as a human being.

Acid, ecstasy, speed, weed, cocaine, GHB, and more... It was all readily available and I consumed as much as I needed or wanted. We would dance until dawn and sleep all day at festivals or dance parties. It was always managed on our part and my partner always kept one eye on me to make sure I wasn't tipping over the edge or overdosing; he was good like that.

We, as a foursome, did witness overdoses and collapses, which were a bit scary at times, especially if you were in the toilets at a party and someone was so far gone that we had no choice but to call an ambulance. I became very good at knowing my limits but even I would get caught out every now and again.

I mentioned earlier that we were in Paris for the 2007 Rugby World Cup and Stephen and I ventured out on a Saturday night to the gay clubs on a mission to "paint the town pink".

We were having such a great time and had met a few locals and were knocking back shots, which a rather lovely French guy insisted on buying us. This rather good-looking young man stuck with us for most of the night and invited us back to his place for more drinks and... Well, I'll leave the rest to your imagination.

As we were walking to his apartment through the dimly lit streets of old Paris, I started to feel a bit woozy but put it down to too many shots. We arrived and our host poured us another drink each. Stephen refused as he had noticed that I was starting to slur my words and was staggering about, so he made me sit down next to him, to stop me falling arse-over-head. I remember not being able to keep my eyes open and kept wanting to go to sleep but my boyfriend was jolting me awake whenever my eyes started to roll back in my head. The French guy was insisting that we stay the night and he would put me to bed but luckily my boyfriend understood what was happening and dragged me up on my feet and announced that we were leaving. There was a heated exchange between our would-be host and my partner and, next minute, we were out the door back on those dark streets.

The icy temperature hit us like a sledgehammer and woke me up immediately and we started walking. Not really knowing where we were, we looked for Notre Dame cathedral, as we knew that the club we were at was close to that, and the Eiffel Tower was visible from around that point, which would lead us back to our hotel. We walked and walked without stopping, chatting constantly to keep us focused on getting to our destination. Paris is a massive city and I think we walked for nearly two hours to get back.

As I started to come out of the mind fuzz I was in, thanks to the cold Parisian night air and active walking, I realized that my man had actually saved me from a really bad situation evolving after our so-called new friend had obviously spiked my drink. His motivation for doing this was scary to say the least and God only knows what he had planned for us. This event reminded me to always be on my toes in this type of social situation and also that I owed my life to my partner on that night.

The regular party events, like Pride parties in Auckland, Mardi Gras in Sydney, Hi 'Bear'nation in Melbourne, were *fabulous* and we attended as many as we could outside family commitments and work. These gathering really did give me that sense of belonging that I had been craving most of my life. Oh yes, I had family and friends but these communities made me feel safe enough to really be myself and the drugs just enhanced this feeling.

Let's remember that we don't live in a bubble and there are others out there that will challenge us at all times through violence and rampant homophobia. Gay hatred and targeted bashings are still part of our world and having a gay son meant I was always worried about his safety when he was out and about.

There are different groups who fuel this hatred of the gay lifestyle and the one at the top of the list for me during this time was the Destiny Church, led by a husband and wife whose actions and rhetoric have attracted critics from the New Zealand media and other public figures. Destiny Church sponsored a nationwide rally against civil unions for gay couples stating that "Enough was Enough" and marching on parliament against our right to marry. But wait, there's more…

These two idiots also sent protestors to gay events, such as "The Big Gay Out", which is a gathering for gay men and women, their families, children and friends. A day full of fun in the park, with music, HIV infection information and testing, fundraising for rainbow community groups and other support groups. Politicians would attend, including the prime minister and leaders of the opposition, as they realized the importance of the rainbow community's voice in society.

I even had both of my sons there on a couple of occasions with Ben doing the tech behind the music and bands and Daniel as an openly gay man, there with his friends.

The Destiny Church representatives would stand dotted around the venue with huge signs stating that we were an "abomination" and how we and all who supported us would be going straight to hell. A lot of people who were there threw abuse at them but they didn't falter or leave, instead they stayed there to make sure their message of hatred was seen by everyone, including young rainbow families and their children. This so-called church's leader, Brian Tamaki, shocked the nation again with homophobic comments that sent the country into a tailspin. Quoting the Old Testament, he said that "sexual perversion" and "homosexuality and acceptance of gay marriage" caused the devastating 2016 earthquakes in New Zealand and that the land convulses under the weight of *certain* human sin.

NZ Herald — 16 November 2016

He later apologized to members of the gay community if we were hurt by his comments about us. This was later reported as cynical and brazen as they had launched a new political party the week before, which his wife fronted, called Vision NZ, which made me laugh hysterically as these were people whose only vision was incredibly blinkered.

The launch press conference around this new party was a circus and cringey to watch and it was reported that those who turned up and were party to it were just being used as part of the political game.

How can we ever grow up and live together harmoniously if people like these ill-informed dickheads preach their hatred against other groups of the human race. I feel let down and disgusted when I see both racism and homophobia used in everyday society. I'm so glad that "gay conversion" — praying the gay away — is now illegal in New Zealand, as it was long overdue.

Stephen and I had started to falter in our relationship and one of the main reasons was mistrust and jealousy, which drove me insane to the point we weren't treating each other well at all. If we were out at a pub or club and I needed to pee he would insist on coming with me. If I was out at work drinks without him, I would catch him driving past to make sure I was where I said I was.

We had agreed a couple of years before that we would "open" our relationship and bring in the odd "third" for sexy fun together and it became a regular occurrence. However, I would get accused of enjoying it a bit too much or he would mention that the other guy was into me more than him. I found this behavior ridiculous as we had an agreement when we embarked on said activity that we would never question each other after the fact as it was just sex and that was the rule.

The fact that I reassured him that he was the only man who I wanted obviously fell on deaf ears, our relationship needed to be a lot stronger to cope with this right from the get-go and it just wasn't. We had blazing arguments and I tried to leave a few times.

My sons were older and had their own lives, working and socializing in their own circles, so my partner and I were alone a lot, which became challenging to say the least. One Christmas morning, I was lying in bed when he got up and walked out to the kitchen. *Great!* I thought to myself, *he's making me a coffee.* But when he didn't return, I went looking. I found him in the kitchen looking through my phone, which made my heart sink and I responded with anger and frustration! Why do that, what they hell was he looking for? Would it make him feel better if he found something?

It was Mardi Gras season and a group of us decided we would head off to Sydney for a week of drinking, dancing and shitloads of whatever illicit drugs we could get our hands on.

We attended the parade and the after-party, which was so incredibly huge with different dance areas and headline acts like Olivia Newton-

John and Cyndi Lauper. It was a mass of mostly gay men dancing and jumping, shirtless, all shapes and sizes, and all races. I had never seen anything like it before and as our drugs kicked in, we merged into the sweaty sea of men and disappeared for a few hours, only stopping to witness Olivia belt out a new rendition of "Xanadu", complete with the most amazing backup dancers.

Getting back to our hotel room in the early daylight hours, I was still too buzzy to sleep so continued to dance to Olivia on my iPod until I finally dropped into bed. We stayed on in Sydney, attending a few more underground leather parties, which were so incredibly raunchy and dark, with drugs again fueling unsafe sex practices. But my man and I always steered away from it as it wasn't our thing and we both had a pact to keep each other safe, especially after our "Paris" incident.

I guess I felt a sense of sadness — not judgement — that a lot of these beautiful men were putting themselves at risk of HIV infection and a death sentence, as it still was before PrEP. Education was still the key and we, as a community, were certainly pushing the message but party drugs certainly seemed to cloud judgment. I was one of the lucky ones who had good anchors in my life, such as my parents and my sons, and flying out of control was never an option for me.

We spent a week in Port Douglas and then flew back to Sydney for a couple of nights before returning to NZ. The streets in the "gay" city, seemed to carry a kind of hangover from the week be fore's, Mardi Gras drunkenness. The mood was certainly more subdued and we lapped up being able to get into any bar or restaurant we wanted.

Returning to our hotel, we passed a certain corner where a tall, younger guy was standing and he made eye contact with both of us, following us along the road to our hotel where he loitered outside to see if we were keen to invite him up to our room. We did and this simple, fun act with this young Italian man and the subsequent sex that the three of us had together wrote the ending chapter in the book of Terry and Stephen.

Bad Romance — Lady Gaga, 2010

Isn't it amazing how one action or event can change your path in life? That's exactly what happened here.

Once again, after the fact, I was accused of liking what went on a little too much and after we returned home to Auckland, our partnership soured even more. We kept in touch with our new Italian friend, Alfredo, via Facebook and Stephen's phone, not mine, which meant I couldn't be accused of crossing any lines.

We returned to Sydney for a long weekend as flights were ridiculously cheap and a certain Italian would be waiting for another hook up with us both. Upon arriving in the city, Stephen's phone wouldn't work so I had to make contact via my NZ number, which meant Alfredo now had my digits. We met up with him again and spent the day and night together, but then my boyfriend stated that we wouldn't be doing it again and had some "other guy" in tow, who he invited to our hotel room after dinner the next night.

After this guy left, I turned to my partner and said, 'That's the last time we do anything like that as I felt as though everything had to happen under his guidance and I no longer had a voice!' I wanted out and I wanted it now.

I told him that I didn't appreciate being pimped out under his ruling with no resistance coming from me so as not to upset him or cause any arguments. Oh yes, I enjoyed the sex, but I needed to have some kind of input as this was meant to be a partnership. 'As soon as we get home,' I continued, 'I'll be moving out and we are done.'

The flight home was hideous as I was so angry that I couldn't talk and the next day, back in Auckland, I packed my bags and left.

Daniel was living in student accommodation by this time but Ben was still at home, along with Sheeba, our collie, so they would stay there until there was a decision on our property and possessions, etc. I think that he thought I was just overreacting and that I would calm down, but I never did.

He was a good man and we had had some great times travelling the globe and dancing around the world. We had shopped in New York, cycled in San Francisco, shopped in Montreal and partied in London. He was a good man but he wasn't the man for me. Letting him go released him (and I) to meet the person that was right for him. He never really spoke to me again and avoided me from then on.

My newfound freedom was interrupted by a certain Italian guy who was constantly on the phone after he realized I was now single. I was flattered after the demise of my long-term relationship. If I could go back now and talk to my younger self at that time, I would say, 'Hang up the phone and *run*!'

But, of course, I didn't, and Alfredo, who turned out to be from Sicily, was soon winging his way to NZ to be with me. I totally was on the rebound but rebound felt good, especially when I was in the arms of a young Sicilian stud like him. Did I really know what I was doing and what I wanted from this? Nope. But I kept going regardless, keen to let loose a bit and just enjoy it.

Alfredo arrived in New Zealand and John and Kim, who had been a great support during my breakup, were there to help me welcome him into the fold. He was a trained masseur and was keen to find work and stay with me as long as possible. We looked for the kind of work he wanted but to no avail, so I found him a temporary job in the TVNZ café on the top floor.

Hitting the gay scene on the arm of my new lover was like having a new red bike that everyone wanted to ride, a new flavored ice-cream that everyone wanted to lick, or a massive, big lollipop that everyone wanted to suck on. They were like flies around shit and I soon became bloody pissed off and annoyed but this was the "scene". Everyone would chase the fresh meat. Unbeknown to me, Alfredo didn't take much chasing and, behind my back, was helping himself to a lot of so-called friends and having anonymous hook-ups.

Being totally unaware, we carried on doing "couple" stuff even a trip back to Tokoroa and Rotorua to visit family and mates. Mum and

Dad thought he was good fun and my friends loved his humor and especially his accent. There was a darker side to this European escapee and I don't just mean him being promiscuous. There was an explosive, violent streak that I began to see more and more of.

It seems crazy to me now (considering how he was behaving behind my back) but he would get incredibly jealous of me talking to other guys and would hit me up about it. One night at Urge Bar, he grabbed me by the throat and slapped me as he thought I was looking at someone else. Just at that moment, Kim walked in and screamed at him to get out and to never hit me again. I was so thankful for that but as soon as I got home, he would convince me that it was all a misunderstanding and sob until I forgave him.

This pattern of behavior was ongoing and was about to get worse. The arguments became a regular occurrence no matter where we were or who we were with, which was followed by sulking and then rage for my noncompliance. Being bloody minded, I would only back down if I absolutely had to and that was mainly for the sake of peace.

The cycle of the opening up of the relationship soon followed and we had no end of guys in the queue, which, again, left me feeling empty and cold. I had gone from one troubled relationship straight into something even worse as it was attached to violence, both emotional and physical.

Alfredo was a very sexual guy and of course he was, being only twenty-six at the time and I struggled that this became our only focus as a couple. I never got romance, just sex. I never got attention, just sex. I never got companionship, just sex. I should've just enjoyed the new plaything and then disappeared but I didn't and now it was time to pay.

There were many phone calls from Alfredo back to family and friends in Sicily and, once again, I had built a kind of relationship with them. A close friend of his wanted to come to NZ and I was all for it as I would maybe understand more about him if I met his mate.

He arrived and was a great guy and I got on so well with him, probably because he was in his forties so I tended to have more in common with him. The three of us were out one night and, as usual, Alfredo became agitated and, by the time we got home, he was bloody angry as I refused to dump his mate and head home with some random from the bar.

I was lying on the bed, drinking a cup of tea — his friend had gone to bed. Alfredo flew at me for spoiling his night and I retaliated by pushing him out of my face so I could get away from him. The tea flew against the wall and he pinned me down on the bed with his hand gripped tightly around my throat and his other hand raised and clenched in a fist. 'I want to fucking *kill* you!' he screamed. I dared him to do it and as his face turned even more red with pure hatred and rage. I managed to loosen his grip and get free. He stood in the middle of the room, glaring at me and shaking with anger.

'Get out of my fucking room!' I bellowed, and after the fifth time of telling him, his friend, Antonio, appeared and managed to get him out. As soon as he cleared the entrance to my room, I slammed to door shut and locked it.

The rest of the night was full of apologies, with him sitting at the outside of the door begging me to open up and eventually he gave up and slept somewhere else. I knew that he had to work that day, so after he left, I called John and Kim for help.

They once again took me in and warned Alfredo to stay away otherwise the police would be called. I also had to return to work and because we both worked in the same building, it was agreed that he would keep his distance. I didn't want to see him, I didn't want to talk about it, I dint want anything from him. It was amazing to me that I had put myself in this position of being abused but there I was and I felt so ashamed and humiliated because I was responsible for him being here and I felt that I was being judged by everyone for that. My inner voice was telling me that I deserved this as I had created it.

Obviously, the separation at work got too hard for him to take and he sought me out. The moment I saw him I freaked and asked him politely to leave me alone, which made him break down in tears, begging me to please talk to him. I declined and backed away, leaving him sobbing in the corridor at TVNZ. Being quite shaken by the confrontation, I excused myself from work and asked John to pick me up from the office.

It was decided that the best place for me was "away" and, as Kim was in Christchurch, working on their new home, I would fly there immediately while John stayed in Auckland to get Alfredo out of the house.

We zoomed around to my home so I could quickly pack a bag and leave before there was any more confrontation. As I was quickly throwing the essentials into a flight bag, I turned to see Alfredo standing in the doorway. 'Where are you going, Terry?'

I jumped as I got such a bloody fright to see him there. 'I'm leaving so please get out of my way, I don't want to talk to you!' I was shaking like a leaf but refused to show him that I was intimidated in any way.

He was sobbing, saying, 'Sorry, sorry, sorry.'

I wasn't buying it and pushed past him and headed toward the car where John was waiting to take me to the airport. The shrieks and wailing that came from Alfredo were deafening as he followed me down the driveway. I jumped into the car and locked the door and John asked me what I wanted to do. 'Floor it!' I said and with that, we roared into reverse, out of the driveway, leaving Alfredo on his knees, screaming at me to stop.

I stayed in Christchurch until the all-clear was sounded from John that he had moved out. That should've been the end of the great Italian story, but in typical Terry fashion, I left the door slightly ajar. I headed back to work and managed to avoid the cafeteria and Alfredo completely, but was as nervous as all hell at the thought of bumping into him. The phone calls and texts started again and were fast and furious. I finally replied, stating that I think he needed to return to Sicily to sort out his life and anger issues and he agreed with me.

The next day, there was a knock at my front door and here was a very sorry Italian, holding a plane ticket home. We met a couple more times after that, before he left to fly back to Europe, and it was very cordial but he constantly declared his undying love for me right to the last minute.

I was coming up to two years in my role at TVNZ and, for me, that was more than enough of the pompous and stiff way of working in media. Alfredo had kept in touch on a regular basis and it kind of worked for me having him at more than arm's-length. He begged me to join him in Europe so I could experience life in Sicily and meet all the wonderful people he had in his life and, of course, his family. The video calls had all of these people on the other end, saying, 'Come, Terry, come to Sicily!'

At first, I laughed the idea off but then I thought to myself, well, I never got to do my OE as I was a parent, so why not go to London and then on to Sicily if I felt safe enough to do so. So, I did! I resigned from my pain-in-the-arse job, made sure my boys were all OK and secure, and flew to the UK.

As the plane took off from Auckland on the midnight flight (in torrential rain), I felt that I was in total control and doing something on my own with no remorse.

Arriving in London, I met up with friends and booked into the small apartment that I had rented in Mayfair as a treat to myself. Mykal was a friend that I had met while he was doing theatre in New Zealand and we had stayed in touch ever since. He was of African descent and had the most stunning dark, chocolate skin and flashy white smile. He wanted to take me out for dinner and dancing in Soho which was dotted with gay bars.

I was in heaven and was like a dog with two dicks, not knowing what to do first. We ended up in a downstairs dance club with great music and beautiful people. While on the dancefloor, I noticed that Mykal had hooked up with some guy and was heading off. I waved and kept dancing. Before I knew it I was flanked by a couple of hot looking Latino guys who had obviously set their sights on me. Not one to be rude, I played along and eventually they signaled me to follow them as they headed to the restrooms. I thought, *what the hell, I'm free to do whatever I want*. There was a security guard on the door but he didn't even blink an eye as the three of us disappeared into one cubicle.

There was a lot of fumbling around until one of them presented a small bag of white powder and then proceeded to line it up on the top of the toilet cistern. Again, I thought to myself, *what the hell,* and waited my turn. We snorted through twenty-pound notes and as I leant over for the second round, I *sneezed*, blowing all this hard-earned cocaine into the air where it sat like a fine mist. I was far from popular and as I was scurrying to escape their anger, I was pulled back and told, in no uncertain terms, that the night had only just begun and as this pure cocaine started to make its way through my system, I quickly agreed. *Welcome to London,* I thought to myself!

Mykal showed up the next day and we exchanged stories over coffee and laughter. He had major concerns for me heading to Sicily in the next week as he was totally aware of what I had been though with Alfredo. I gave him my word that I would reach out if I found myself in any danger. After a few more nights out and some shopping trips, I booked my flight to Catania in Sicily. Alfredo had been constant with text and calls to keep tabs on me and my intended arrival date, which I hadn't confirmed at that stage.

I managed to get a room at a transit hotel by Heathrow as the flight I finally booked was early in the morning. It was there, as I was laying on my bed preparing for an early night, that I got the word that my dear Aunty Joan, my friend and ally, my aunty with the movie star looks and who's time in Wellington during the war changed our family forever, had died. She was gone and I was on the other side of the world, alone in this room. I was devastated and felt so far from home.

The flight the next morning was certainly an experience, with an older plane that rattled and groaned whenever we hit turbulence. The landing at Catania airport felt like we had been dropped out of the sky, as we hit the runway with a loud thud and seemed to bounce to a stop. As we taxied to the arrivals building, I caught a glimpse of Mount Etna puffing black smoke into the hot, hazy sky. It was the biggest active volcano I had ever seen.

We disembarked and were bussed to another terminal where we waited for the luggage and the tension started to build as I knew Alfredo would be waiting for me just through the next set of doors.

My bags came into sight and I grabbed them and walked toward the doors to the outside and as they were self-opening. All of a sudden, there he was, standing there grinning his head off that his Kiwi lover, friend, partner was here in Sicilia.

We embraced and he guided me to where his car was parked. No sooner were we in the vehicle than he launched at me, kissing me so hard and long that I thought I'd pass out from lack of oxygen. He explained to me that here in his country, homosexuals were to be despised and so was any public displays of affection between them.

At flat out speed in his Fiat Pinto, he took me on a whirlwind tour of Catania and stopped at a bookshop, which he disappeared into and then returned with a *Travelers Guide to Sicily* book, which outlined everything this island country had to offer.

We eventually arrived in the village of Zafferana on the slopes of the great volcano, Etna, where his family lived. I was introduced to his parents and extended family. Some of the neighbors even came to the house to meet the "Kiwi", fresh from New Zealand. Those who spoke English spoken it so broken that I had no idea what the hell they were saying, which makes your brain work overtime, trying to decipher each sentence. As a rule, 90% of Sicily's population don't speak English at all and won't really engage with you if they even have to try.

I settled in and the first task I had to complete was to write a eulogy for Aunty Joan, which would be read out on my behalf by my sister, Gloria. I included things that Joan only told me and said that she would be a part of me forever. I hated not being there and when I eventually made it back to New Zealand, I sat on her grave and cried and chatted with her until I felt that I had said goodbye enough for me to be at peace with her passing.

Catania and Zafferana were like stepping back in time thirty years. Nobody wore seat belts and sometimes had their kids on their laps while driving. Petrol pump attendants would smoke cigarettes while filling your car. The roadside service stations not only sold coffee but had a bar and sold take-out liquor and the Church, and associated saints, ran the country. Weddings took place every day of the week as there was such a backlog of people who wanted to tie the knot, and the Mafia was everywhere you looked. If you were parking in town for dinner, in a school car park, a hospital park, or anywhere that people gathered, there would always be a Mafia representative there ready to take your money to ensure you and your vehicle's safety when you returned. As you can imagine, my eyes were out on stalks. It was advised that I keep my heavily tattooed arms covered when out as the Mafia could see it as rival gang-related, so I covered up as much as I could in forty-degree heat!

At lunchtime every day, the entire village would close down — shops, cafes, petrol stations, everything — and then reopen at four p.m. so all the locals could avoid the dry heat of the middle of the day. I would sit there when everyone would disappear to bed, twiddling my thumbs, as I found it difficult to sleep during the day, so while Zafferana slept, I sat up like a bloody morepork, sipping endless cups of coffee.

I was paraded around all of Alfredo's friends and extended family and constantly showered with gifts, so I felt very spoilt and lucky to be so included in everyday Sicilian life and culture.

I was called "beddu" — a Sicilian term meaning "darling" or "beautiful", in the male sense — by one of his grandmothers who we visited in hospital. Every time I saw her after that she would summon me forward to her, saying, 'Beddu, ah, beddu.'

I would walk through the piazza (village square) and I would hear, 'Hey, Kiwi!' from the odd person I had met earlier through the family. That was the only English words they knew, of course, but I loved it.

We walked on the ancient lava flows of Mount Etna, banging a stick before us to shoo away any hidden snakes that were highly poisonous. Eek! I had eyes in the back of my head that day.

On a Friday night we would wash out a couple of glass flagons and head to the next village and stop out front of a villa, rang the bell… Quite a few times… Then an old *senora* would slowly open the door, asking us what we wanted. After a rather heated exchange between her and Alfredo, she would let us in and we would follow her through her small, tiled piazza and on to a courtyard where her chickens would scatter as we walked through. At the end of that makeshift chicken yard was a large shed, which she unlocked, struggling with the large wooden door but declining any help to open it. Inside was a huge tank and she turned, signaling us to give her the flagons which she placed under a large old tap and turned the handle. The *vino rosso* (red wine) that flowed into our glass vessels filled the space with the most amazing bouquet and I couldn't wait to taste it.

We left after paying her a few euros in coins and carried on to the party. This vino was totally organic and apparently the *senora* had been brewing it for decades but wasn't that keen on selling it, hence the agreement at the door. We must have worked our magic on her a little bit as we soon became regulars at the front door of her villa. However, she was always grumpy, no matter what.

Buying weed was so much more difficult and any purchase was handled by gangs and or Mafioso so was a very underground activity. We'd drive to a certain area in Catania at night and would pull up in the Pinto and stop where a young guy would be standing and Alfredo would say what we were after and he would wave us on to the next guy, where you could pick up the goods and pay. Sometimes, if they thought you were a bit suspect, you would be sent around and around the block a few times before the transaction was complete. It was like a bad festival movie and there I was, right in the middle of it — very serious stuff.

At all times, my tattoos were covered so as not to cause drama that could've resulted in the dealers thinking that we were another gang on their patch, which would most definitely result in having our throats cut. Scary but true. The saddest part of this drug circle was that most of these delivery posts were manned by really young guys whose lives would probably never get any better. I hated it but Alfredo insisted I was with him each time.

We travelled around ancient villages, visiting extended family and witnessing some activities that were as old as the villages they took place in. I was so fascinated with all of this ancient history that dated back to pagan civilization and it's all still there, slowly crumbling into the ground. Compared to our history in NZ, this was absolutely mind-blowing and I was so engaged, hanging off every word that explained the current surroundings.

One of my favorite places we visited was a small fishing village called Marzamemi, on the southern tip of Sicily, facing the Mediterranean Sea. It was so beautiful and quaint, just like a postcard, and we ate and drank the night away before heading back to the campground a few kilometers out of town. The camp was complete with open-air showers and squat toilets that are definitely a challenge if your aim was off!

Marzamemi fishing village — Sicily

We spent the days swimming in the Mediterranean Sea and soaking up the sun. We walked out to an old salt mine on the point and found a place that you could dig the mud out of the bank and smear it over your face and entire body. This mud was full of minerals that were good for your skin so we did that and waited for it to dry, then washed it off by swimming in the sea's warm clear water. I was in heaven.

I guess you can say that "what goes up, must come down", and that's what was happening in the background, right throughout this amazing experience. Alfredo's behavior had deteriorated and the old patterns were starting to emerge and I became more and more anxious around him. I knew that this was inevitable and I totally knew what I had signed up for but thought that maybe I would get some more time in before it all went tits up.

It started with anger and then mistrust and then, once again, I found myself in the position that I was offered up as a sexual sandwich between him and some old fuck buddies he had waiting, and he became angry when I wouldn't comply. My self-worth started to hit an all-time low and I began to feel extremely alone, being stuck in a small village in the middle of a country, whose language I didn't speak. My phone calls home to Mum, Dad and my boys were always upbeat as I didn't want anyone to worry about me or, even worse, say, 'I told you so!'

The arguments were becoming more frequent between us and sometimes he would even turn on his parents, which sent the entire household into one big screaming match, which I regularly removed myself from hiding in the downstairs rooms. His mother would apologize to me profusely for her son's actions after each fight and follow me around with plates of food, trying to feed me and diffuse any ill feeling. 'No more war, no more war,' she would say, and I felt so sorry for her as none of it was her fault.

Alfredo's friend, Antonio, who had stayed in Auckland with us during the violent outbursts earlier that year, had hosted us for dinner a few times during my stay and had introduced me to a lot of his friends who were more my age. A lot of them spoke English, which was so refreshing after struggling to learn Italian on a daily basis. He had decided to have a midsummer party with a "flower" theme and I was excited to attend and catch up with the group. Alfredo was not so keen and most of that was driven by his lack of ability to control me in that environment, as I could speak to a lot more people and hold my own.

We arrived and the whole villa was dripping with opulence, society's beautiful and successful people, and champagne galore. We were greeted by Antonio, who quickly whipped us around the crowd, introducing us both until Alfredo, who had a face like a smacked arse, bailed out of the lineup and headed to some guys he knew in the bar area. I was loving the whole atmosphere and would check in with Alfredo to make sure all was cool, just to keep the peace and avoid any conflict.

As the evening continued, the angrier Alfredo got, as I was having my own conversations and obviously having a ball, which infuriated him. My toing and froing to ensure he was OK and feed his ego just made the situation worse and, without warning, I was grabbed by my shirt and dragged down the gilded, marble staircase and out to the Pinto. 'Get in the fucking car!' he screamed and when I refused, he pushed me into the open door, smacking my head on the opening. With that, he squealed out of parking area and away from any help I may have needed.

The short car ride through Catania's narrow streets was filled with abuse thrown at me about how I was flirting and making eyes at all the other guys in the room. This was all total crap but in his mind that's all he saw. 'I will kill you!' he screamed while holding me by the scruff of the neck with one hand and steering the small car with the other. I was terrified of what he would do once we hit the *autostrada* (motorway) and accelerated to a higher speed, so the closer we got to the on-ramp, the more I realized that I needed to get out of this bloody car somehow.

The abuse was at an all-time high when we turned the final corner and he slowed down a bit... *This is it,* I thought to myself, *my last chance to get the hell out of here.* And with that thought, I grabbed the handbrake and pulled it for all I was worth. The car came to a griding halt as I held that brake until we were totally stationary and flung the passenger door open to get the hell out. I was half out of the car when he grabbed my foot, snapping my jandle, which made me hit the sealed road headfirst.

Stumbling to my feet, I was set to run when he again grabbed me and ordered me back into the car and when I refused, he swung an almighty punch at me, which I managed to deflect. The thought that he wanted to knock me out made my blood boil and I felt a huge amount of anger building up inside me that had been stored up over the past few years of putting up with his shit. Out it came and I erupted, pushing him back and flying at him straight on (with one jandle on), stating that I was so sick of all the shit he had put me though and this is where it ended. The impact from my push back was so hard that he lost his balance and fell backwards. 'Now leave me the fuck alone, you immature bastardo!' I bellowed just before I turned to run. He grabbed me again, forcing me to the ground and holding me there.

By this time, some people had started to come out of their houses and questioned what was going on. *'Non preoccuparti, e ubriaco!* (don't worry, he's just drunk!)' he yelled to them so they would stay away.

'No, no, no, help me!' I screamed but they turned and went back into their houses.

By this time, I was bleeding from my head and I could feel my eye starting to puff up from the impact on the road. I can't remember how I managed to break free but there was no way that this boy from Tokoroa was going to die on this dirty back street of Catania. As I got my balance and started to run, I felt my last jandle snap but just kept going at lightning speed.

I ran around the nearest corner where I nearly ran smack bang into a family enjoying a late-night dinner out the front of their villa. It must have been terrifying seeing this foreigner running toward them, bleeding, no shoes and a ripped shirt. 'Please help me,' I pleaded. 'Please, I need help.' But they refused to engage with me at all and quickly packed up and moved inside, slamming the door behind them.

I continued on, not knowing where I was or what directing to flee to. I heard Alfredo's car coming around the corner so I ran down the nearest street to get off that particular road, hiding behind a long line of vehicles to avoid detection. He drove slowly past and I saw the headlights slowly pass over the cars in front of me. Once he was gone and I was again in darkness, I started running through the grotty and littered streets, looking for anything familiar, but to no avail. I took a wrong turn and ended up on a dead-end road and before I could get out of it, Alfredo's car appeared, blocking the only escape route. He got out and ran toward me and I fled in the opposite direction, coming to a stop at a massive set of iron gates where a dog was barking uncontrollably at all the commotion. I held onto the gates for dear life kicking alfredo away as he tried to prise my fingers off the steel rods. Once again, a resident appeared to see what was happening and, once again, Alfredo told him that I needed help as I had too much to drink.

As he pulled me free from the gates, he spun me around, grabbing me by the throat again and lifting me off the ground. There was nothing I could do other than to spit in his face so I hoicked up as much phlegm as I possibly could into my mouth and spat it right into his eye.

He was so shocked by this act of defiance that, after spitting back into my face, he dropped me like a stone. As soon as my feet hit the ground, I sprinted passed his parked car and into the night.

Having no idea where I was headed, I started to worry that I would have to stay on the street until someone came looking for me, but right at that moment, I recognized a set of large bins that we had parked next to when we arrived at Antonio's soiree. Running through the front door, I made my way up the glamourous stairwell and into the arms of Antonio, who screamed, 'He did this to you again?'

He ordered the front door locked in case Alfredo returned and put me into a spare room to clean me up. I was helped into the shower and offered a new set of clothes as mine were bloodstained and ripped. I heard the commotion at the front door when my attacker arrived, demanding to see me. When they refused, he started to kick the door until they mentioned that the *polizia* would be called if he didn't piss off.

The next few days were a bit of a blur and I just stayed inside Antonio's apartment with the curtains drawn to lick my wounds and take in all that had happened. I was on the phone to my family, informing them of what had happened and planning my next move. John and Kim just happened to be on their way to Europe via Copenhagen, where they were boarding a ship destined for the Baltics on a *gay only* cruise.

'Come with us!' they said excitedly and I agreed that I would fly to meet them via London. It had been months since I had seen them and a friendly face from home was all I craved.

All of my possessions where still in Zafferana, so Antonio organized that we would head over there to pick them up and I could say goodbye to Alfredo's family. That was such an awkward visit as I whisked around, packing up my stuff and saying my goodbyes, looking like I just survived a massive bullfight, complete with black eyes. I could see the hurt on his parents faces but his narcissistic behavior also had them tightly under his control as they said nothing at all about my injuries. After he had discovered that I had been there, the texts and calls started with gusto, offering me everything from remorse and apologies to more abuse and character assassination.

Antonio saw how distraught I was and insisted that I get out of the house and enjoy some of the summer weather to make me feel better. I agreed and here I was, on the back of his Vespa, flying through the streets of downtown Catania towards the rocky beaches. I spent the day on the beach, basking in the sun on the massive rocks and swimming in the cool ocean. Then, at the end of the day, Antonio would pick me up and take me home.

I repeated this most days until Alfredo somehow got the intel that I was spending my days at a certain beach and, much to my horror, he showed up, sitting down next to me on the beach. I felt defiant and powerful as I was no longer taking any more of his shit and it showed. I told him that he needed to leave and to leave me in peace before my imminent departure to London in a few days. Of course, I made sure that I dropped in the conversation that I was heading away on an "all gay" cruise with the boys from NZ. He was calm and accepted my words until that point, then got up, telling me just what he thought of that idea and left.

More text and calls came over the next hours and days, begging me to see him and not to go on the cruise as this disturbed him no end. 'Please see me one last time,' he begged, stating that he had something to give me from his parents. I finally agreed under Antonio's watchful eye.

This guy was a master manipulator who always got his own way and couldn't cope when he didn't. He used his smoldering good looks and sex to get what he was after and, time after time, I fell for it, again and again, until I had finally had enough.

He came to the airport the day I left for London, offering me the gifts from his family. I accepted gracefully and walked away toward the departure gate without looking back.

That wasn't the end the of Alfredo story, as the communication went on for years until it finally petered out. I heard through some friends in later years that he was doing gay porn on various sites and when they offered to show me his wares, I respectfully declined.

Do we ultimately learn from our mistakes or go on to repeat them? I'm not sure, but I tell you this… I made my decisions with the resources I had at the time and now I choose to regret nothing.

I met with the boys in Copenhagen and boarded the ship for the cruise. The three of us had our picture taken on arrival but because of my still very black eye, we all thought twice about ordering a copy. The ship travelled to Estonia, Helsinki, St Petersburg — where we ate some hideous red cabbage soup — then Stockholm, before coming to an end in time for gay pride in Amsterdam.

The three of us didn't remember much about the latter, as we were so munted on weed from various coffee shops and, on one occasion, John overdosed on mushrooms, spoiling our night as he was totally out of control.

We had danced and partied hard all around the Baltic Sea and I really felt as if they had saved me from a massive cloud of depression that followed the events in Sicily. I had a moment of total reflection when I was dancing on one of the top deck dancefloors at around one a.m. I looked up skyward and out to sea, noticing that we were so far north on the earth's surface that it wasn't even dark, more like twilight. At that moment, I felt so far from my family but in awe of what I was seeing and would probably never see again in this lifetime.

The boys left for NZ and I boarded my flight back to London where I had arranged to meet with Rashika, who had broken up with her longtime partner in NZ and was struggling to cope. 'Come see me. I'll meet you in London.' And that she did!

I arrived a few days before her and planned to meet Mykal for a catch-up before any activity with Rashika. The anger from my experiences in Sicily had passed and now I just felt sad. Sad that I had failed at another relationship and sad that I had actually allowed myself to stay and return to my abuser time and time again. I was to meet my friend in Piccadilly, so I took the walk from Buckingham Palace, across Green Park, toward Mayfair and The Ritz. It was during this slow walk that all my emotions came to the surface and I broke down, trying to hide my sobs from the many people out catching the rays of sunshine during their lunch breaks. It felt good to let it all out and by the time I got to the top of Green Park, I felt a sense of euphoria and resolution. I soon spotted my friend's welcoming smile which quickly turned to anger when he saw the traces of violence still marking my face.

'I'll bloody kill him,' he said. But he agreed with me that one day all of the shit that this particular Italian had inflicted on all around him would indeed be his downfall.

Rashika arrived and it was so great to see another face from home, making me feel calm, safe and relaxed. We spent a few days in London to plan where we were heading next and what she wanted to see. Again, as always, we hit the pubs around this magic city, seeing the sites and showing her all the hot spots and places of interest as it was her first time. We trawled around the front of Buckingham Palace, shook the gates, walked around Harrods and had the hottest curry in Brick Lane. She already had mates in London so we hung out with them as well, which was really refreshing for me.

Because I'm a good mate, I thought that getting fucked up in Amsterdam would be a great distraction from her life back home, so we booked the flights and headed there… It was later known as "Amster-damage" — it didn't disappoint.

There was a major event in the city when we arrived and all hotels were full so we had to go to a hotel agent to see if we could find a bed in the city somewhere. It was literally the last bed in Amsterdam so we grabbed it as sleeping on the street was something we both weren't all that OK with. It turned out that our room was on a houseboat… Well, kind of a floating B & B, run by a couple of young entrepreneurs, who welcomed us along with their other weary guests. It was quite a walk from the old city but beggars couldn't be choosers. We walked over the rather narrow gangplank and were shown to our room, complete with a couple of single beds and en suite — choice!

After dropping our bags and freshening up, we walked back into town to have a few drinks and something to eat. After a bit of compulsory shopping, we ended up in one of the notorious "coffee shops", which is always funny when you first walk in as there is no noise, no conversation, as everyone sitting in there is so stoned that they just can't manage to string any kind of sentence together. We opted for some cake, which worried me a little as you never really know what you are getting and how strong it will be. We took our wee morsel and drinks outside to sit in the fresh air and both agreed that having just half would be a sensible idea. After a while and no reaction, I was talked into eating the other half (didn't take much convincing, to be honest).

We left the bar as Rashika desperately wanted to see the red-light area at night, with the ladies posing in the windows for customers, and as it was now dark, off we trotted. I can't really remember how it happened and at what point, but as we made our way around the crowded, famous area of the "ladies of the night", the cake kicked in. I noticed something was up when Rashika turned to me and said, 'There's that dog!'

I replied, 'What bloody dog?'

'It's the same dog that I've seen about three times!' With that, we stopped still on the spot.

It turned out that we were so stoned that we were just going around in circles, around the same block over and over. We both absolutely lost it and were crying with laughter but then the reality set in about how the hell were we going to find our way back to this bloody boat as, if you have ever been to Amsterdam you will know, these streets are on a grid system and all look the same!

'OK,' I said, 'give me a minute.' I really concentrated on the landmarks and where the Centraal Train Station was because if I could find that, I knew that the boat wasn't far from there on the right-hand side.

We trotted off, which must have looked hilarious as I had my *stoned but concentrating* face on and Rashika was trailing a couple of steps behind me with her handbag clutched tightly under her arm as paranoia had kicked in with her, making her think that someone was about to snatch if from her at any moment.

By the luck of God knows what, we stumbled onto the train station and I announced that we were on the right track and nearly home.

Turning right, we followed the waterfront and the long walk to the next set of buildings, which had our accommodation hidden behind it. The walk, of course, seemed to take forever in our vacant state and I was having a conversation with my mate about how I may have to lay down for a few minutes but not to panic as I would be OK after a short rest and then we would continue on our way. It turned out that Rashika was having a conversation with me, also only in her head, that somebody was following us and wanted her handbag that was clutched under her arm so tight that her knuckles were white. Of course, none of this was out loud, which we laughed about later but somehow it managed to kill some time as we turned the corner and there was the boat!

'Oh my God!' I exclaimed to my partner in crime. 'There's a bloody party happening on the front of the boat!' It was right where we had to walk the plank and we weren't that steady on our feet by this point.

'Hi there!' we both said as we approached the dreaded narrow plank and everyone turned to say hi back. We both stepped on to the narrow entrance, trying to act as normal as possible, which was damn near impossible by that point but somehow, we managed to pull it off and then disappeared below deck, falling into our beds fully clothed and eventually kicking the door to the room shut.

Waking the next morning, we made our way to the upper deck for a much-needed breakfast but walking into the breakfast area, we found that we were the only ones up. Turns out that the other guests had partied to the wee small hours and we had slept through the entire thing, hearing nothing!

Eventually one of the owners appeared, looking like a wet bag of dog shit with eyes redder than the surface of mars, apologizing for the lack of service. We didn't care, just got cooking as we were so hungry that we thought we were going to die. One to tell our grandchildren, we joked as we looked at where to head next on our next adventure.

It was decided that Barcelona and Paris were next, so we hunted for flights and trains to get us there. We flew to Spain on a random airline that I can't even remember the name of and it was probably one of the scariest flights I'd ever been on as, once again, the old plane rattled and shook and was lucky to even get up in the air. It was as though all the old planes went to these smaller airlines in Europe to die! But thank God, we made it to Barcelona in one piece and found a train to take us further out to Sitges, which had amazing beaches, shopping and a fabulous gay community and night life.

Hitting the beach, we found ourselves faced with a certain dilemma... There was a "straight" family beach and just over the rocks there was a "gay" beach. The "straight" beach had a few couples dotted about and the "gay" beach was chocka full of people with music pumping and even food being sold. It was definitely a no-brainer, huh, and we found ourselves a small spot surrounded by about a thousand beautiful men. I was extremely happy to say the least and Rashika was happy to look at all the beautiful bodies. The only straight man on this beach was a young Spanish guy selling ice blocks and he spotted the only straight girl next to me within minutes and spent the day flirting with her continuously. It was so cute to watch a couple of heterosexuals going through the motions!

After a few hours on the beach, we walked around the village, taking in all the sites and trying to get a glimpse into real life as opposed to just the tourist traps. By pure accident, we came across a wedding that had just finished and the happy couple had just exited the church, into the arms of their family and friends. It was as you would expect — an ancient white church with a steeple set against the calm blue sea. A single bell was ringing out in congratulations to the most handsome couple I think I had ever seen. Rashika and I stood there in the crowd, just watching, taking photos and drinking in the "movie-like" atmosphere. We both agreed that, when we met the right guy, we would both come back here and get married!

Night fell and the small village came alive with the restaurants and bars heaving with gay men, all races, all shapes and all sizes. As we walked down the street to pick a venue to eat, we noticed that all of the seating was set to face the walkways on both sides so anyone at the bars and cafes wouldn't miss out on perving opportunities as people walked past. It was so unashamedly obvious. We laughed about it but felt completely on show, which was a bit awkward, so we picked a café and took a seat.

Ordering drinks and dinner, we settled in for the evening, enjoying the music, food and sights of people walking up and down on show and doing a better job of it than we did.

Across from us, there was a rowdy table of guys and one of them in particular had me in his sights, smiling, winking and watching my every move. Rashika was pressing me to "go say hi", which I swiftly replied to with a 'Hell no, not with my track record!' So we carried on just enjoying each other's company and taking in the activities unfolding around us.

Eventually, the loud table of guys left, including the smiling, winking guy that I was trying to ignore. We also finished our drinks and decided to move on to a bar and were drawn in by the music to one just a few doors down. We stood at the bar with our rather expensive cocktails when "smiley guy" just so happened to be standing next to us. Rashika gave me a push and I said "gidday" in the most terrible, clunky accent.

His name was Unal, from Germany, and he was on holiday with a friend so we stayed chatting and drinking with him and his group. The copious amount of liquor was starting to take its toll so it was decided that Unal would walk us back to our hotel and then taxi back to where he was staying. We arrived and decided to have a nightcap in the foyer of our accommodation and during that time, he put the moves on me. I was so tempted as he seemed kind, polite and genuine.

'Right!' Rashika piped up. 'You can go with him *(pointing at me)*, but I want all your details *(pointing at Unal)* and contact number, just in case you are a serial killer!' Grabbing the opportunity, he presented everything, including his driver's license and once she approved his documentation, she went up to bed and Unal and I jumped in the nearest taxi and headed to the country retreat where he was staying. It was so rural that the cab could only get to the bottom of the rugged driveway and we had to walk the rest of the way up. The villa was stone and decorated with the most amazing fixtures and furniture and the bed was fit for a queen, or in this case, two queens.

We awoke in the morning and Unal insisted on getting up early and taking me to the breakfast area, which was a short walk up a cobbled path. When we got there, my jaw dropped open. It was set on a terraced area dotted with beautifully set tables and overlooked the Spanish landscape and out to sea. It was like a page out of a travel magazine and here I was, drinking it all in. Unal escorted me back to the hotel and a waiting Rashika, who wanted to know all the details and she wanted to know it now!

It turned out that he was heading back to Barcelona for a few days and offered us accommodation and whatever else we needed. We accepted and upon arriving back in Barcelona, he set us up with somewhere to stay and took us out on the town. Rashika was with some friends of his and I was with him in a rooftop apartment with the most hideous staircase that was eleven flights and no lift.

We arrived at a bar that was owned by a friend of his and we all sat at the bar, ready to order drinks, when he disappeared out the back, only to appear a few minutes later, signaling us to join him out back. Cocaine was rife and a drug of choice for the area, so I went after him, while my Kiwi mate opted out, to keep her head in case I lost mine. The night was electric and I had one of the wildest times in my life (apparently). I was walking along to the next club when we passed a lamp shop on a corner and I stopped to discuss all the way that lamps and lighting could be used in one's home. 'I love lamps!' I proclaimed, and Rashika never let me forget it, bringing it up in conversation for years to come.

This was right before we lost her as she had other plans with a hot bartender that we had met a few days before and argued about which was he swung. She won that bet.

Paris was waiting for us and we stayed in a B & B that a friend of mine owned and it was so beautiful and extremely Parisian, however, as he was fully booked, we only had a few days there and had to find alternative accommodation after that. All I will say is the next B & B had a door that fell on my head, loose plumbing that I had to fix, and, to top it all off, we caught bugs from the beds which gave us terrible rashes on Rashika's hands and arms and all over my face. Attractive, much!

From there, we headed back to London, meeting up with Mykal and taking in shows and catching up again with her mates. It was at that time that Rashika got the news that her dad in NZ was fatally ill and wasn't expected to survive. She was devastated and had to plan to leave for NZ as soon as possible and I was going to miss her terribly as she had become a lifeline for me but I was determined to stay in the UK for as long as possible as I didn't feel ready to go home.

Staying separately in London, I got a text from Rashika saying that her dad had just passed away and she was so distraught. I caught the tube to Brixton where she was staying and upon seeing her there, was no way that I would let her take the long flight back to New Zealand alone, so I decided to put myself second and go back home with her and return at a later date.

As our flight descended into a rainy Auckland, we looked at each other and held hands as the wheels hit NZ soil, knowing that our lives would be different as soon as we walked out of the airport. Hers, with having to deal with the death of a parent and the aftermath and mine, trying to settle back into life at home after such a huge journey, not only in miles but in life itself.

Within months, Rashika not only had to deal with the death of her father but also the disintegration of her family, along with the premature death of her ex-boyfriend at only thirty years old.

She later went on to find a good man, marry him and have her own family. We never did get back to Sitges together to have that wedding in that particular church as we had planned all those years ago.

It felt strange to be at home after all the time away but good to see my sons and close friends. Sheeba, my collie, refused to have anything to do with me and gave me a wide birth — abandonment issues?

I kept my arrival low key and a secret mainly from my parents and siblings, as I just didn't know what I was going to do long-term and I really didn't want to see many people at all at that time and my anxiety around being home was at an all-time high.

I was embarrassed about what had happened in Sicily and what people would say. I had put my friends and family through all that drama and I was ashamed. I wasn't looking forward to the "I told you so" comments.

A couple of weeks passed, and with my family and friends down the line in Tokoroa and Rotorua still thinking that I was on the other side of the world, I received a phone call from Gloria telling me that Mum had a fall and was in Waikato hospital.

This incident was to bring me out of hiding and back into the real world. I slipped out of Auckland and headed south to Hamilton and the Waikato hospital. It was the first time I had entered the hospital since I had my tonsils out all those years ago. I parked and started the journey to search out Mum in the massive concrete structure, managing to get lost in the long corridors and different wards. After asking for directions twice, I finally found the right ward and walked up the long hallway until

I found a familiar name written on the door whiteboard — "Myrna Fergusson".

Noticing that she was sharing the room with three others, I tiptoed in to not disturb her elderly roommates and to try and surprise her. Her bed was by the large window looking over the trees and onto the lake. She was asleep and looked so small and old. I took a seat next to her bed and quietly took her arthritic, twisted hand and held it softly. Slowly she opened one eye and look straight at me. 'What the hell are you doing here?' she exclaimed. 'When did you get back, you bloody little sneak!' I giggled as it was so nice to hear her voice and see the expression on her delighted face. She told me of her fall and the coinciding operation, detail by detail, as only Mum could.

I explained that I was going to Tokoroa to surprise everyone else and she promised not to say a word to anyone until I got there. This was not a simple task for Mother, as her nickname was "eyes and ears of the world", and with good reason.

After spending the time with Mum and telling her all about my travels and what I had seen and done, she wanted to sleep so I left and headed back home to Tokoroa to see Dad and the rest of the family.

It was such great fun to surprise everyone and give them a hell of a shock. When I walked in to see Dad, the Bushman was lost for words, sitting in his La-Z-Boy chair with his mouth dropped open, mimicking exactly Mums response — "what the hell", etc.

Gloria was the best one, as I called her from the bottom of her driveway, saying that I was calling from London and I was walking to the local Tesco for some milk. As she was chatting to me, I walked in her front door. She looked at me then looked at the phone and then looked at me again. 'You bloody bastard!' she screamed before we ran toward each other to squeeze the living daylights out of one another.

Throughout all of these reunions, I felt a sense of home and it felt so good to be back home surrounded by all that I knew.

Back in Auckland, I was offered a contract to return to TV3 and run the direct sales team so I jumped at the opportunity to return to familiar surroundings and the people that I had started my media career with. Looking back, I can see now that it was a lot about bedding myself back into my former life and feeling safe and secure with all my anchors intact. My boys were happy with Dad in the country again so I was at their beck and call, and Sheeba was slowly warming to me, although I could see a lingering look of uncertainty in her eyes.

I also noticed that our "Sheebee" had slowed down a hell of a lot and had literally gone stone deaf overnight. Her beautiful, trusting big brown eyes had become cloudy and she slept most of the day. I was abruptly woken one morning before work when Daniel yelled into my room, 'There's something wrong with Sheeba!' Leaping out of bed, I found her staggering on her feet with her eyes flicking from side to side, so we rushed her to the vet.

She was fourteen years old by this stage and having fits and strokes for a collie of this age was to be expected. We were so distraught by the news, as I guess we thought that we would have her forever. I have always stated that I never understood why our pets can't live as long as we do, as it would save us a hell of a lot of heartache and grief losing them, as they become part of our family. The vet explained that the medication he gave us for our girl would chill her out and slow any seizures she may have.

We all returned to our daily routine and work hours while Sheeba stayed home, minding the house but sleeping most of the day away. I would return after work, open the door to a sleeping doggy then manage to step over her without waking her up. I'd be home at least thirty minutes before she realized I was upstairs and would then give me a late, but very sweet, "welcome home".

It was Mum's birthday and we were all getting ready to leave for the day when Sheeba gave me a look… A look as if to say, *I've had enough, Dad, and I'm so tired.* I called the vet who told us to bring her in but to prepare ourselves that it would probably be the time that she had to be euthanized.

It was December and our Christmas tree was up and our very tired girl had decided that she would lay down next to it, making herself comfortable. Daniel and I took turns at sitting with her, chatting to her and telling her how much she was loved and that we would be taking her to the vet soon to help her feel better. I was on the phone to my boss when Daniel turned to me and said, 'Dad, I think she's gone!' I knelt down next to her and felt for a heartbeat. She had gone in her own time, in her own way, in her own home, right under that Christmas tree, with us at her side as if not to cause any fuss or commotion. I felt so incredibly grateful that she had waited until I was home from Europe before leaving us. It was a good death after a good life and she left such a huge gap in our everyday life — sleep on, dear Sheeba.

Over the next couple of years, I enjoyed being single and home alone mostly, as Ben and Dan had both moved out to go flatting with partners and friends. I was back to circulating on the scene at bars and clubs and using the internet or the local sauna on a Sunday arvo to satisfy my sexual needs. In a big city like Auckland, it wasn't that hard and I had decent pickings when it came to men. I also dated a few who wanted more but I was unsure and dated a few more who were unsure about me. A lot of the guys I hung out with were already coupled up and I was often the old maid when we all hit the town… In other words, couple, couple, couple, me!

I was briefly seeing a guy that I really felt that I could do something long-term with and we even moved in together, which kind of gives you hope that there is someone out there for you after all. It was going well until our sex life abruptly stopped and shortly after, I picked up the wrong phone to see a text from someone he had met that day for sex. I was upset but not overly devastated as this is what I was getting used to when having a partner within the scene or gay community. It really did feel as though everyone and anyone was fair game and, as I mentioned previously, "fresh meat" was always on the menu.

I moved into my own apartment and purchased a large bach on Waiheke Island, where I spent most of my weekends and had regular visits from family and friends.

During a visit to Rotorua one weekend, I stumbled on an open home sign that led me straight to my Aunty Joan's old house at 9 Dawson Drive in Ngongotahā, where she had lived with husband, Andy. I knew it was on the market as my cousin, Val, had sent me a newspaper advert, showing all the details. I decided to have a look around and see what had changed, etc… It was empty, dark, smelly and cold in the extreme. It was a home that they had loved so much during their decades living there and now it was an empty shell that hardly resembled anything I remembered. One of the only things that remained untouched was Joan's coal range, still intact and in working order. The gardens had all been removed, leaving a large parcel of land resembling a stark rugby field.

The agent was pleasant but I could tell she wanted to get the hell out of there as soon as she could. It was up for auction and being slightly tempted, I told her to keep in touch if it didn't sell.

A week later, the phone rang and of course it didn't sell, due to the terrible state of the property. I made an offer and picked it up for a song as I could see the potential due to its location being close to Lake Rotorua and the huge parcel of land it sat on.

After a couple of drunken painting parties and help from Val doing touch-ups when I went back to Auckland, it was ready for a new tenant. Even though I was advised by everyone to *not* touch it, it turned out to be one of the best decisions I had ever made in real estate and I wanted it, regardless, knowing for sure that Joan and Andy would've been pleased that I saved their beloved home and was bringing it back to life. I was lucky enough to get a long-term tenant and it managed itself for the next few years with a great return — phew!

After a few years in my role at TV3, the entire structure changed due to the network being sold to an overseas interest and I struggled with the new management… Well, to say that was an understatement as we all seemed to be dropping like flies, so I thought I would jump before I was pushed. My buddy, Sharon, media queen extraordinaire, who had been at TVNZ and TV3 with me had moved to Sky. She personally hand-shook me through to the right people and I landed a management role at Sky TV, which would see me through for the next nearly five years.

My mates, John and Kim, had returned to Auckland from Christchurch a few years before, and I loved being around them again. So, on the weekends I wasn't on the island, we would spend together getting up to all kinds of mischief. Kim and I would hit the gym together when possible and walk to stay as fit and slim as possible. He would also sit in as my plus-one if I ever wanted to go to the odd show or opera and didn't want to do it on my own. And John was certainly OK with that as it wasn't really his thing!

They were both a fantastic support and truly great friends, who I shared so much history with. They had been together for over thirty years and I had been on and on at them to make it official since gay marriage had finally been passed in parliament. I even said to them, if they ever did get married, that I would wear the bloody dress!

They eventually weakened and applied for the marriage license. When it came through, we picked a date and booked the venue and caterers. The date was Kim's sixtieth birthday and the invites went out announcing a massive birthday party with no mention of a wedding. The theme would be "white" and *still* no one clicked that there could be something else happening, but I guess that no one would even suspect as they had both been so adamant that getting married was never a priority. Even John didn't say a word and he was even worse than my mother at keeping a secret!

It was decided that we would break the boredom of winter in Auckland and celebrate us organizing the entire wedding without detection by going away on another "gay only" cruise but this time around on the Mexican Riviera. The tickets were booked and we flew to LA, where I had organized a limo driver to pick us up drive us to Long Beach where we had booked to stay on the original *Queen Mary,* which was now a floating hotel. After my bag going missing, an argument between the guys, and the limo driver going to the wrong terminal, we finally made it to our floating paradise.

It certainly was an experience staying on this old bucket, as she was totally original, right down to the beds and toilet fittings! The floors sagged and there were parts of it that I was surprised hadn't rusted off and fallen into the water, however, she was steeped in history and the displays, including some of Diana's dresses, saved the day. We wined and dined most evenings and spent the days walking and cruising around long beach.

The ship seemed to be a place that couples would have hen and stag functions and even weddings, so it happened that we ended up in the middle of a hen party that was being held in a top bar situated on the ship's bow. We dirty-danced, joked with the bride and her bridesmaids, even helping ourselves to their very generous bar tab that an unaware groom must have been footing the bill for. Towards the end of the night, I called Mum and Dad to tell them where we were and how much fun it was. I would always do this when I was travelling as it not only kept them informed of where I was in the world but it kind of let them experience stuff they never got to do through my eyes. 'You boys bloody behave yourselves!' she said before I hung up.

It was the day of the cruise and I had stashed as much booze in my suitcase as possible to save us money on drinks so we could preload in our room. Kim, being our self-proclaimed "company secretary", was in charge of all bookings and when we eventually got to our room, we hurtled abuse at him as it was so small with a tiny window, a double bed and a pull-down bunk above. Our bags arrived in the room and you can imagine the disappointment when I found a note from the ship's security saying that they had confiscated my booze, which put an end to my cunning plan!

I pulled out the bunk bed and put up the ladder, it felt as though we were on school camp but the difference with this one was that we had lots of bars instead of campfires, so off we went.

There was the usual scene with all the pretty boys with muscles, aka, the plastics, all around the pool with their deck chairs and sun loungers all pre-booked. The older gays in the theatre or casino. The bears and otters around the stern pool and everyone in between wandering around to see who would talk to them. If you were a bit horny later at night, all you needed to do was head to the very top deck and onto the observation deck for a hook-up or quick blowie. Not being the sort to be put in boxes, my besties and I wandered around talking, swimming and drinking with everyone and having an absolute ball.

One of the ports we first got to was Puerto Vallarta and we decided to disembark to have a look around but avoided the traditional bus trips to the sugar-coated tourist areas.

Crossing a busy highway and probably guilty of blatant jaywalking, we found ourselves in a Walmart carpark and because none of us had ever experienced a Walmart shopping experience, we excitedly entered.

It is like The Warehouse and Kmart had a baby, complete with a pharmacy and grocery but on a huge scale. John thought it was a good idea to head to the pharmacy to see if we could get anything to spice up the trip. He had heard somewhere and from someone that, in Mexico, all you needed to do was rock up to the pharmacy and say that you had a very sick cat and they would give you ketamine. Kim and I were mortified as John made his way to the pharmacy, ignoring our calls saying that it wouldn't be true and he would get in trouble. I had visions of us all being locked up in some filthy Mexican prison with no windows and a bucket to piss in.

Kim and I were hiding in the isles, getting as far away from John and the pharmacy as possible. He reappeared moments later, telling us what a waste of time that was as the pharmacist didn't speak any English and he got tired of trying to explain what a cat was. After nearly wetting our pants at the outcome, we made our way to an adjoining mall and found a great Mexican restaurant. It served jugs and jugs of margarita, which gave us enough inner fuel to again cross the busy highway and get back on the ship.

The cruise ship was a much smaller version of the one we had been on a few years before, so we got thrown around more when out at sea, and what were the odds of us hitting a big storm? The odds were pretty slim but hit a storm, we did, and the swelling seas threw our ship about to the point that a lot of passengers got violently seasick, including me.

I spent two days in bed, missing a lot of the random dance parties and group gatherings. Not being able to hold anything down, including water, John called the medic who had been flat out trying to keep up with the demand. A young and very handsome doctor appeared in our cabin and instantly I felt better, even before he gave me the jab in my bum to stop the nausea and vomiting. Within hours, I was up and ready to party again.

It was the night of the massive "white" party and the boys had three amazing white tutus made for us to wear, which were amazing and stole the show — well, at least *we* thought we looked good!

Wanting to get totally messed up, I produced some valium that I used for long-haul flights, so we popped one each and hit the dancefloor.

John and I were having such a great night, but Kim started to stagger around, losing his footing and banging into groups of people. Not a good look when you're sixty years old, staggering about on the dancefloor, wearing a white sparkly custom-made tutu. We dragged him off the people around him and steered him back towards our room.

John and I decided to stop at the late-night snack bar for a bit of a post-dance feed and Kim kept walking and stating that he knew where the room was and how he needed to get to bed.

After the gorging of the most fabulous paninis, we arrived at our cabin door, but when we tried to open it, there was something blocking it. I kept pushing enough to get my head in the door enough to see the obstruction — Kim was laying, passed out, on the floor, having not quite made it to the bed. 'He's not dead,' I informed John, as I could hear him snoring. We both pushed on the door, moving his limp tutu-clad carcass enough so we could enter. Of course, we never let him forget this and still bring it up to this day.

The rest of the cruise was so much fun, complete with more eating, more drinking, more parties, and even a wee shipboard romance for me, which was a lot of fun.

We attended daytime T-dance, where the crew appeared with massive fire hoses that they blasted us all with while on the dancefloor. It was crazy fun, but all good things must come to an end and the damage that was caused by the storm we hit cut out some posts and destination from the itinerary and we soon found ourselves back in LA, ready for the next adventure.

We picked up our rental car and John volunteered to drive along the massive freeways with only a GPS with a rather annoying accent as a guide. Our next destination was Palm Springs, and the trip there was again full of adventure and hilarious moments. We must have looked like the bloody Keystone Cops trying to find our way out of LA but after a wrong turn in front of a highway patrol officer, illegal turns, lane changes and a little off-road experience — we made it.

Palm Springs, set in the middle of the desert, was the place that old-time movie stars had their holiday homes. Stars like Bob Hope, Lucille Ball, Dean Martin, Marilyn Monroe and more. I was totally in awe as this was really my kind of town, complete with shops that sold vintage movie memorabilia. Shopping, eating and drinking was, again, on the menu. We even found an outlet store out in the desert, which excited Kim and I so much that we ignored John's pleas to please return to our motel as the Thai food he had the night before was only a clench away from disaster!

Finally understanding the urgency of the situation, we ran for the car and zoomed back to our room but, alas, too late for poor John, who had no choice but to leave his mark on the car seat. Oops.

We had the most amazing, fun time, full of laughter and special moments, which will always be tattooed in my memory. Home was calling and we arrived back in the country, telling all who would listen about our great trip away.

Royals — Lorde, 2014

The boys' wedding was fast approaching and, still under the guise of a sixtieth birthday party, we began the final set up details. I made the wedding cake, which I stored in the fridge at SKY TV and, as I am a man of my word, I went searching for the dress that I promised I would wear if the boys actually tied the knot.

My buddy, Denise, and I were in stiches in Save Mart as she handed me selections of wedding frocks, veils and gloves. We found just the thing.

The big day came and everyone turned up wearing their interpretation of a white outfit to try and outdo each other. I was appointed the HBC for the night, which translated means "Head Bitch in Charge", so I was right in my element, having been sewn into my gown by sister, Gloria, who adorned in a Snow White costume.

The evening was really gaining some traction when I was given the thumbs up to change the music to "Chapel of Love". Then John and Kim appeared, hand in hand, having gotten changed out of their original outfits and into their actual wedding suits. An astonished crowd parted to let them through, and they were married in front of a gawping and pleasantly shocked party of their good mates and close family. We did it! And right up to that point, nobody had even an inkling that this would be the outcome of the night.

Before Christmas that same year, I had decided to sell the apartment and move into a small villa in Grey Lynn, complete with a small yard and good living space. It gave me the space to once again entertain and have family to stay if I wanted without having to get out of my own bed. The nights after work at Sky with my staff became legendary and regular BBQs with my boys were always on the cards.

Denise and I were still the best of friends and would go to the concerts that no one else would want to go to — Dolly Parton, Spandau

Ballet, Ricky Martin, etc., and we loved it. Being together at these events, however, we soon found out that we weren't the only ones getting together. It soon came to light that my son, Ben, and her daughter, Casey, were an item, which of course we were delighted about but had to make sure that no matter what happened between them, it would never affect our friendship. Family get-togethers now included Denise and her hubby too, which was so comfortable as we had all known each other for the longest time.

Daniel had married his boyfriend so everyone was all loved up except for me, which I had finally come to terms with and was enjoying my time alone.

I had mentioned the idea of getting some kind of pet as living alone can be tiresome and lonely at times. John took that conversation literally and arrived with a cat in a cage, looking for a forever home. His name was Horace and he spent the next two weeks under the beds, hiding, only coming out to eat and then disappearing again. His aloof nature and uncaring attitude only made me more convinced that he was not only homophobic but also socially inept. As a result of this, I started calling him "Doris" because of his attitude and the name stuck. Having another living being in the house at night and when I get home was life-changing and we ended up being a perfect match. Occasionally, I would even take him with me to the bach on Waiheke.

Mum was thrilled that I finally had a pussy in my life, but not the type she really wanted me to have… She loved cats and would always ask how the cat was before asking about what was happening in my life.

My anxiety and depression, for some reason, started to hit me hard — was it because I found myself alone again, with no partner in sight, or was it my job that was getting me down? As part of the management team at Sky, I began to get shut out of meetings and left out of any strategic planning or information. I was always a strong, loud voice that insisted on having my say on work matters, so I can only put it down to the two at the top being threatened by me and wanted to keep me in my box. It was an incredibly weird place to work because of a very "us and them" childlike management style. I had also lost my ally, Sharon, who had got me the job there in the first place.

Suffering from mental illness was something I had spent most of my adult life fighting and I wasn't putting up with it any more. The darkness in my mind was always hiding just under the surface and it made me either angry and hot-headed, or deathly quiet. No more was I prepared to suffer with this so I made an appointment with my GP and after a couple of trials, I managed to get on the right medication to keep me on an even keel.

My life was different as soon as they started to kick in as I found myself being able to see things rationally and clearly enough to make a qualified decision without losing my head. Yes, it affected my sex drive but I looked at that as a positive because I had become extremely promiscuous.

I always felt that something inside me was a bit broken and now, with this medication, I started to think, *wow... Is this how normal people feel?* I could control my moods and responses to different dilemmas that in the past I found impossible to deal with.

I was then looking for something to fill my nights and weekends and decided that I would pick up the paintbrush for the first time in decades and start to create my own style of portraiture. I purchased canvases and a wooden easel and started my journey into art. Now, I'm not saying that my meds were the reason for my rediscovered passion for art, and talent to do it, but it certainly cleared my cluttered mind enough for me to stay focused on each project.

I started by using a mixture of photography and acrylic on canvas to capture the essence of the subject, and I fell in love with the process and was overjoyed with the results I was getting. I created a few portraits using vintage photographs of my Mum, Dad and Gertie, which I sent to Gloria. Her response was, 'Shit, that's good!' So I carried on.

I was struggling with how to sign off my work as I thought that plain old *Terry Fergusson* was just a little boring, and my years of media training was telling me to search for a brand that I could use instead, but I just couldn't seem to crack it.

With the portraits of my parents ready to be shared, I loaded up the car and headed to Tokoroa to show them off directly to the subjects themselves. As usual, the traffic out of Auckland at the end of the week was horrendous so it was a long, slow journey. I was still wracking my brain when I was coming through Tirau, of all places, and on the crest of the hill opposite the old hotel was a small shop called The Carpenter's Daughter. Slowing to a crawl, the words, "The Bushman's Son" came into my mind.

My dad was a bushman, as was his dad, and even his dad. A bushman and fine art don't really go hand in hand, but I saw this as a positive, and my edge, my point of difference. Boom, there it was... A brand that I could use that not only would get noticed but was absolutely who I was as an individual.

To test my talent, I entered a piece depicting Aunty Joan during the war, called *Beautifully Complicated,* into the Titirangi Emerging Artist Awards and got a finalist placing. I was so bloody stoked that it was recognized as being worthy enough to go up against other artists.

I soon had my small studio — the spare room — full of images that I had created and started asking people I knew or worked with to pose for me for totally original pieces. Again, I was so please with what I was turning out and moved my studio into the garage to give me more room to create and display.

Close to where I worked at Sky was a small gallery, which I would frequent and purchase items and pieces that caught my eye. I pitched my portfolio to them, along with other galleries in Auckland and Wellington, leaving examples and contact details, hoping that the phone would ring. It didn't.

The Auckland gallery that I had frequented had another arm, situated in Wellington, so in between work appointments in the capital city, I fronted up, asking if they had actually taken a look at my work examples but getting ready to be blown off as just another try-hard.

'Yes!' replied Ron, the owner. He was planning that he would be in Auckland the following week to meet with his colleague, Ngaire, at the gallery for a show opening and they both wanted to come and see my work after that. I was on my way to being represented by two people that new their stuff.

The stage was set, well, it was my living room at home that was set up like a gallery, featuring every piece I had strategically placed through every inch of space. Upon arriving, they both looked over the collection carefully, curiously and quietly at first, but then piped up, 'Wow! This is great! Real and raw — you have an exhibition right here and we'd like to hang it in our gallery!'

'What? Really? This stuff? My stuff?'

Did I hear that right? They loved my work and wanted to represent it, and me? It was real, and the three of us had a few rum and cokes, to celebrate. It took a bit of convincing to explain my "Bushman's Son" brand and what it meant to me that it be used on all media and promotion around my art. I explained that it was a nod to my past, upbringing and my parents. It was a brand that is totally Kiwi and would stand out like dogs' balls in the art world. Slowly but surely, they agreed to take it on and respect my position and bigger plan for the brand.

My bushman dad seemed to be quietly thrilled with his involvement and presence within my art brand, but it was hard to know as he really was a man of few words when it came to any sort of acknowledgement or praise. It felt like for most of my life I had tried to get his attention or to find some common ground between us and this was something that made me feel closer to him without any words being uttered.

I decided to create a piece featuring my parents as they were in the present day, like a snapshot in time that would depict who they are and who they were after they were long gone. The day I asked them to pose I got a "no way!" from both of them but managed to talk them around. I took a series of photographs with them kissing, embracing, but couldn't quite get the money shot I was after.

'Dad,' I said, 'make her laugh!' With that, he leaned in close to her face and said something that no child wants to hear their parents talk about and with that statement, Mum roared with laughter and — *click* — I had it.

Feeling a bit cheeky, I entered the piece into the NZ Adam Portrait Awards and it was accepted into the finals, being one of fifty selected for the judging. I didn't win the big prize of $25K, however, the piece I named *Still Mine* won the overall People's Choice Award, which meant so much to me as an emerging artist. Gloria and I flew to Wellington to accept the award and celebrate. Of course, Ron and Ngaire from the galleries where thrilled that I was getting acknowledged and noticed, as this would help sales of my other work and bring interest to my first exhibition. The stars align...

I named my first exhibition *Raw,* which, in my mind, meant... raw talent, as I was emerging and raw material, meaning that this was my first work and would never be as raw again.

Right when an exhibition date was set for the Auckland gallery, I was called into a meeting at work and was invited to bring in a support person. *Here we go*, I thought to myself, *please make me redundant!* I had done my dash at Sky and a major change in broadcasting into the regions had made me kind of surplus to requirements. I was actually so thrilled that I was given a way out and could plan in time what to do next.

At this time, I started to notice that Mum had changed, and it became more and more evident with each visit and phone call, but I couldn't put my finger on what it was. She had a knee replacement the year before and Dad had noticed that she wouldn't or couldn't do the exercises and would fly off the handle at him when he tried to question her. Her cooking and cleaning became more and more infrequent, with my ex-bushman dad picking up the slack, much to our surprise. They finally gave up sleeping together in the same bed as Mum just couldn't settle at night and was up and down to the toilet frequently. They had been married around sixty-five years and held each other's hand every night (unless Dad was in the shit for being out too late at the club again) but finally something had to give.

It got worse and Mum would have Dad up and down all night, demanding to be placed on the loo and then back to bed and even then, she wouldn't sleep, insisting that our father adjust her pillows and straighten the sheets over and over. Her paranoia became unbearable, for not only Dad, but for Mum herself as she knew that something was definitely wrong in her head and even her face had changed to resemble a wooden type of stare.

She was diagnosed eventually with Parkinson's disease and we were all so shocked and saddened. It wasn't the Parkinson's that you associate with tremors, etc., but the one that eats away at your brain and changes the way you look and who you are. Our father was amazing, stepping up to aid his ailing wife with everything she needed, but we could see that the effect on this elderly man in his late eighties was just too much.

She fell over frequently and even with home help, ended up in the local hospital to calm her down and tend to her injuries. The medication she was taking was the strongest available to help control the diseases hideous symptoms. If she was even a little late being fed these drugs, she would change... Her eye would twitch and she would cry or scream out uncontrollably.

We were all called to a meeting at the hospital with Mum and Dad to discuss options for Mum's ongoing care as going back home was not an option. We all had to vote on her future as she sat there in front of us in her favorite dressing gown. Our hearts were broken but so was our Mum — she was a broken woman because of this disease that was destroying her mind and changing her from the fun and witty mum we all knew and loved. It was Gloria's turn to vote and she turned to Mum in tears and said, 'No Mum, I don't want this...'

With that, Mum put her hand on her hand and said, in a moment of absolute clarity, 'I think it's time, it's OK.'

We all agreed with her but putting a parent into care is one of the hardest things you will ever have to do. Before we left to make the arrangements and before I headed back to Auckland, we all stood together for a photo. This would be the last picture ever taken of us as a complete family.

All of the beds in the aged care facility in Tokoroa were full so our mother was placed initially in a home in Rotorua until a space became available. She hated it and would always ask us to sneak her out and take her home, also asking what she had done so wrong that would make us put her in there. It was extremely heartbreaking to see her so frail and vulnerable.

With all of this a priority, my redundancy coming through, and my art and the pending exhibition potentially becoming a revenue stream, I made a decision that made all my Auckland friends and colleagues *gasp* in shock. I had decided to go home, back to Rotorua, to be closer to Mum and the family and use my art as income. I even had somewhere to live as my long-term tenants in Joan and Andy's house had given notice to leave. It was as though the universe was saying *come home, boy,* so that was my plan.

I decided that the week after my exhibition launch, I would pack everything up and go, so the truck was ordered and John found a tenant for my house in Grey Lynn until it was sold. I had my last day at Sky TV and walked out feeling bloody great and so relieved to be out.

With all my moving jobs in place, I started to get all the selected work ready for *Raw*. The catalogues were printed, the invites were out, the advertising was done and all I had to do was finish packing up the house and wait.

I sent the invitation out to my siblings and Dad, thinking that there was no way that he would come with Mum being in care and, besides, he didn't really like to travel far, but he said yes and was catching a ride on the day with my brother, Ray. I was so excited, as my dad was coming to something that I really needed him to be at so maybe he felt that somehow. My sisters arrived also, with aunties and cousins surprising me, along with old friends, new friends and the general public. The venue was so full that there was a queue at the door and I, along with Ron and Ngaire, was completely overwhelmed.

It was a Tuesday night but that didn't seem to matter to anyone as the wine flowed and the beer was guzzled. Art was flying out the door and at the end of its run, *Raw* was labeled a sellout exhibition. I was interviewed by different magazines and newspapers and even had a television interview outlining my background and motivation behind the exhibit. It was absolutely awesome to have that kind of exposure and it certainly did spread the word and definitely helped my brand.

During the night, I had a friend open with a Māori blessing and he even sang opera, which left everyone in awe. It was speech time and my gracious hosts opened with some kind and encouraging words of support for me and the art that adorned the walls of the gallery. I responded by giving thanks to all the subjects I had used and to my sons and the rest of my family. I then called up the bushman himself to stand next to me while I thanked him publicly, not only for the bushman name, but also for his and my mum's support.

My mother not being there was so incredibly hard as she couldn't even be told of the event because she would have spun out of control about not being able to attend and would try everything she could to escape.

When the bulk of the guest started to leave, it was decided that we would all head back to my house for a celebration. I was still trying to get to my home when the bulk of the people were already there so the neighbors unlocked it, put on the heating and made sure all was ready when eventually I arrived.

It was such a happy, festive environment with champagne flowing, more opera singing, dancing and right in the middle of it was my dad, chatting and using his wit to entertain all who would listen. Last drinks were poured around four a.m., and Dad went to bed about an hour or so before that.

So there it was, I had achieved the status of an exhibiting artist and I had sold a shitload of work and even picked up some commissions though the exposure on social media and my website. The only thing left to do was wait for the truck and load up all my possessions, throw Doris in his cage, and head down to Ngongotahā to start the next chapter of life — a quieter life close to my parents. It was hard to say goodbye to my kids, but they had their own lives sorted so I was good to go.

Hello — Adele 2016

It was a cold morning when the truck arrived at 38 Cooper Street and lowered its back deck to start loading my life inside. Slowly, my wee house got more and more empty and the reality of leaving my sixteen-year life in New Zealand's biggest city hit. Wanting to beat the traffic and arrive in Ngongotahā before the truck did, I frantically finished cleaning and then tried putting Doris in his travel cage, but he wasn't having a bar of it, scratching, clawing and holding onto the sides so I couldn't close the lid. After losing what felt like a few pints of blood, I loaded him and the last of my things in the car and hit the motorway, south, towards our new home. I guess I felt numb leaving my big city life behind but excited more than apprehensive about living back in a smaller place.

Even though I had to experience Doris screaming and howling for three hours, the drive seemed to go reasonably quickly, probably due to my mind being preoccupied with all that was going on.

Pulling into the driveway of our new home, Doris suddenly fell silent, as if he knew we were finally home. With him in his cage and me fumbling with the keys, I managed to get the back door open and walked into the kitchen, stopping alongside the coal range that had been long since cold, unlike in the days that my aunty always had it constantly red hot with pots of soup or casseroles bubbling furiously on the top. Now it was a cold, empty room that echoed with a still silence and smelt dusty, damp and dirty.

For a moment, I was lost for words, even though I knew what I was up for, coming to live here, but the reality was a bit of a shock. Before I could feel even sorrier for myself, I heard the truck arrive, so placed Doris in the bathroom with a litter tray and shut the door.

I flung open all the doors and windows in the house and slowly the stale smell started to disappear. The appliances and furniture were all placed, and this empty shell slowly started to resemble a home — our home.

Settling down for the first night in our old but new home, I released Doris from his bathroom prison so he could explore the new surroundings room by room with all the familiar smells of our own furniture. I fired up the coal range until the oven dial couldn't go any further and then bled the water cylinder to get rid of the rusty water that would've been sitting in the pipes for years.

However, I forgot that if you left it all boiling for too long, the pipe on the roof would explode with an overflow of scalding excess water. First, I heard the rumble coming through the pipes, then into the walls and room... Then, Boom! It exploded through the pipe in the outside roof, heading skyward like a geyser. All I could do was run the inside and turn on all the taps, just as I was taught as a kid, and wait for it to stop. My new neighbors must have cracked up at the site of me running in and out of the house, trying to defuse the situation.

I spent the next month or so painting and wallpapering, gardening and dragging this once great home's carcass into the twenty-first century. Doris was in his element, catching rats and mice galore as the place was majorly infested by the rodents and even had opossums nesting in the roof space. I would open my pantry door on occasion and be greeted by a large rat sitting there, staring me out, so I would scream in shock, which sent Doris skidding and broadsiding towards the kitchen door and outside. A bloody great help he was — not!

In between my jobs at home, I would pick up Mum's only surviving sibling, Velma, and take her to the Rotorua Care Village to see her baby sister. Mum would spend the time chatting about going home and when she was leaving, and Aunty Velma would try and correct her, saying, 'Sorry, Myrna, but you need to stay in here as you're not well.' Mum would grumble under her breath and look the other way.

On another occasion, when I delivered Velma to Mum's room, she (Mum) turned to her (Velma) and said, 'Oh, Velma, you here to take me home?' When Velma said no, Myrna replied, 'Well, you might as well fuck off then!' We were all so shocked at her gruff statement that laughter was the only response we could manage and even Mum saw the funny side to her outburst and giggled along with the rest of us.

Dad would drive from Tokoroa three days a week to spend time with his wife, which left our mother wondering where he was and what he was doing on the days in between. The paranoia, which was a major symptom of her disease, really ramped up and she would throw all kinds of accusations at him as soon as he walked into her room. Seeing other women, being out in other rooms with underage girls, and more. She really believed that Dad was up to no good in her absence. Poor Dad, he was mortified but saw the funny side of it, which helped him cope with his wife's decline.

Eventually, a room opened in the Tokoroa facility and Mum was transferred by ambulance to her new care home. This meant that Dad could see her every day, along with the rest of us, including some of her friends that were either in the home with her or in the same town. She seemed more relaxed there, but the disease was advancing at a rate of knots. Her room was always full of people, which she loved at first but she would become tired quickly and fall asleep while everyone was there. She was no longer able to feed herself or even hold a cup for water, so needed more and more care.

The level of care in this place wasn't great and we were constantly looking for staff to help our mum to the toilet or to turn her when she was in pain. If she was up and sitting in her chair, then deciding she needed to get back into bed, it was almost impossible to find someone to do the deed, so a couple of times we ended up carrying her to bed ourselves. I understand that these places are also a business and are often run on the smell of an oily rag, but surely the standard of care shouldn't suffer because of that, but that's exactly what we experience as a family.

Mum ended up with the most horrific bed sores on the base of her spine as she wasn't moved enough or washed enough and would sometimes be left sitting in her own urine for lengths of time, which made her sores sting, and she would howl in pain.

My favorite times to visit her was first thing in the morning, when the ward was quiet and most of the residents were asleep. I would tiptoe into the room so as not to wake her and pull up a chair next to her bed, taking her toasty warm hand in mine and sit quietly, watching her breath. Eventually she would wake up and ask me for water or to adjust her pillow. They were really special mornings as she was so calm and sleepy and there would be moments that I would see the old mum that we all missed so much.

Returning one lunchtime, I was appalled to see our frail mummy propped up in her bed, bib on, spoon in hand and the lunch tray set up in front of her. The staff knew that she was unable to feed herself by this stage but had just left her to fend for herself. After feeding Mum as much as she would take, I marched to the office, demanding an apology to Mum and all of us. It was so cruel and sad to see her sitting there, not being able to even complete one of life's basic tasks. From that point, I made a small sign that I stuck above her bed that stated, *"My name is Myrna Fergusson. I am now unable to feed myself so will need help to eat when you deliver my food. Please respect this. Thank you."*

A week or so later, Mum 's color changed and she developed a cough which quickly turned into pneumonia because of her frail state. Her intake of food had declined even more due to her inability to swallow, which was a major symptom of her disease. She became so thin and small almost overnight and without her false teeth in, she became almost unrecognizable.

The doctors were so thin on the ground that it took days for her to be seen and diagnosed. We gathered as a family to make sure she was never alone, and special and close relations rushed to be near her also. Most of us were braced for the inevitable, while others were in a state of denial. I sort of floated between the two. I didn't want her to leave us but this person in the bed, moaning in pain and discomfort, wasn't my mum any more, she needed to be released and rest as she would have wanted.

The doctor pumped her full of strong antibiotics, and the rest home finally gave her an air mattress to take the pressure off her bedsores. We waited patiently, talking to her, giving her water and then, by some miracle, she woke one morning and started chatting as if nothing had happened.

We fed her up as much as she could take and wheeled her out of the room she had been stuck in for weeks, passed the room we called "Death

Row", through the dining room, past the nurses' station, outside, and into the sunlight she missed so much. This little outing was more for us than her as it created a sense of normality around our mum that we had desperately missed.

She signaled shortly after to go back inside where a cousin sat with her, played the ukulele and sang a song, which Mum joined in with, knowing every word. We were all so relieved to have her back although we knew she was still so gravely ill.

It was at this point I shared some exciting news with her — I was going to be a grandfather! Ben and Denise's daughter, Casey, were expecting a baby and it was a boy! Mum was so pleased and happy and congratulated us all. Remember that babies and cats were her passion in life. I was so afraid that she wouldn't recover and I would never have had the chance to tell her and she would never have known that there was a new generation of Fergussons, coming through me.

With Mum being stable, we all seemed to get on with life around her. Dad with his daily visits until four p.m., and the rest of us in and out of her small room on a daily basis. Older brother, Ray, continued with his (and partner's) plans to go on safari in Africa and I needed to head to Waiheke Island to put the bach on the market so I could buy something in the bay. It seems crazy, but I think we were all drawn into a false sense of security with our mum being up, about and communicating with us again.

I packed up the car with Doris in his cage, as I knew that I would need a couple of weeks on the island to whip the house into shape to go on the market. Before leaving, I spent time with Mother before saying goodbye and that I would see her as soon as I got back.

I was leaving her room and turned to wave at her as she was sitting up in her chair, but she was distracted, asking Dad to do something for her. That image of her not seeing me wave goodbye has stuck with me for years, as it was the last time I would ever see my mummy alive.

My parents' sixty-sixth wedding anniversary was looming and our mother was aware of it somehow as she was insisting that her room was kept tidy as the party would be on soon.

Mothers Eyes — Six60, 2016

The island was a welcome escape and I had fun catching up with a few regular visitors. I was so looking forward to attending my friend Rashika's wedding on the coming Saturday in Auckland city, along with catching up with all my old "working in television" mates.

I felt somewhere deep down inside that it was probably time to head back home soon so I spent the day gathering up my things and putting the final touches to stuff that needed doing. I had even prepared Doris' cage for the impending drive back home. Call it a premonition, intuition, I don't know, but I was motivated to prepare to move.

The phone rang on the Friday night, just as I sat down for my second glass of wine. I was alone as all my guests had gone home, so I was enjoying the peace and quiet. It was Gloria on the other end of the line. 'I'm with Mummy,' she announced and told me that she was listening on speaker. Mum's voice had all but disappeared and was reduced to just a soft whisper. 'Get here,' she whispered softly.

I replied with, 'Yup, I'll be there soon.' And I told her that I loved her very much.

Dad had spent the day there, along with other welcome visitors to acknowledge the big sixty-sixth wedding anniversary, so Mother was quite worn out.

Gloria stayed with her until dark, chatting and holding hands. Dad had gone home hours before and every other visitor had left for that night. Being Mum, she told Gloria to leave as she didn't want her to be leaving in the dark of night as she feared for her safety even then. Finally convinced, as Mum said she wanted to sleep, closing her eyes, Gloria kissed our mum goodnight and quietly walked out the door so as not to wake her up. She stood outside for a few seconds then peeped in to see her laying there calmly, but now her eyes were open and looking skyward. What could she see? Something we couldn't? After a few minutes, even though she didn't want to leave her, Gloria left for home.

It was just after four a.m. that the still quiet and darkness of my room on Waiheke Island was interrupted with the sound and light that erupted from my mobile phone that was sitting on the table next to me bed. I must've been in such a deep sleep as, for a few seconds, I couldn't understand what was happening. I heard Gloria's voice and even though I subconsciously knew what this call was about, I asked her what had happened. 'It's that phone call,' she replied, 'our mummy is gone.'

I needed a moment so said that I would call her back. Jumping out of my bed in the dark, I ran up the hallway, yelling for Mum and going round in circles. I just really didn't know what to do, how to act and what I was feeling. I was calling for her as I felt so very far away and lost.

Turning the lights on and taking a breath, I called my sister back to learn more and make some plans. Mum had died while a nurse was checking her sores and was gone with just a breath. By the time Gloria and Desma had arrived, she had been changed and redressed in day clothes. My sisters laid on the bed with her, cuddling her and kissing her as she was still so toasty and warm. Dad and the rest of the family were on their way. Ray was away in some remote villages in Africa and I was stuck on the island, not knowing what to do next.

The ferry terminal wasn't open until around six thirty a.m., so I finally pulled myself together, loaded up the car, put Doris in his cage and rang the terminal over and over again but with no reply.

'Fuck this!' I said, locking the house up, jumping in the car and heading to the wharf, where a long line of cars were banked up, waiting to get on the next harbor crossing. I begged the woman in the office for a space for us and it seemed to take her forever to check with the ferry staff if they could squeeze me on as it was fully booked. After adjusting some vehicles forward into a tighter fit, I was able to board the ferry to the mainland. The entire crossing and trip back to Tokoroa was done in silence, no radio, no phone, only Doris howling from his cage.

I cried and stopped, stopped and cried but mostly felt numb all over, as the whole thing felt totally unreal and extremely foreign.

I roared into Tokoroa a few hours later. Pulling into the carpark at the care home, I recognized all the cars that belonged to our different family members. I had organized for my mate, Karen, to come and collect Doris and take him home to Ngongotahā as I knew that I wouldn't be returning there anytime soon.

I sat in the car silently, attempting to move, to get out, but I bloody couldn't. My legs just wouldn't move and I guess I thought if I just stayed in the car without heading to my mother's room, the whole thing wouldn't be real. I called my sisters to come out and get me so I had no choice but to make a move and within minutes, they were there, tapping on the driver's window of my car.

We embraced and wept as they walked me into the familiar surroundings, passed the nurses' station, through the dining room and "Death Row", arriving at the entrance to Mum's room where the door was closed with a sign asking for quiet and respect for the family. This shit got so suddenly real but I wasn't quite ready so I insisted that we take just a few minutes to sit and chat before going in.

I signaled that I was ready and we made our way to the door and it was opened, revealing Dad sitting in the middle of the room, with everyone else surrounding him. I walked forward to shake his hand, trying not to look left to where Mum was still lying in her bed. There were lots of kisses and hugs from everyone and when I was ready, I turned toward my mum, where a couple of my nieces where sitting, still holding her hand.

The sight of my mother lying there, mouth open, cold and dead, was overwhelming and I felt a massive bubble of grief rising up in my body and expelling a type of wail that made it so hard to catch my breath and to even stand. I sat down next to Mum's grey corpse and put my head on her chest, trying to stop the sounds of grief and the tears but it just wasn't possible… Well, not just yet.

We played Mum's favorite music and took turns at sitting with her until the undertaker arrived to tell us what would be done next. They were so gentle when they lifted off her bed and onto the stretcher, placing a Perspex sheet over her face so the cover wouldn't touch it. We then followed Mum's body out of the room and out to the entrance where the staff were standing as a guard of honour, which was so touching even though I'm sure they did it each time someone passed, but to us it was really respectful.

It was decided that Mum would lay at Rex's house for the next few days so, later that evening, we got the word that she was ready to be dressed, made up and handed back to us.

We were all waiting in the family room when my son, Daniel, walked in, having driven from Auckland to support me as we had discussed. The girls had brought Mother a complete, new outfit, and we were eventually ushered into the dressing room where our mum was waiting. Her hair had been wet so was straight and combed back from her face, which was as white as the sheet that covered her from the chest down.

The face of death is not pretty but when we looked closer, we could see remnants of our mum, so proceeded, through clothing and make-up, to bring her back.

Us boys left while the girls placed her in her undergarments then we all helped with her new outfit. The undertaker then explained the applying of make-up and with her hair done in the usual way, Myrna reappeared before our eyes. We, along with Dad, had chosen the casket so we gently placed her in it and then into the hearse for the drive to Rex's.

Everyone left to prepare the space and I was left to ride with my mum. So, as the funeral director was rummaging around in his office, I sat quietly in the hearse with her, telling her that she wasn't alone and where we were going. It was the last time I would get with her alone forever, so I chatted and wept quietly until he returned and we drove off.

The next few days were a blur of people, food, flowers, music and more people. Mum's Jolley relations all started to gather and Aunty Velma, the only surviving sibling, came to spend some time with her baby sister. She was alone now, without any brothers or sisters, and told me often how she hated being the only one left. We forget that when you are that old, it's not only your family that disappears but all your friends as well, leaving you completely alone.

A steady flow of people came to bid Myrna farewell and, as a family, it gave us comfort to know that our mum was so loved and extremely popular. Dad took it all in his stride, drinking with Rex and his mates most nights. I realize that alcohol can be a cover for grief but my brother made sure it was top of the menu every night, which really pissed me off. Here was our mum, lying cold and stiff upstairs, while he was parting every night with the music on full tilt. I just avoided any conflict for Dad's sake, staying out of the way and with Mum as we all had an agreement that she would never be left alone.

John and Kim arrived on the last night before the funeral, which was full of singing and stories, remembering all the good times. Dad took his place next to the casket, to spend as much time as possible with his wife. John, after a few wines, asked Dad if he could kiss Mum goodbye, and because her casket was on the floor, he had to lean forward, putting his hand on both side of the box to lean down. He managed the kiss and, as he pushed himself up, I had visions of the side walls of the flimsy box breaking off, landing John flat on top of my mum. Instead, he made it, but the motion of his movement rocked poor Mum's head from side to side rigorously. We all chuckled then made sure we had an early night to prepare for the big day tomorrow.

Sleeping next to the coffin on mattresses, in a room full of about ten people, made the snoring horrific to the point I expected Mum to sit up and scream, 'Hey! Shut up!' In the dead of that night, having not had much success with sleep, I reached my hand over the side of the coffin and held onto Mum's knobbly, arthritic hand and held it until if got warm again, but this time it was from my own body heat. I miss that now, holding her hand and talking shit, arguing about the weather or asking how that cat was before asking how I was. She was gone and soon her body would disappear too — forever.

The time came to say our final farewells and close the lid on her beautiful face. Here was this old woman lying in her casket with a room full of people of all ages broken by her departure, watching as she had her hair done for the last time as the rays of sunlight touched on her still face.

I wrote the service for Mum to be factual but entertaining to reflect her personality and I even dropped the odd F-bomb accidentally. The laughs came thick and fast, and it truly ended up being a celebration of her life, complete with guest speakers and props. There weren't enough funeral sheets or food as the place was so full of family and friends. We waved her goodbye after our dad had closed the back of the hearse, while we released a multitude of colorful balloons with "MYRNA" written on them. Goodbye, Mum, rest well.

Myrna Jolley, 1950, Mamaku. My mum.

Life went back to as normal as it could do and once the ashes were returned to us, Mum took her place under Dad's TV for the next few years, moving only to be dusted or to do the rounds of each of our homes on dates we wanted. Eventually, our father insisted that she needed to stay home with him from then on.

Dad told me that, not long after the funeral, he dreamt that she had come into his bedroom to kiss him goodbye and to tell him how much she loved him. There were tears welling up in his eyes, something that I had never witnessed in my entire life, but there he was, this nearly ninety-year-old bushman, still grieving for his lost love. 'How did she look?' I asked.

He replied, 'She was so young and beautiful, just like when he married her.'

I could see that this gave him peace and acceptance and even made the rest of us feel better at coping with this massive loss.

My relationship with my dad was never easy as we were still so different and he would play up to anyone who was in the room to ridicule me, especially when Rex was around as he would make homophobic remarks about me. Dad would buy into it, making me feel ridiculous and now I had no mum to pull them into line, saying, 'Hey! Stop that, I don't like that word,' or 'Cut that language out now!'

I was on my own with this and I found it hard to cope with, especially when the faggot word was broken out (that's the word that Mum just couldn't cope with) or the jokes about what may have been happening in my bedroom and who with.

The first Christmas without her was difficult enough and, come Boxing Day, I'd had enough of all the bullshit that was being flung at me. Dad was in amongst it but, to be fair, was always kinder if it was just him and I.

I stayed away from him for the next few months so I could avoid any confrontation or unnecessary arguments.

The portrait of my parents that had caused so much of a stir in the NZ Portrait Awards, and also online, was tucked away in storage and gathering dust. It even made the cover of the *New Zealand Artists*

Magazine, with a cool write-up inside that followed my journey as a self-taught artist and the reason behind the piece.

I eventually collected it and hung it in my home, but it was too God damn powerful and beautiful for it to be not shown off. Beautiful in a way that it showed an everlasting love that needed to be celebrated, it solely belonged in Tokoroa where most of that love took place. I spoke to the Tokoroa council, who were really open to taking it off my hands on an indefinite loan, along with another sole piece depicting my dad as a real Tokoroa bushman, complete with hard hat. They nearly bit my hand off at the opportunity to show art that depicted lifelong residents by an artist born in the town.

It was decided, after a couple of meetings, that both portraits would hang in the foyer of the new South Waikato Events Centre, where they could be viewed and appreciated on a regular basis. The council invited the entire family, and friends of Mum and Dad's, to a commitment ceremony where the pieces were unveiled and blessed. As we were standing in the center, which overlooked the local sportsgrounds, there was an amazing rainbow that appeared as if to say that our mum approved. From that moment on, my parents would always be visually part of life in Tokoroa, especially where sports and recreation took place, and Dad, being Dad, didn't say much but we could tell he was pleased as punch to leave that legacy.

I was approached by a local media company, which owned the *Daily Post* newspaper in Rotorua, along with the radio station I had worked at for decades before. Cash was getting low and I thought that I would be better to go back to work for a few months to top up the funds.

The day I started, I walked into that same office where I had started my media career in the late 1980s. The crazy thing about it was that I was sitting not far from where I use to sit and there was my old mate, Chrissie, who had stayed with the company for the last thirty years. It was as if we picked up where we left off so long ago and became the best of mates almost immediately. The overall team made me feel so welcome and it was bizarre but really comforting to be back! Here I was, back on the streets of Rotorua, touting for media business with some familiar faces who I had had a relationship with decades before.

I thought that leaving Auckland could possibly hurt my "Bushman's Son" art brand. However, because I was now in the regions, it made me more active on all social media and resulted in more enquiries, followers, commissions and sales. People still wanted what I was turning out so it was encouraging, however, my Auckland and Wellington exhibitions had slowed and I was starting to get negative feedback from the gallery owners. I know that I haven't got an art degree and that I break every rule when it comes to what the art world expects but I am true to myself and my "Bushman" brand, so I pulled away from the red tape of being represented and produced what I wanted, when I wanted. Maybe it was my pig-headedness, but it felt good to stand up for what I believed and go my own way.

Off the back of all of this happening, I was introduced to a community foundation that allowed you to build a fund locally within the Bay of Plenty to help at a local level.

In my case, it would be an art foundation that would give emerging artists a leg up to create and get started, as I understood how bloody hard that was. Putting the word out there for donations was like getting blood out of a stone so I decided to hold a series of local exhibitions as fundraisers to get the fund to the threshold so we could start asking for applications and gifting to successful applicants.

The first show was held at the local art village, which started the trickle into the fund, which was disappointing, so I pitched to the community fund organisers, saying that if they backed me with a little funding, we could do something special.

Taonga, The Exhibition was held in the local civic theatre to huge crowds and generated a great lump sum for the fund, which definitely got us on track. It was based on images of Māori that hadn't been seen for more than a thousand years and were lifted from original glass plates from a private collection. The identities of those depicted were a mystery but I worked hard to give them a voice and face for the twenty-first century.

Eventually, the entire collection sold out and all monies went to the fund but again we weren't quite there so I pushed on and a year or so later, I decided to put up for tender every piece I had created at a charity event called Essential Pieces. The result blew us all away and raised more than the amount we needed to hit the mark.

The poster girl for this event was a young Aunty Joan, named *Forgotten Casualty Of War,* which sold on the night as well, much to my horror, but I'm sure she would have been OK with the fact that the money went to a good cause.

My brand was intact, we had raised the amount needed to gift to local artists and The Bushman's Son legacy was secured for generations to come. My dream would be to have my sons, grandsons and great grandsons to manage it and add to it in the name of my mum and dad.

My first grandson, James, was born late in November, followed by Oliver in 2018. These two little guys gave me a boost and amaze me each time I see them. The really cool thing is that I share these two with my old buddy, Denise. It's unbelievable that we are grandparents together and there is a piece of each of us in both of them.

After moving from Auckland, both of my sons joined me in Rotorua so now we are all back exactly where we started but each live our own lives, coming together as often as we can.

Living alone, with Doris at my side, and living between home and Papamoa, where I brought a beach house after selling the bach on Waiheke Island, was total perfection. It gave me time out from work and allowed me to chill out on the beach, at the pub with mates and hook up with guys when I needed. Again, the apps and internet were the only way to really meet men out of the main centers, so I made sure I had my money's worth.

Again, the only thing that happens when it's just about hooking up for sex is that is the only thing you get and, as time went on, I was more and more OK with that. I could pick and choose who I wanted and block all of those who became annoying or stalker-like. Fun was fun and I was happy with my lot. I was never any good at relationships anyway so it was good that I was avoiding any related heartache and this helped keep my anxiety in check. It was coming up to five years being alone and my mother's words echoed in my memory: *You need someone in your life as you get older, you can't be alone forever!*

However, my life was filled with family, good friends and my beautiful grandchildren, so I really did feel complete on most levels. I'm not saying that I didn't get lonely at times, because I did, especially through winter. But Doris and his antics kept me entertained and busy with picking up dead mice, rats or bits of birds that he insisted on bringing in to show me at every opportunity and at all hours!

It was during this time that I had been chatting online with a couple of guys in a relationship who wanted to hook up for some fun. The three of us had tried over a year or so to get together but it never seemed to work out. Until one weekend, when I was alone at the house in Papamoa, and they popped up in the same area, so we exchanged messages and decided to meet up for a coffee to see if we liked each other enough to "get it on"!

I drove to the venue and spotted the two guys sitting at table outside so endeavored to saunter over towards them, trying to act as cool as possible. After the introductions, we all sat down for coffee. The attraction was immediate but, as happens when hooking up with couples, the attraction was really strong between myself and one of them more than the other. As a couple, this is the risk you take when opening up your relationship and probably need to expect it will happen from time to time. If you are strong and solid as a couple, there shouldn't be any problems, but if the relationship is fragile… Well, it could spell disaster.

We chatted and even though I was drawn to one more than the other, we all got on so well together and really enjoyed each other's company, so it was decided that we would meet again next time they were over my way. A week passed and they were back in Papamoa and we decided that the time was right to get together for a sex marathon. I gave them my address and jumped in the shower, scrubbing everything that I may have needed to use!

I was really nervous when they arrived and as I met them at the door, one of them — Kyle — blurted out, 'I've had a lot of sex in this house!' When I questioned his statement, it turned out that he lived in this very house with his ex-partner and an old friend of mine who I had purchased the house through. It turned out that we had both stayed here during the

243

years my friend owned it but never met! It was no wonder I liked him a little more than his current partner and put it down to just being familiar.

Without wanting to beat around the bush too much, I said to them both, 'Oh well, coffee or a fuck?' That certainly broke the ice and we got down to business. The three of us got on so well and they ended up staying for hours. We ended up inviting some mutual friends over for drinks and it turned into a bit of a party, with everyone leaving in the wee small hours. Going back to work on Monday, I sat down with Chrissie and told her of my weekend antics and what had gone on and she replied with, 'Oh well, as long as you're having fun and know what you're doing.'

'I am and I do,' was my response.

The following weekend, the three of us got together again and we were really gelling as a threesome — lots of laughs, drinks, fun and sex. It wasn't until my mate, John, and sister, Desma, commented that they could see an attraction between Kyle and I, which I wasn't aware was showing in any way. But there it was, and as soon as it was said, the attraction started to grow.

I found myself wanting to be around Kyle but, at the same time, I felt so bad that I had the hots for him behind his partner's back. Not an ideal situation.

The three of us continued to have shitloads of fun together but I started to feel a bit uncomfortable as my feelings grew for Kyle and not knowing how he felt was driving me batty. It was a beautiful weekend afternoon in Papamoa as the three of us decided to listen to music over a wine or three. Kyle and I were on the sofa, exchanging facts on favorite music we had in common, while his partner went outside to take a phone call. Without even thinking about it, I just blurted out how I was feeling about him and *only* him and all the time apologizing as I knew that this could end everything, including our friendship. He turned to me and uttered, 'I feel exactly the same!'

Now, can I just say before I look like I am committing relationship sabotage, that I had noticed that when we were together in the bedroom there was absolutely no interaction between them as a couple. I had even mentioned it to John for his take on it.

Kyle explained to me that his relationship was crumbling, coming to an end, and he seemed to be really genuine about it. He said that once he sorted it all out with his partner that he would like to pursue me, but not before he had put a full stop on his current commitment. This made me admire the guy even more and I was completely hooked.

Our communication wasn't regular at all; however, I was still hearing from his partner and, put it this way… He wasn't exchanging recipes with me and the pics he sent weren't of scones, if you know what I mean. It was so obvious that they were not communicating with each other at all and they both were interested in me. This actually made me feel better about what was happening between Kyle and I.

Being caught up in the middle of a broken couple isn't nice but after they had split, it seemed to be OK as Kyle had come clean about his feelings for me and the answer from his ex-partner was, 'Well, if you don't pursue him, I will.' So, as far as we knew, it was all good to go.

With all break-ups, it turned on its head and the nastiness started. Kyle was even sleeping in the caravan in their driveway as a statement that the relationship was done. However, for reasons that I tried to stay out of *(failing miserably)*, it all went tits up and has never really calmed down since, with the ex, using everything he could to character-assassinate Kyle, even though he himself had started a new relationship. It seems to me like an incredible waste of energy, making someone pay for something forever… Go figure.

My adoration for this new man in my life grew stronger and stronger and soon the adoration turned into a feeling of love. I'm not talking about love as I knew it, but an all-encompassing feeling of being totally captured and "in love".

I cared about this guy, liked him and fell in love with him. His family were wary of me and I get that, but I'll leave them all to make their own decisions about us and either come along for the ride or not. Kyle used up a lot of energy to keep everybody happy and in harmony but you just can't force people to do something that they just don't want to do.

Him being a family-orientated guy was really attractive to me and I introduced him to my vast family at every opportunity. I always say to him that it was such a shame that he never got to meet Myrna, my mum, as she always had a soft spot for a nice-looking young man and would've loved him! He also missed Aunty Velma as she passed away less than two years after Mum, so the entire Jolley family were gone.

There was one guy from that generation still here and I couldn't wait to get this really important guy in my life in front of Stubb — my dad — the bushman himself.

Dad, now living on my brother Rex's farm in the cottage, was coping with life without Myrna, and seemed to be getting on with his regular routine... Club on a Friday until four p.m., which he always called "a *very* important meeting" that he just couldn't miss. Club again on a Monday for the lucky number (cash) draw and work he did for my brother's mowing company, which made him a regular attraction on the tractor, mowing local school fields and sports grounds. He was a regular on the open roads about town in his high-viz vest on his push bike, clocking up between ten and sixteen kilometers a day. 'Use it or lose it,' he would always say and would put that down to him managing to get to the age he was.

Dad greeted Kyle on the day they met in the usual way by trying to beat him with the hard gripping "Stubb" handshake, which he used on all of us to squeeze our fingers until they hurt, saying, 'Gotcha!' They got on well and I was really pleased — it was me that Dad didn't understand, not any of my partners or friends.

Being in a strained relationship with my father for most of my life wasn't great and was constantly there, in the back of my mind, nagging at me. Those close to us would always say that our father never had a problem with me or my sexuality, however, they weren't the brunt of the *poof* jokes whenever he was around mates or my brothers, as my sisters didn't like that kind of talk much. I loved him a lot as he was my dad and it was nice when we were alone together talking and hanging out but I grew tired of being the target of ridicule so my visits waned. I know he is old... I know he's never been any different, I know what I'm up for if I'm in a crowd with him but it hurts because of all of that... He's my father and I can take a joke but the joke just got too old.

As time went by, I picked up the phone more often to say hi to Stubb and our arguments and banter about the weather dominated our conversations, then he would have a little bit of gossip and I'd reply with what we'd been up to. After Mum died, it was him that picked up the phone and called me on my birthday, which had never happened in my entire life, but as Mum was gone, he felt that it was his duty... 'Myrn would want me to ring ya for your birthday so... Happy Birthday, OK!' That was so cool and he did it to all of us, stepping in for Mum, which was really awesome.

Even though I felt poles apart from Stubb, when it came to our father and son relationship, we did enjoy some quiet but special moments. Mum's death really did soften his hard exterior to the point that he would say out loud that he loved all of his family — everyone! He would tell all the females as often as needed, but the males not so much, but you know that he did feel it.

On one of the rare visits to me in Rotorua, he had in his possession a small metal cup, explaining, 'This is for you!' It was a silver cup with his name, "Neil", engraved on it as he had won a baby competition in 1930. 'I've given Ray a chopping trophy and Rex my rugby trophy and I thought it was only fair that I give you this one.' It was such a cool moment for me that Dad actually included me alongside my older brothers. It felt good and I felt as visible as them for the first time in decades as it was always my mother who insured I was counted in and never my father. I thanked him and I treasure it to this day...

It came as a surprise to me when my father summonsed me to Tokoroa to help sort out all his finances, lock them away into term deposits and to sell the unit that me and our mum had owned. I secured the buyer, completed the paperwork and took direction where Dad wanted what to go and where. If any other family member queried any of this interaction, he would simply say, 'Talk to Terry, he's my agent!' This made me chuckle with a certain importance, of course!

He then made me joint executor of his will and final affairs with my oldest brother Ray, which was a job that I never really wanted as I knew deep down inside that there would be problems around this, especially between the six of us, who were all so different and strongheaded.

Kyle and I continued our relationship, with him still working and living in Hamilton but being home with me in Ngongotahā from Friday to Monday, which worked mostly, however, we were put through our paces and had lots to face as part of our relationship. We went through some traumatic experiences but always managed to find our way back to each other and it all seemed to make us stronger as a couple. My anxiety around being in a relationship and always striving to get it right was sometimes off the Richter scale. This caused Kyle to go the same way, although his anxiety was diagnosed years before and was mostly managed. Through discussions about it and his experience, I now had a name for what I had been dealing with for most of my adult life and it was treatable, not only through meds, but also through discussions and counselling on how to manage it.

My GP adjusted my depression medication and in a few weeks of going through the mental fog once again, I felt so incredibly good. A lot of people see the taking of medication for mental health as weak, but I contest that as someone that can now feel normal in society and cope with everyday activities, friendships, relationships and even conflict. Again, I thought to myself, *wow, so this is what it feels like to take everything in its stride and not get tied up in knots over the smallest things!*

This became my new normal and, *no*, I don't feel numb to any feelings at all, and I can still laugh and cry… It's just that I now have the ability to take a breath and work with what I have in front of me. Oh, I don't get it right every time and I still have my moments of madness, however, now it's not the end of the world and I feel I can find my way back from it.

As a result of this, I feel, as a couple, Kyle and I have grown so much and every day I love him a little more. This finally is the person that I love unconditionally, and I can see myself growing old with. My grandsons are so cute around him — unable to pronounce "Kyle", they ended up with the nearest thing they could say, "Carol", and it stuck and he absolutely loves it. My man and I made more and more appearances together, and he was now my plus-one when I had work functions, instead of using my ring-ins! After five years of being single and being totally accepting of that, this man had stolen my heart and made me feel special every day, so I always strive to make him feel the same way.

The continuing problems we had with my new partner's family, driven by his ex-partner, amazed me and bothered me more than him as it was all unnecessary but still continued regardless. You would think that such hatred would run out but it still was running on a full tank, which was continually filled up by others without a life of their own — sad much!

Much to my work buddy, Chrissie's, horror, I decided that a few months of work, turning into a few years, was probably enough. My buddy and I had become a great team, achieving great results in our sector and were visible in the marketplace as we attended every business event we could, to build our brand. Of course, we were there for the booze and food as well but work was always on our mind — mostly!

I had so enjoyed my time back in the old *Daily Post* building, surrounded by old and new mates, but it felt as though I was battling against a massive machine that started to treat us more as numbers than actual employees. I had questioned a few decisions from those at the top who, bleated on about how proud they were to have a "Rainbow Tick", meaning they embraced their LGBT employees, but at the same time produce a wedding magazine titled *Mr & Mrs!* Um, really?

So what they were saying is that marriage was still only recognized between a man and a woman. I jumped up and down about how, as a gay community, we fought tirelessly for the right to marry and this was an insult to all of those who participated and won. I remembered being in that pub in Auckland when the Homosexual Law Reform was passed and the celebrating that I witnessed and here I was, over thirty years later, still defending the issue.

The reply was, 'Oh, there's a gay section within the magazine.' What! So why call it *Mr and Mrs*?

It was this kind of contradiction that really pissed me off and I unfortunately had my guard up from then on.

So, the date was decided when I would vacate my seat and leave Chrissie to continue alone, but that date was moved out so many times that it felt like I'd given notice decades before. I was sad when I left, as the team of people I worked with, had become like family, but it was time to try retirement once again.

My art was in demand and I had decided to add being a celebrant to my portfolio of skills so I could legally conduct weddings and host funerals. It felt so good to be busy with all my new ventures and the wedding bookings in my long-term calendar were building up.

My Uncle Rex in Auckland had lost his wife, Eunice, decades earlier, and now was about to turn ninety years old, a few months before Dad did the same. They had been such good mates over the years, through pig-hunting, deer-stalking and also now losing their wives. Yes, the years were catching up with these two, with Uncle Rex using a walker and mobility scooter to get him to the bowling club, and he had full-time care at home. Dad, still living alone in the cottage, was still reasonable active but was definitely slowing down in all areas.

These two guys, at ninety years old, *both* wanted a party (each) and wouldn't take no for an answer. So Rex's family flew into action with the preparations and we all attended, including Dad, who travelled to Auckland from Tokoroa to see his old mate turn the grand old age. The night was so much fun for all the family and was full of music, dancing and singing, and the two old mates sat there, drinking and lapping it all up. Here they were, the two of them, Rex and Stubb, watching us playing up and drinking way too much but not so long ago, it was them and their wives doing the partying and we would be sneaking out of bed to watch them dance and giggle to the wee small hours. I felt sad for them but thankful that they were still with us.

Dad's ninetieth party was next and it was decided that the local events centre would be not only big enough but also well-heated for the elderly attendees and us. This was the very place where Mum and Dad's portraits were hanging in the foyer, which made it even more special. A lot of my brothers' mates came along and they so admired Dad, calling him an absolute legend as he showed so little sign of slowing down, in fact, it seemed as though he would last forever! It was midwinter in Tokoroa and the ice was thick on the ground but we managed to get Uncle Rex and Dad in and planted on their seats, close to the bar, the food and the toilets. Again, they both had a great night and sat taking in all the conversation and atmosphere.

Before midnight, Rex signaled that he was tired and wanted to return to the motel where they were staying, so we all went along to escort him along the short track back to the accommodation. The frost was heavy and as Kyle pushed the wheelchair over the uneven ground, cutting through the frost covered grass, he said, 'Kylie, if anyone needs to find their way home… Tell them to follow the tracks!' This statement along with calling Kyle "Kylie" stuck and was used regularly to reminisce about that fun night.'

Uncle Rex went downhill not long after that and never recovered due to his ailing heart and general old age. We made it to his bedside on the Saturday and in the early hours of Sunday morning, he went to be with his Eunice again.

Telling Dad that he had gone was hard as, once again, he was becoming more and more alone, with his family and friends departing after similar long lives. He would always joke that he was still here and not planning to go anywhere but the separation from more and more of the old familiar faces had to be taking its toll. He chose not to attend Rex's funeral and we all totally understood why.

Kyle and I had so many plans to travel and do lots of cool stuff as a couple, but the rise of Covid-19 seemed to have other ideas. We first heard of this new disease, which had potential to spread fast and furiously, through human-to-human contact, on the TV news. They stated that it had its origins in China's wet markets and had started to get out of control. Brushing it off as something that would eventually be contained, we got on with our lives. Then it hit — we were informed by the prime minister that the situation with Covid-19 had become dire and there was going to be announcements around our NZ response over the next few days… "Locked down" — it was a term that we became quickly aware of and used to, as it dictated our everyday lives for the next wee while.

Every cloud has a silver lining and this lockdown meant that Kyle could work from home with me in Ngongotahā as an essential worker. He would get up, get dressed and head out to the caravan to attend Zoom meetings and complete his working day. I would have the coal range red hot, producing scones, soup, stews and whatever I could muster. The only real trips out were to the supermarket where everyone's patience was tested due to the queues of people waiting to get in and the restrictions on certain items when purchasing your weekly groceries. Items such as soap, cat food, toilet paper and, the worst of the lots — alcohol! Only three bottles at a time! We were bloody horrified but managed to adjust.

Getting out and about and exercising was a must for the two of us and we hit the empty streets daily to make sure we kept our sanity. People out and about seemed nicer and greeted you wherever you went, as they were all in the same boat at the end of the day… Stuck in their homes without much social interaction. Cycling and walking around the deserted roads was movie-like, as it was as if everyone had just disappeared, gone. And here was the empty highway, CBD, carparks, all deathly quiet, other than Kyle and me, chatting as we rode by. It's a piece of our local history that we were living through and will be etched in my memory forever. The daily updates on cases and deaths were a must-see for us so our day was planned mostly around that and we had even turned the lounge into a second bedroom, almost like camping out, much to Doris' delight.

I would call Dad regularly and we would joke about who would catch "the Covid" first, him or me, and how Mum would not have coped living through a worldwide pandemic as she would have been so paranoid about catching it that she probably wouldn't have even answered the phone in case of infection!

He seemed to be coping OK with the isolation although I could hear the loneliness in his voice. Not only had he lost his wife but now everyone had to stay away as he was in his nineties and extremely vulnerable. Looking back now, we could see that this separation was taking its toll and he was extremely lonely, just sitting in his chair, watching TV and sleeping most of the day, and not even able to go to his beloved club as it too was shut down due to the pandemic. Our phone conversations seemed to be getting shorter as he would be heading to bed earlier with every passing week.

Lockdown was over and we were slowly all reunited with our loved ones and Dad had no shortage of visitors, which started to really wear him out. He became too tired to even attend the draws at the club, stating that he didn't think that he would be going back there again — ever.

Dad asked for help one morning, asking my brother, Rex, to call an ambulance as he couldn't walk and was visibly shaken by how frail he felt. We were all told that he had been admitted and was undergoing tests, etc., but what we didn't know was that the problem was far greater than our father ever let on. He had been in pain for some time but, typical Dad, had played it down to be nothing more than a scratch, but it seemed that a tumour on his kidney had grown at a rate of knots, along with more cancer spreading through his body. Being as deaf as a post, he would sit in the doctor's office, just nodding and not hearing a bloody thing, so we never knew what was actually going on with him but the change in his face made it obvious.

He was taken to Waikato hospital for more tests and after a week or so, was released to my brother, Ray, who drove him back home to Tokoroa. Ray had talked to the doctor and was told that our dad would probably not survive what was happening to his body. Being defiant, Stubb sat at home again in his chair, insisting that the doctors had "a plan" for him and that he was only thinking positively, so we backed him all the way.

His face changed daily, getting a little gaunter each day, but his puku (belly) was so distended with whatever was happening within. The word got around that this old legend wasn't doing too good, so Dad's house and driveway was constantly packed with cars and his tiny living room bustling with kids, grandkids, great-grandkids, extended family and what little good mates he had left. This left him exhausted but he loved every minute of it. My son, Ben, would take my grandkids to see him at least twice a week and he loved seeing them and all the other mokos as well.

Right through this time, he was still adamant that the doctors had a plan and that he would fight it until he won.

Dad would often comment on the nausea that plagued him and had to admit that the pain was starting to niggle at him but you never really knew how bad it actually was as this old bushman was so staunch and never wanted us to worry about him not coping. But eventually we saw right through this facade. Morphine was offered in small doses but there were also talks about medical marijuana to ease any discomfort. The first round worked well for him and he slept like a baby but after the next lot, he announced that he wouldn't be partaking in any more of that wacky baccy as he hallucinated that he was being chased by birds! Not the ones in short skirts and high heels but big feathery bastards! So that was the end of that!

We know that sleeping was so difficult for Dad during this time and I can only imagine what was going on in his head. Well, actually, I can imagine this ninety-year-old man climbing into his bed at night, trying to sleep, knowing that something in his body was trying to end his life. Regardless of this, he insisted that no one stay the night as he was OK on his own. Maybe he liked the quiet after his action-packed days full of a never-ending line of visitors, or maybe it was his time, late at night, to think about what was next. Whatever it was, he played it very close to his chest, as he always had, and we as his family knew we had to respect this or else.

Visiting him one afternoon, we had noticed an even more rapid decline, even though he was full of conversation and cheek. As I started to leave, waiting for the others to tell him he was loved and kiss him goodbye, I hung back. I stood over my father as he sat in his comfy chair and without any words being spoken, I sunk to my knees and put my head on his shoulder. Without hesitating he placed his head on mine and I told him how much I loved him and he agreed with me, in Stubb's way.

Walking out, I had to try and fight back the tears and my heart felt so sore I thought it would break, it was as if I knew that would be the last time, I saw my dad alive… And it was.

Kyle and I ended up in Papamoa for a quick stay and we had arranged for my old workmate, Judith, to join us for a night. It was set to be full of good wine, great food and the usual conversations. It had been ages since we had all caught up so we were all extremely excited. Kyle and I had made the beds at the bach, ready for our visitor, and the wine was chilled, ready to go.

Judith arrived, and after she unpacked the many nibbles she had brought with her, we sat down for a well-deserved glass of vino. Dad and his condition was the topic of conversation when my phone rang.

It was Gloria and she was on her way to Hamilton as Dad had been taken via ambulance after having another incident with not being able to walk or even function. The conversation around this was very definite — everything that could've gone wrong with Dad, had happened, and she would call me back as soon as she knew more.

He was admitted and was told that he wouldn't have long to live and wouldn't be leaving the ward alive. Gloria, brother, Ray, and my nephew, Nick, were the only ones with him because of the Covid restrictions that were still in place around the hospitals.

I hung up and grabbed my vino, taking a large sip... I filled Kyle and Judith in on what I had just been told and we all sat there, silent, for a few minutes. I got up and walked into the kitchen for absolutely no reason at all, other than to take in all I had just heard. I felt so far removed from what was happening and sitting around eating and drinking in Papamoa didn't feel right or where I needed to be.

'I'm so sorry,' I announced, 'but I wanna go home.' We all agreed that it would be the best thing to do so we all packed up, Judith went home and Kyle and I drove back to Ngongotahā. At no time did I think that we should all rush over to the hospital in Hamilton as we wouldn't have access to Dad anyway because of Covid, so home was where I needed to be... Closer to everyone and everything.

The drive home was reasonably quiet as I was still trying to process what had actually been said and what would happen next. The evening was overcast and bleak, which matched how I was feeling and what was about to come.

It felt good to be home and to have all the familiar sounds, smells and things around me, which sounds kind of weird, I know, but it really did give me comfort.

My brother, Ray, had accompanied our dad in the ambulance ride to the hospital and was still with him when Gloria and her son arrived. She found him still on the hospital gurney, which was proving way too uncomfortable for this ailing nearly ninety-one-year-old human. He was very chatty with everyone, even at this stage, but had already been told down in the emergency room that his card was marked and that this would be his last journey. As always, our dad took it in his stride and said nothing to anyone. Thank God Ray was there to witness what was said and what to expect.

He looked at Gloria when she arrived and looked relieved to see her there. 'Is Terry coming?' he apparently asked her, and when she replied that I would be there in the morning, the look he gave her was a look that the morning would be too late.

He had been there for a few hours before Gloria even got there and still nobody had given him any pain relief at all, probably because Dad had told the doctor, when asked, 'Any pain, Mr Fergusson?'

He replied, 'No, not really, I'm OK.'

Typical that he wouldn't say yes in case it was seen as weak, or he genuinely coped with the level of pain he was experiencing. With our father, it could've been all of the above!

My sister queried the lack of pain relief regardless, and shortly after, the nurse turned up with a couple of paracetamol… Paracetamol!

Eventually the nurses arrived with a special vibrating mattress, which was designed to be extremely comfortable and pressure point-free. After that, he really relaxed without any discomfort.

At this point, they asked Stubb, if there was an emergency with him and he stopped breathing, did he want to be resuscitated, to which he replied with a definite "nope", and added, 'I can't stay here forever!' He definitely knew that it was his time to go…

The comfy mattress enabled him to sleep, only breaking to open one eye to make sure Gloria was still there and then doze off again. Ray decided to whip back to the motel where he and his partner were staying close by.

The chatting ceased and the room fell quiet… The eye contact stopped and Dad lay there with both eyes open, looking straight ahead as if in a sort of waking coma, as my sister described it. The staff insisted that if there was anyone else that needed to be there that she should call them now. She phoned our brother and he started to make his way back to the hospital.

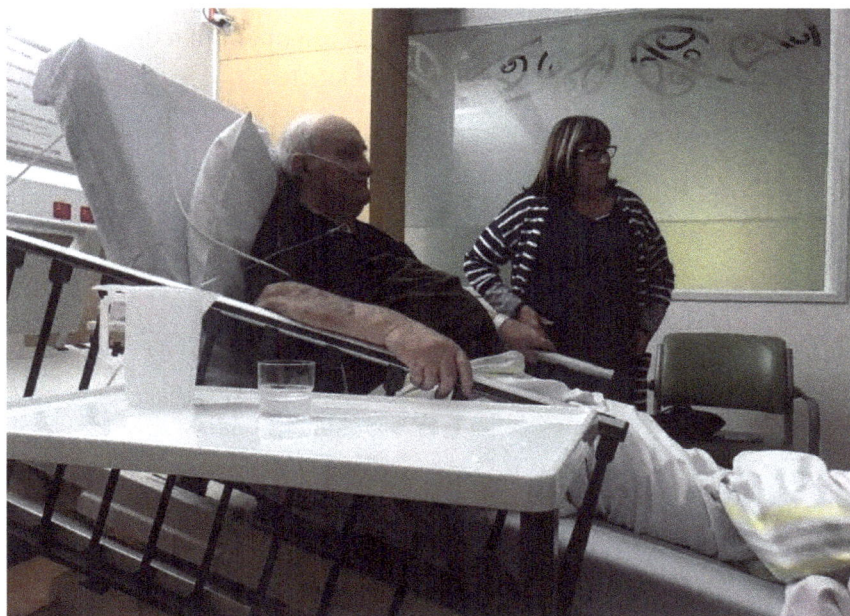

The last photograph of our bushman dad with Gloria.

Signaling Nick to come and hold his other hand, they watched as his breathing change, his breaths getting longer and slower, but all the time still talking to him to ensure he knew that he wasn't alone. Gloria told him how much we all loved him and the both of them, with one hand each, never left his side, even though at this point there were no responses.

As he started to struggle and wince, she leaned forward, saying, 'It's OK, Dad, go be with Mum… Go be with Mum.'

Screwing his face up a few more times and without even a whimper, our bushman went to be with his Myrna, the love of his life, who he had missed so very much, or at least that's what I hope and none of us really know. Dropping his hand, Gloria ran out to find the staff to confirm what she already knew — he was gone.

They laid his bed flat and Gloria gently closed his eyes and rolled up a sheet to place under his chin to keep his mouth closed before his body temperature dropped and it was impossible to shut. Nobody tells you this shit but we learnt this the hard way after our mum died.

Ray arrived at the room but it was too late.

Four a.m.

The phone rang, breaking the night's silence and as I glanced through the darkness to see the caller ID, I knew straight away that it was over. Gloria's voice was calm and soft as she told me that our dad had passed and even though it was expected, it was still so shocking that his cancer had taken him only three weeks after the final diagnosis. It was a good death, an uncomplicated death, without hassle or drama, just like Stubb himself.

Kyle and I stayed up and decided that we would pour a rum in Dad's honor and toasted him and his life and all he meant to all of us.

This bushman's wishes were, firstly, no funeral, as he didn't want to lay around in a box for days on end with everyone filing in, looking up his nostril. No embalming, as he certainly didn't want to be pushed, prodded, pumped, cut or sewn in any way. We decided that, as soon as his body arrived back in Tokoroa, we would prepare him ourselves and send him away quickly to be cremated.

Kyle and I were ready early and we drove toward Tokoroa, via Mamaku, where my parents had lived married and started a family. We stopped on the road halfway up to the village and I, with Kyle checking for cars, cut a mass of fern and punga leaves to adorn our bushman dad, instead of a coffin lid, which was also on his list as a definite no-no, along with the rest of the box.

It was difficult driving down his driveway, seeing his car parked where he had left it and the gathering family wandering about, not really knowing what to do next. Walking into Dad's cottage, we were confronted with my brother, Rex, and his drunken mates, who had pushed on through with their drinking from the night before and were absolutely paralytic.

I should have expected that but thought that maybe this time we could actually be a family and forge a plan together to carry out Stubb's wishes… But no.

We were greeted by my brother, who stated that Dad didn't like faggots, but he really liked Kyle. With this statement and a couple of other swipes, we left for the main house to get some clarity and left them to it.

Dad's body was released after a few phone calls from me to get him back to Tokoroa, otherwise we would collect him ourselves. It was around eight p.m. when we finally got to dress him and made sure he was good to go, which meant that he needed to stay in the funeral home overnight. We decided that between nine a.m. and eleven a.m. the next morning, we could spend some time with him, bring the kids and say goodbye each in our own way and that's what we did.

There he was, still on a hospital trolley, dressed in his high-vis with his track pants on and terrible old sneakers that he refused to throw away. He even admitted to wearing them to town on the odd occasion, much to our horror!

The grandkids and great-grandkids were talking to him, kissing him, sharing their hunting and sport stories with him and it felt right, almost as he wanted. After a few short words and a lot of emotion, it was time to say goodbye…

Ray and I helped the undertaker to wheel Dad through the soft, velvet curtain and into the prep room, where the other men in the family were waiting.

We jointly lifted his body off the gurney and into a small MDF box to keep him stable on the final journey to the crematorium. After placing a soft cloth over his face, we covered his entire boy in the leaves that I and others had collected, until we couldn't see him at all. It felt almost like a tribal ritual for a great *Rangatira* and I guess for us that's exactly what it was. The bushman had returned to his craft and was at rest under the greenery of the native bush he loved so much. He really did go bush for the final time, on his terms, in his own way.

The Bushman's Son

It's funny now, when I look back at the time I created the pseudonym that I used to sign my paintings, as it became a vehicle for many things to honor my father.

He understood it and enjoyed it and, for me, it brought me closer to him and part of his life without uttering a word.

We didn't understand each other but we both understood this and that made it even easier to let him go as he wanted and he will live as long as it exists.

We die twice in this life — the first when our physical body dies and the second is the last time your name is spoken on earth.

Of all the things I had been through with my bushman father, his death was the most significant as it taught me how much he actually meant to me and how to accept not only his death but also my Mum's, as I had struggled so much with that. It certainly is a special kind of lonely when you lose your parents. I like to think that he is with her now, so it taught me to let go. Be sad but life moves on, with or without you. I am so bloody thankful that, in the end, he gave me that moment of total acceptance that many gay men never get from their fathers and, whether or not it was planned, there was a final absolution.

Little did I know that my father's death would spark a chain reaction that would unexplainably destroy close relationships in my life… friends, brothers, sisters, sons, and grandsons… amazing that our family can treat us the worst in life, and it's true friends that always have our back… but that's a whole other story…

The End

261

The award winning portrait of my parents 2016

"Long casting shadows slowly creep on the wall as the shining spring son comes up. Its rays, shine down on the flowers and seeds and the cool green grass grows hot. The leaves sprout the flowers bloom as they take in the sun that shines. But in the evening breeze the sun disappears, leaving the world quite blind."

Terry — 1975

Lightning Source UK Ltd.
Milton Keynes UK
UKHW020607110722
405674UK00001B/11

9 781800 163607